CAMPAIGN
FOR
REAL ALE

D1734852

CONTENTS

This is the third edition of the East London & City Beer Guide. The area covered is huge, from Fleet Street eastwards to the boarders of Essex, and from the Thames northwards to Chingford: over 1000 pubs in all.

DEDICATION
This guide is dedicated to those stout people (in more ways than one) up and down the country, who like ourselves have had to survey some absolute dives in order to produce a beer guide. Particular thanks to Adrian Hall and Maxine Cooper without whose inspiration the last two guides would not have been possible. And to those former East London & City Branch Chairmen who are no longer with us: Dave Wakefield, Jack Long and Brian Marsh.

PUBLISHED BY
The East London & City Branch of the Campaign for Real Ale Ltd, 34 Alma Road, St Albans, Hertfordshire AL1 3BW.

ISBN No.1 85249 055 1

PRINTER
Calvert's Press, Workers' Co-operative, 31/39 Redchurch Street, London E2 7DJ. tele 071-739-1474. fax 071-739-0881.

DISCLAIMER
While every reasonable care has been taken in the production of this Guide, we cannot be responsible for or guarantee accuracy as there are continual changes in the type and quality of beers and other facilities offered by pubs. The opinions expressed in this Guide are those of individuals and not of CAMRA as a body and we cannot be held responsible for these or any errors.

FURTHER COPIES OF THIS GUIDE...
May be obtained from Keith Emmerson, 111 Ordell Road, Bow, London E3 2EQ. Please allow 60 pence for post and packing.

The Campaign began in 1971. A group of drinkers in the North-West decided that something had to be done about the declining quality of the beer available in most pubs – fizzy, cold, bland and overpriced. It was in sharp contrast to the reasonably priced ale still available in the pubs owned by independent brewers.

The new organisation was called the *'Campaign for the Revitalisation of Ale'*. Its officers all volunteers, produced a newsheet called *'What's Brewing'*, and visited breweries in an attempt to find out what was going on in the industry.

It was a disturbing picture. Mergers and takeovers since the 1950s had created six brewing combines responsible for over 80% of beer production and controlling more than half the pubs in which beer was sold. The brewing giants – dubbed the 'Big Six' – were Bass Charrington, Allied Breweries, Courage, Whitbread, Watney and Scottish and Newcastle. Together with Guinness, they were responsible for close on 90% of the beer brewed in Britain.

This domination of the industry cut down consumers' choice. Within the 1960s the number of beers produced in Britain had been halved from 3,000 to 1,500. In area after area, small local breweries producing beer that suited the local palate had been phased out and replaced by the new, heavily promoted national keg beers. In most parts of the country, the majority of pubs were owned by the Big Six – in some areas one of the giants had a virtual monopoly of pubs – and so the drinker had no choice but to drink the national kegs. In this way, scores of traditional ales were replaced by the new processed beers and the big brewers claimed that they were merely following 'demand'. Using their monopoly strength, the big brewers charged several pence a pint more for their beers than the remaining independents.

When the founders of CAMRA publicised these facts in *What's brewing'*, the campaign's national monthly newspaper they found there were many drinkers who were equally disturbed by the change in the quality of beer and the state of the brewing industry. Soon a flourishing national organisation started to take shape. A conference was called, membership cards produced, a small subscription levied, and the name changed to the more manageable *Campaign for Real Ale'*.

Membership soared to 1,000 – then 10,000 and finally to more than 20,000. Full-time staff had to be taken on to cope with the demands of a mass membership (28,000 strong in 1991 and still rising).

The big brewers found they had a fight on their hands. Their manipulation of the market was being challenged by a growing number of disgruntled beer drinkers. The Campaign denounced their keg beers as weak, tasteless and over-priced. They tested them and found they did not compare well with the traditional ales of the small brewers, most of which were better quality and better value for money.

CAMRA's technical research on the materials that go into beer left them far from happy with the ingredients used in many national keg beers. Malted barley, the traditional cereal used to brew beer, was being adulterated with such inferior ingredients as malt extract, flaked maize, rice grits, potato starch and pasta flour. True hops were also being replaced or mixed with hops were also being replaced or mixed with hop extracts. Chemicals were being introduced into the brewing process to give beers fake sparkle and false foaming heads, and some brewers were experimenting with new devices to speed up the natural brewing process. All of these processes gave the drinkers poorer beer - but the brewers bigger profits.

When CAMRA revealed this type of information it quickly became recognised as the beer drinkers' champion and an organisation with authority and expertise. Even the most dedicated keg drinkers heard of CAMRA and grasped its basic ideas, while lovers of traditional beer gave enthusiastic support to its beer festivals and marches, demonstration and meetings throughout the country.

CAMRA has never claimed to represent all beer drinkers but it can rightly say that it is the only organisation that speaks for those on the customers' side of the bar. While the major plank of the Campaign is the fight for traditional beer, it also demands choice for all pubs so that drinkers can find a range of beers, both processed and real. The Campaign has attacked the tarty modernisation of many pubs, ripping out out of public bars and the introduction of expensive electronic machines that replace the centuries-old genuine pub games. It has produced a series of reports for government bodies and official inquiries, aimed at giving *all* beer drinkers a better deal.

How beer is brewed

How beer is brewed

Ingredients: Malted barley (partially germinated barley which has been heated to produce sugars vital to the brewing process), water, hops, and yeast.

Method: 1. Malted barley is ground into a coarse powder called grist which is stewed with hot water (known as 'liquor' in the trade) in a large vessel called a mash tun. Quantities are carefully measured and balanced for each individual brew and different malts and barleys are used for the various styles of beer; Mild, bitter, stout, porter etc.

2. The resulting thick liquid (wort) is left to stand so that it absorbs the sugars from the malt. It is then run off into a large kettle called a copper and the remaining grist is sparged (sprayed with hot water) to extract any last sugars, which are added to the copper. The grist is spent and sold off to farmers for animal fodder.

3. The wort is boiled with hops for about two hours. The hops, which later act as a preservative, here add bitterness, the boiling killing off bacteria at the same time. The wort is then passed through a giant strainer, called a hop back, cooled and run into fermenting vessels, where yeast is added (pitched).

4. Yeast is a one-celled fungus that multiplies in sweet liquids. The yeast converts the sugars in the wort into alcohol and carbon dioxide gas - a process called fermentation. A thick creamy head of yeast forms on the wort, which is skimmed off and reused. Enough yeast is left in the liquid for fermentation to continue. About five days after fermentation starts the sugars in the brew are almost exhausted, the yeast sinks to the bottom of the tank and primary fermentation is finished. As the yeast multiplies with each brew, the same strain is often used for many years. The surplus is sold to such companies as Marmite.

5. The rough or green beer is now run into conditioning tanks, where the yeast continues to work on the remaining sugars.

6. The beer is then put into casks. Finings (normally a fish extract, but occasionally synthetic) are added to draw the yeast to the bottom and so clear the beer. Sometimes extra sugars are introduced to encourage a strong secondary fermentation. The casks are then read for delivery.

7. Real beer has to stand for up to 48 hours in the pub cellar while the sediment settles. A tap is knocked into the cask ready for serving the beer and a soft wooden peg is driven into the shive hole (a small hole in the top of the cask) to let out the

naturally occurring carbon dioxide. Once the beer is ready to serve, the soft peg is replaced by a hard one which regulates the escape of gas. However, once a cask has been tapped and air is allowed to enter its beer will only remain drinkable for a few days.

Keg beer: Keg beer follows the same procedure as above, up to point 5. Here instead of conditioning and running off into casks, it is chilled, filtered, usually pasteurised and then run off into containers called kegs. These have just one opening into which carbon dioxide is introduced to force the beer to the bar when the tap is opened. Keg beer, being a dead product, does not continue to ferment or condition in the container and does not need to stand for any length of time.

Lager: Lager follows a similar procedure, too, up to point 4. But different malts provide the wort and the strain of yeast used sinks to the bottom, rather than floating on the top of the wort. Thus, lager is bottom fermented. During fermentation, the vessel is kept at a lower temperature than for ale.
             After fermentation true lager are left to condition at the brewery for several months in cold (around 0^0 C), sealed containers. Very often, in Britain this process last only weeks and then the lager (commonly many degrees weaker than its European namesake) follows the same schedule and serving procedure as keg beer. On the Continent many lagers are not pasteurised or filtered, and are dispensed without the addition of gas, relying instead on the pressure of their own natural CO_2 output.

CASK SIZES & MEASURES

Butt	108 gallons (no longer used)
Puncheon	72 gallons (no longer used)
Hogshead	54 gallons (now rarely used)
Barrel	36 gallons
Kilderkin or kiln	18 gallons
Firkin	9 gallons
Pin	4½ gallons (now rarely used)
Yard of Ale	41/4-4½ pints (not standard)
Gallon	8 pints
Quart	2 pints (a quarter gallon)
Pint	20 fluid onces
Nip	Third of a pint (a common bottle size)
Gill	5 fluid onces (a quarter pint mistakenly a half pint in some areas)

Scoure: The Good Beer Guide

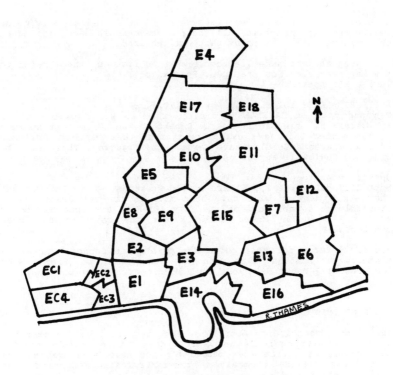

Area covered
by the Guide

We decided not to re-invent the wheel so the format of this guide is the same as last time. All the pubs have again been plotted on our maps so an A-Z is once again not required.

Following the pub name are some bracketed figures, these refer to the map reference for that pub. For example:
In the EC1 section -

ARTILLERY ARMS: 102 Bunhill Row. (D1/02).
The pub name in CAPITALS indicates that is sells real ale. D1 indicates that the pub is in the D part of the EC1 map in section 1. The number 2 is it's exact location in that section. Prefixes such as The, and Ye Olde have largely been ignored. Therefore 'Ye Olde Red Cow' will appear under R.

Opening hours:
Most City pubs (EC1, 2, 3, 4) are closed weekends. Where this is not the case a mention will have been made in the pub description. Similarly most pubs outside the City (E1-E18) are open on Sunday 12-3 and 7-10:30. Where this is not the case it has been mentioned.

Regular updates for this guide are printed in London Drinker a monthly publication that can be subscribed to from: Stan Tompkins, 122 Manor Way, Uxbridge, Middlesex. £6 for one year.

SCOPE OF THIS GUIDE

This East London & City Beer Guide includes all public houses but only those with real ale get a full description. Establishments that demand an entrance or membership fee have been omitted as have those calling themselves brassieres/restaurants/bars that sell no real ale.

The area covered is from the City postal districts EC1 to EC4 and from E1 in the west to E18 in the east. Though three pubs in E4 are uniquely also in Essex, pubs in Essex are covered by the Essex Beer Guide, a new edition for 1991 is available from the address below.

No comment has been made regarding the quality of the beer sold. The publication "The Good Beer Guide" covers this aspect of real ale and can be bought from CAMRA Ltd, 34 Alma Road, St Albans, Herts AL1 3BW.

EC1

Stations - Angel (Northern), Old Street (BR/Northern), Barbican and Farringdon (BR/Circle/Metropolitan).

A mixed area extending from Smithfield and the Barbican up to the City Road and including all of Clerkenwell but only the fringes of the City. For the most part it is residential and there are a number of good locals pubs. In the evenings a surprising number have live music on offer.

Smithfield and the area near Farringdon Street station are the best for finding the regional brewers' pubs, although in these days free houses are cropping up all over the place. Smithfield also offers a range of places with early morning opening for the Market. Strictly speaking you should have business there, but most pubs are flexible about this.

In parts of this area the pubs serve mainly the office trade and you should check opening time carefully, particularly on Saturday when those in this category may be shut. In the more residential areas there may be afternoon and early evening closing on a Saturday. To help you in this respect treat all pubs as being closed at weekends unless otherwise stated in the pub description.

ANGEL: 73 City Road. (D1/1) *Ind Coope Taylor Walker.*
TAYLOR WALKER BEST BITTER, TETLEY BITTER, IND COOPE BURTON ALE, YOUNGS SPECIAL. See John Thirkell's write-up of the pub (by the staircase). A delightful one-bar pub which will send your food and drinks up to you to the upstairs restaurant that doubles as a function room. Hot meals at lunchtimes and by request in the evenings. Snacks at all times. Darts upstairs except when there are functions there. Opens Monday to Friday 11-11 and closed weekends.

ARTILLERY ARMS: 102 Bunhill Row. (D1/2) *Fullers.*
FULLERS LONDON PRIDE, ESB. Small ex-Hanbury Buxton Truman pub. Very keen darts house. A tradition of live piano on Wednesday evenings with jazz on Friday night. There is food at all sessions and a feature is roast Sunday lunch. Open Monday to Friday 11-11, Saturday 11-3 and 7-11 and normal Sunday hours. Function room/restaurant.

BARLEY MOW: 50 Long Lane. (C2/3) *Whitbreads.*
FLOWERS IPA, MARSTONS PEDIGREE. Extensive wood panelling in a natural finish gives this market pub along with the bric-a-brac an air of cosy comfort. Children and function rooms. Food at lunchtimes. Open 11.30-9 Monday to Friday but closed weekends.

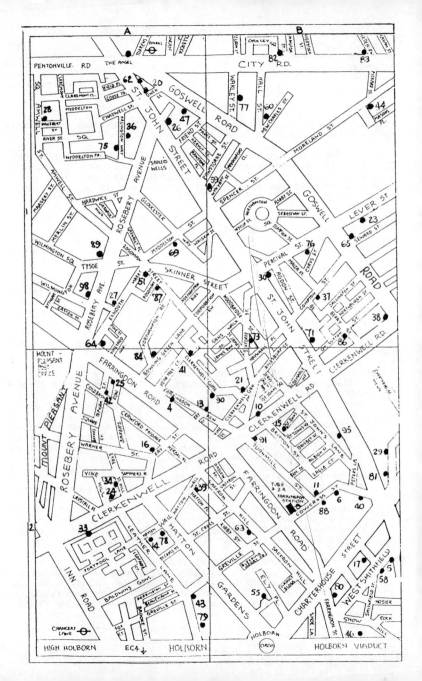

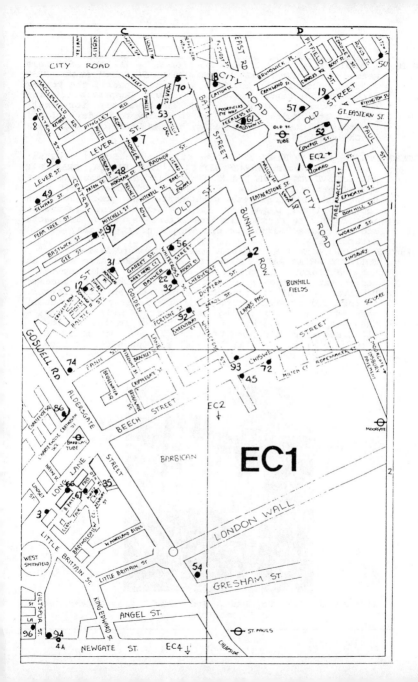

BETSEY TROTWOOD: 56 Farringdon Road. **(A2/4)** *Shepherd Neame*. *SHEPHERD NEAME MASTER BREW, SHEPHERD NEAME BEST BITTER.* Formerly the Butchers Arms and latterly the Betsey after the Dickens character in David Copperfield. Wine bar, and function room which is available for small parties etc. Hours: 11.30 - 11.00 Monday to Friday closed Saturday but open normal Sunday hours. Darts. Cooked meals lunchtimes.

BILBO BAGGINS BEER & BANJO EMPORIUM: 122 Newgate Street. **(C2/5a)** *Free House*. *ADNAMS BITTER, TETLEY BITTER, BRAKSPEAR PA, GREENE KING ABBOT ALE.* Former Indian restaurant that opened early 1991. Now an up-to-date luncheon spot with downstairs bar complete with darts and pool. Function room. A stones throw from the Viaduct Tavern. Brakspears is a favourite of the licensee Peter he of the moustache and antipodes (Kiwi) accent. Open Monday — Friday 11-11 Saturday 11-3.

BISHOPS FINGER: 8 West Smithfield. (B2/5) *Shepherd Neame*. *SHEPHERD NEAME MASTER BREW BISHOPS FINGER.* Also known as the Rutland. Large one bar pub with upstairs restaurant/function room. Name recalls that which used to be given in Kent to signposts shaped like an index finger. Largest and clearest price list we've ever seen, no doubt here what you are paying, no need to hide the area's cheapest pints outside of happy hours. Darts. Snacks at all times with cooked meals at lunchtime. Open 11.30-10.30 Monday to Friday. Sat 11.30-3. Closed Sun eves. Postmen in uniform may not be served! I'm surprised they get any mail.

Blue Angel: 415 City Road. *Ind Coope Taylor Walker. Pub demolished.*

BLUE POSTS: 86/89 Cowcross Street. (B2/6) *Bass Charrington.*
CHARRINGTON IPA, BASS. Blue posts marked a boundary or area in the open air market. The pub has a curious ceramic frieze depicting waves occasionally surmounted by a red tulip or rose styled flower. Food at all times. Open 11-11 Monday to Friday. Closed weekends. Darts.

BRITANNIA: 94 Ironmonger Row. (C1/7) *Whitbreads.*
WHITBREAD FLOWERS ORIGINAL. The present building dates from 1939. Darts and live music Friday, Saturday and Sunday are the attractions in this pub with a circular bar where the original doorways to the snug and saloon remain. Cooked meals lunchtime and snacks are available in this friendly local which is open Monday to Saturday 12-11 and normal Sunday hours.

BRITISH LION: 155 Central Street. (C1/8) *Whitbreads.*
WHITBREAD FLOWERS ORIGINAL. This is one of the few out and out music pubs. Monday night is talent night with music for everyone Thursday, Friday, Saturday and Sunday evenings. Hot and cold food available at all time weekdays. Open Monday to Thursday 11-11, 11-1am Friday and Saturday and normal Sunday hours.

Bulls Head: 125 Central Street. (C1/9) *Bass Charrington.*
No real ale!

BURGUNDY BENS: 102/108 Clerkenwell Road. (B2/10) *Free House.*
DAVY'S OLD WALLOP. Has an outside drinking area. Cellar bar marks another Davys of London pub where Courage Directors and Kronenborg masquerade under house names.Cooked food in the restaurant from 11.30-3 and 5-8. Open Monday to Friday 11.30-8.30 and closed weekends.

CASTLE: 43/5 Cowcross Street. (B2/11) *Bass Charrington.*
CHARRINGTON IPA, BASS. Large busy semi-circular bar: a pawnbroker's sign and a large painting commemorate a former licensee of this pub lending George IV money for a bet with a watch as security, upon the successful outcome of which he accepted as reward the right to practise as a pawnbroker which of course has not been used for many years. Darts, pool and function room. Snacks at all times and cooked food lunchtime. Open 11-11 Monday to Friday but closed weekends.

CHEQUERS: 44 Old Street. (C1/12) *Whitbreads.*
FLOWERS IPA, WHITBREAD FLOWERS ORIGINAL, BODDINGTONS BITTER. One-bar pub that is a real local. Cooked meals lunchtime and snacks at all times. A very cosy atmosphere helped by the lack of any drastic changes over the years. Open all permitted hours.

CITY PRIDE: 28 Farringdon Lane. (A2/13) *Fullers.*
CHISWICK, FULLERS LONDON PRIDE, ESB. Formerly the White Swan (Charrington), a Toby house bought by Fullers and expanded to take on neighbouring premises. Bright and friendly. Function room with dartboard. Food at all times including Sunday. Open all permitted hours.

CLOCK HOUSE: 82 Leather Lane. (A2/14) *Bass Charrington.*
CHARRINGTON IPA, BASS. Cooked food and snacks are available weekdays at all times in this pub which has a most unusual mirrored ceiling. Darts and pool. Function room available. Open Monday to Wendesday 11-3 and 5-11, Thursday and Friday 11-11, Saturday 11-3.30 and 8-11 plus normal Sunday hours.

COACH & HORSES: 2 St John's Square. (B2/15) *Whitbreads.*
WHITBREAD WETHERED, WHITBREAD FLOWERS ORIGINAL, BODDINGTONS BITTER, BRAKSPEAR PA. This Baldwin Inns pub has an outside drinking area. Darts. Hot and cold food at all times. Open Monday to Friday 11-11. Closed weekends but the function room is available at all times.

COACH & HORSES: 26/28 Ray Street. (A2/16) *Ind Coope Taylor* Walker. *IND COOPE BURTON ALE, TAYLOR WALKER BEST BITTER, TETLEY BITTER, YOUNGS SPECIAL.* Must be one of the nicest looking pubs both inside and outside in the area. Cooked meals lunchtimes snacks at all times. Garden and darts. Now open all permitted hours but closed on Saturday evenings.

COCK TAVERN: East Poultry Avenue-Central Markets. (B2/17) *Free* House. *COURAGE BEST BITTER, JOHN SMITH'S BITTER, BODDINGTONS BITTER.* Basically a large restaurant comprising of two rooms along which runs a bar. Children are welcome in the restaurant which is named 'Steakmaster'. Karaoke on Friday night till 11pm. Breakfast is served from 5.30-9.30am and re-opens 11-4 or later as custom dictates. Closed weekends except for functions.

COLONEL JASPERS: 190/196 City Road. (D1/18) *Free House.*
Sells Davys Old Jollop which is not unlike Courage Directors. Comfortable no frills cellar bar where children are catered for in the restaurant. There is also a function room. No-music policy and the beer can be bought by the gallon and port by the pint. Open Monday to Friday 11.30-4 and 5.30-8.30, closed weekends.

CROSBY HEAD: 243 Old Street. (D1/19) *Grand Met-Trumans.*
WEBSTERS YORKSHIRE BITTER, FULLERS LONDON PRIDE. Live Country and Western music on Saturday striptease on Thursday and Friday and if that isn't enough entertainment darts and pool are available. This one bar pub provides hot meals at lunchtimes and snacks at all times. Open

Monday to Friday 11-11 Saturday 11-3 and 7-11 with normal Sunday hours.

Crown & Woolpack: 394 St John Street. (A1/20) *Courage.*
No beer - closed.

CROWN TAVERN: 43 Clerkenwell Green. (B2/21) *Ind Coope Nicholson Free Hse. TETLEY BITTER, IND COOPE BURTON ALE, ADNAMS BITTER, WADWORTH 6X, GREENE KING IPA.* The change in beers reflect the 'ownership' of this smart, friendly bric-a-brac festooned three-bar pub. Look for the snob screens. Restaurant doubles as a function room. Opens Monday to Friday 11.30-11. Saturday 12-11. Closed Sunday.

DRUM & MONKEY: 167 Whitecross Street. (C1/22) *Whitbreads. WHITBREAD WETHERED, FLOWERS IPA, GREENE KING ABBOT ALE.* Formally the British Queen. Recently refurbished inside and out. Darts and pool. Restaurant doubles as a function room. Open Monday to Thursday 11-7, Friday 11-11, Saturday 11-5 and closed Sundays.

DUKE OF WELLINGTON: 21/25 Lever Street. (B1/23) *Ind Coope* Taylor Walker. *TETLEY BITTER, IND COOPE BURTON ALE.* Beers the same price! On Friday, Saturday and Sunday a quartet and singer provide the entertainment, almost a big band in today's era of the disco. Hot and cold food at lunchtime and by request in the evening. Darts. Open Monday to Thursday 11-3 and 5-11, Friday and Saturday 11-3 and 8-12 with normal Sunday hours.

DUKE OF YORK: 156 Clerkenwell Road. (A2/24) *Grand Met-Watneys. WEBSTERS YORKSHIRE BITTER, RUDDLES BEST RUDDLES COUNTY.* Due for refit. One bar pub decorated in Laura Ashley/Habitat style. Cooked meals at all times. Open all permitted hours except Saturday and Sunday evenings when it is closed. Function room.

EAGLE: 159 Farringdon Road. (A2/25) *Free House. SHEFFORD BITTER, RUDDLES BEST.* Free house with a bottle tie to Watney. The food is based on European Farmhouse style. Upstairs is an art gallery. Open noon to 11pm Monday to Friday. Closed weekends.

EMPRESS OF RUSSIA: 362 St John Street. (A1/26) *Whitbreads. WHITBREAD WETHERED, WHITBREAD FLOWERS ORIGINAL, CASTLE EDEN, MARSTONS PEDIGREE.* Food is available six days a week (not Sunday). Darts and pool played here and a function room is available. It is rumoured that a certain part-time editor of Whats Brewing has been barred from here. Open Monday to Friday 11.30-11. Saturday 11.30-3 and 6-11. Normal Sunday hours.

EXMOUTH ARMS: 23 Exmouth Market. (A1/27) *Courage. COURAGE BEST BITTER.* Darts are played except at the weekends when the disco is on the oche. Hot and cold food lunchtimes and evenings, restricted menu at weekends. Open all permitted hours.

FOUNTAIN: 68 Amwell Street. (A1/28) *Ind Coope Taylor Walker.* *TETLEY BITTER, IND COOPE BURTON ALE.* An unspoilt pub in central London with many original features to make it a gem. Snacks lunchtime. Still retains its public and saloon bars. Darts. Open all permitted hours.

FOX & ANCHOR: 115 Charterhouse Street. (B2/29) *Ind Coope Taylor Walker. TETLEY BITTER, IND COOPE BURTON ALE, YOUNGS SPECIAL.* This pub has an exceptional frontage where the name has been worked into the wall and floor in a most unusual style. It can be seen that the central windows have been doors possibly indicating that this was a three bar pub. Restaurant/function room. Open Monday to Friday 6am-3pm.

GEORGE & DRAGON: 240 St John Street. (B1/30) *Grand Met-Trumans. WEBSTERS YORKSHIRE BITTER, YOUNGERS SCOTCH, RUDDLES BEST, RUDDLES COUNTY.* One of the few pubs where the range of beers has increased, albeit to detriment of the Truman beers. Scotch currently 99p. This managed house has an outside drinking area, darts and pool (upstairs). On Sunday evening jazz is played by a group from the nearby City of London University. Hot and cold food available at all times. Tiles depicting St George and the Dragon. Open Monday to Thursday 11-3 and 5-11, 11-11 Friday and Saturday. Plus Sunday.

George IV: 39 Goswell Road. *Courage.*
Pub demolished.

GOLDEN HIND: 58 Old Street. (C1/31) *Whitbreads.*
CASTLE EDEN, FLOWERS IPA , WHITBREAD FLOWERS ORIGINAL, MARSTONS PEDIGREE. Formerly the Vertical Refreshment Co. and Golden Cock. Roof garden. Darts can be played upstairs. Children's room available when function room is not in use. Snacks and cooked meals available at all times. Open Monday to Saturday 11.30-11 plus permitted Sunday hours.

GREEN MAN & STILL: 161 Whitecross Street. (C1/32) *Courage.*
COURAGE BEST BITTER, DIRECTORS BITTER , YOUNGS SPECIAL. This market pub has an outside drinking area but the upstairs room is not in use. One-bar pub with darts and pool. Hot food available lunchtimes. Open all permitted hours.

GRIFFIN: 125 Clerkenwell Road. (A2/33) *Grand Met-Watneys.*
WEBSTERS YORKSHIRE BITTER, RUDDLES BEST. Stands on the site of Reid's Griffin Brewery. Two bar pub with darts and pool. Tongue-and-groove panelling give this pub a particular welcoming atmosphere. Live music at weekends. Darts and pool. Food at all times. Open all permitted hours.

GUNMAKERS ARMS: 13 Eyre Street Hill. (A2/34) *Bass Charrington.*
CHARRINGTON IPA, BASS. Cat swinging still not practical. Snacks at all times - cooked meals lunchtime. Darts. Clerkenwell's heritage of world renowned clockmakers who in some instances manufactured gun mechanisms is remembered in this delightful pub. Open all permitted hours.

HAND & SHEARS: 1 Middle Street. (C2/35) *Courage.*
COURAGE BEST BITTER, DIRECTORS BITTER. This pub was closed late 1990 for six months whilst supportive repairs were made to this listed building. Panelling had to be taken out and replaced. The standard of work was very high and to a casual glance no changes are visible except for a short door. There is now an upstairs bar in the restaurant/function room bringing the total of bars to four. Darts. Open Monday - Friday 11.30-11 and Sunday lunchtime.

HARLEQUIN: 27 Arlington Way. (A1/36) *Grand Met-Watneys.*
WEBSTERS YORKSHIRE BITTER , RUDDLES BEST. Hot and cold snacks at all times bar Sunday. Look carefully and note many original features. Open Monday to Saturday 11.30-3 and 5.15-11.30 and Sunday lunchtime only. Try celebrity spotting here.

Harrow: 64 Compton Street. (B1/37) *Grand Met-Watneys.*
No beer - closed.

Hat & Feathers: 2 Clerkenwell Road. (B1/38) *Ind Coope Taylor Walker. No beer - closed.*

HAT & TUN: 3 Hatton Wall. (A2/39) *Bass Charrington.*
CHARRINGTON IPA. It is always a pleasure to return to this pub where many original features remind one of how pubs used to be. The carved wood surround at the back of the bar is worth a visit. Snacks at all times and hot food lunchtime and on request in the evenings. Function room available. Open Monday to Friday 11-11. Closed weekends.

HOPE: 94 Cowcross Street. (B2/40) *Grand Met-Watneys.*
WEBSTERS YORKSHIRE BITTER, RUDDLES COUNTY YOUNGS BITTER. c1855 bowed and curved, etched windows, silver inlaid mirrors mark move of live animal market to Caledonian Market. Built as an inn during the days between the medieval and modern market in an area which was then parkland. It is alleged that the pub was erected over the Path of Hope leading to a sanctuary church, which condemned prisoners from Newgate Prison were led, if they received a last minute reprieve. Restaurant. Function room. Open Monday - Friday 6.30 - 9.30 and 11-6, closed weekends.

HORSESHOE: 24 Clerkenwell Close. (A2/41) *Courage.*
COURAGE BEST BITTER, DIRECTORS BITTER. Many original features under threat of refurbishment. Function room and garden. They hope to extend cooked meals to the evenings. Snacks at all times. Open Monday to Friday 11-1 Saturday 11-3 and 7-11. Closed Sundays. A keen darts pub.

Horseshoe & Magpie: 5 Topham Street. (A2/42) *Grand Met-Watneys. No beer - closed.*

Joint & Gem: Cowcross Street. *Grand Met-Watneys. No longer a pub.*

KING OF DIAMONDS: Greville Street. (A2/43) *Ind Coope Burton.*
TETLEY BITTER, IND COOPE BURTON ALE. An unusual feature of this pub is the upstairs patio garden (open from Easter) which overlooks the market. Children welcome. Two function rooms and a restaurant which is open at lunchtimes only. Darts. Open Monday to Friday 11-9, Saturday 11-3. Closed Saturday evenings and all Sunday.

Kings Arms: 18 Moreland Street. (B1/44) *Banks & Taylor.*
No beer - closed.

KINGS HEAD: 49 Chiswell Street. (D2/45) *Whitbreads.*
WHITBREAD WETHERED, WHITBREAD FLOWERS ORIGINAL, BODDINGTONS BITTER. A 60ft extension is proposed that will become a restaurant and will double as a function room at other times. When you leave note the Victorian flush post boxes to the right of the Chiswell Street exit. Open all permitted hours.

KNIGHTS: 54 Holborn Viacuct. (B2/46) *Free House.*
RAYMENTS SPECIAL, GREENE KING IPA, GREENE KING ABBOT ALE. A recent if pricey addition to the ranks of real ale establishments. This very smart and relaxed pub also boasts a restaurant which doubles as a function room seven days a week. There is an outside drinking area. Cooked meals lunchtime snacks at all times. Hot food evenings on request. Open Monday to Friday 11-11. Closed weekends.

LADY OWEN ARMS: 285 Goswell Road. (A1/47) *Ind Coope Burton.*
YOUNGS SPECIAL. No longer really a public house as it charges an admission charge. For punks.

Langton Arms: 1 Norman Street. (C1/48) *Bass Charrington.*
No beer - closed.

LEOPARD: 33 Seward Street. (C1/49) *Free House.*
COURAGE BEST BITTER, DIRECTORS BITTER, GREENE KING IPA GREENE KING ABBOT ALE, CORNISH DRAUGHT STEAM BITTER. There has been a pub on this site since 1740. It is still possible to make out where the dividing walls were for off sales, public and saloon bars. Garden. Darts. Food available lunchtimes. Open Monday to Friday 11.30-3 and 5.30-11. Closed Saturday but open on Sunday lunchtime.

London Apprentice: 333 Old Street. (D1/50) *Free House.*
No real ale!

LONDON SPA: 70 Exmouth Market. (A1/51) *Free House.*
DIRECTORS BITTER, BASS, CHARRINGTON IPA. Reasonably priced Finch's pub that locates the site of the entrance to a once popular open air resort. A rare pub to find where public bar prices are 3p cheaper. Three function rooms also mark this wall-tiled pub as unusual. Hot and cold snacks are available at all times but restricted menu at

weekends. Darts. Open all permitted hours. Stop Press: Finch's pubs bought by Youngs August 1991.

LORD NELSON: 17 Mora Street. (C1/52) *Grand Met-Watneys.*
WEBSTERS YORKSHIRE BITTER, RUDDLES BEST, RUDDLES COUNTY. Noted stripper house lunchtimes and every evening except Sunday. DJ every night also except Sunday because the pub is closed. Snacks available at all times from four bars. Pool has a bar for itself away from the other distractions. Open Monday to Friday 11.30-3.30 and 5.30-11, Saturday 12-3.30 and 7-11, Sunday 12-3 only.

LORD NELSON: 262/4 Old Street. (D1/53) *Grand Met-Watneys.*
WEBSTERS YORKSHIRE BITTER, RUDDLES BEST. Nelson memorabilia and photos of the locality decorate the walls of this two bar pub that has a function room. Darts and pool. Food lunchtime only. Opens Monday to Friday 11-11. Closed weekends.

LORD RAGLAN: 61 St Martin's-le-Grand. (C2/54) *Courage.*
COURAGE BEST BITTER, JOHN SMITH'S BITTER, DIRECTORS BITTER. Called the Bush and then the Mourning Bush until its reconstruction in 1855. Multibar pub with eating and drinking on about four levels. This pub was once entitled to open 24 hours a day by royal edict after the landlord opened to King Charles II in the early hours of the morning. The present name is in memory of a hero of the Crimean War. Opens 11-9 Monday to Friday. Closed weekends.

Metropolitan Tavern: 95 Farringdon Road. *Free House.*
Pub demolished.

YE OLDE MITRE TAVERN: Ely Court. (B2/55) *Ind Coope Friary Meux.*

FRIARY MEUX BEST BITTER, TETLEY BITTER, IND COOPE BURTON ALE. Ask for the handout on the history of the pub. Darts are played upstairs and hot and cold food at all times. Function room and outside drinking area. No music. Open Monday to Friday 11-11. Closed weekends.

MOLLY BLOOMS: 142 Whitecross Street. (C1/56) *Grand Met-Watneys.*
RUDDLES BEST, RUDDLES COUNTY, FULLERS LONDON PRIDE. The pub now houses the HQ of Saxon Inns hence there is no function room now. Formerly the Spread Eagle. Refurbishment has introduced a separate eating area for the cooked meals served lunchtime. Snacks are also available at this time. Live music Friday evening (folk rock). Now only one bar. Outside drinking area. Open all permitted hours.

MURPHYS TAVERNS: 1 Vince Street. (D1/57) *Grand Met-Watneys.*
WEBSTERS YORKSHIRE BITTER, RUDDLES BEST. Formerly the Gluepot. A two-bar pub that has live music for the family on Saturday night. Darts and pool. Hot lunches and snacks

at all times. There is also an outdoor drinking area in this one of three pubs belonging to Murphys Taverns. Open Mon to Fri 11-11   Sat 11-4 and 7-11 and open Sundays.

THE NEW MARKET: 25 Smithfield Street. (B2/58) *Bass Charrington. CHARRINGTON IPA, BASS.* This pub has had three name changes in the last 6 years, from the 'Newmarket Hotel' to 'Newmarket Tavern' and now the 'The New Market'. An interesting collection of bummerees (market porters) badges. The name bummeree is supposed to have originated from Billingsgate Fish Market, when porters who served the bum boats, became bummerees. Function room, darts, food at all times. Upstairs ladies loo. Open 6.30-9.30am and 11-11 Mon-Fri. Closed weekends.

NEW RED LION: 292 St John Street. (B1/59) *Grand Met-Watneys. RUDDLES BEST, YOUNGS BITTER.* Three dart teams and two pool teams. TV in the public bar. Used by the City University staff. Amazing collection of Guinness and celebration ales. Cash register which was last repaired in 1915 only goes to £5.3.11 three farthings. Hot and cold food Monday to Friday lunchtimes only.   Open all permitted hours. Enjoy the garden.

OAKLEY ARMS: 32 Hall Street. (B1/60) *Grand Met-Trumans. WEBSTERS YORKSHIRE BITTER, RUDDLES BEST, FLOWERS IPA.* A very large pub which has a tiled exterior and style of glazing that has almost disappeared from the London area. Darts, pool and jukebox are played here. Hot food and snacks at lunchtime. Open Monday to Saturday 11-11. Closed Sunday evenings.

OLD FOUNTAIN: 3 Baldwin Street. (D1/61) *Whitbreads. FLOWERS IPA, CASTLE EDEN, WHITBREAD FLOWERS ORIGINAL, WINTER ROYAL (WINTER ONLY), BODDINGTONS BITTER, MARSTONS PEDIGREE.* This 200 year old pub is one of the few in the East London & City area selling Castle Eden. It may well get its name from a local well or fountain in an area that was noted for underground rivers. The old style of the pub has been well kept up and there is a preservation order on the building. Hot food lunchtimes and snacks at all times. Open Monday to Friday 11-11, Saturday 11-3 only, normal Sunday hours.

OLD RED LION: 418 St John Street. (A1/62) *Bass Charrington. CHARRINGTON IPA, BASS.* Pool is very popular in this two-bar pub. The long bar is separated by a most unusual engraved glass partition. Snacks available at all times. Open all permitted hours.

ONE TUN: 125 Saffron Hill. (B2/63) *Grand Met-Watneys. WEBSTERS YORKSHIRE BITTER, RUDDLES BEST.* Surveyor asked to leave which makes an unpleasant change from the hospitality from most of the other pubs in the area. Probably one best avoided.

PENNY BLACK: 106 Farringdon Road. (A1/64) *Grand Met-Watneys.*
WEBSTERS YORKSHIRE BITTER, RUDDLES COUNTY. Very popular pub and at the current prices why not? Two bars, darts and pool in the public bar. Hot and cold food available at all times. Function room. Open all permitted hours. It used to be called 'The Clerkenwell Tavern'.

PHEASANT & FIRKIN: 166 Goswell Road. (B1/65) *Free House.*
WEBSTERS YORKSHIRE BITTER, RUDDLES COUNTY, PHEASANT, BARBARIAN, DOGBOLTER, REAL CIDER. Ex Bruces pub now owned by Stakis Leisure, formerly the Old Ivy House (Charrington). All beers are now cask conditioned. Disappointing to see 'Watney' beers in a pub like this. Hot food lunchtime and on request in the evenings. Cold food at all times. Darts. Open Monday to Thursday 11.30-3 and 5-11, Friday 11-11, Saturday 12-3 and 7-11 with normal Sunday hours. The cider is from Westons.

YE OLDE RED COW: 72 Long Lane. (C2/66) *Grand Met-Watneys.*
WEBSTERS YORKSHIRE BITTER, YOUNGS BITTER. Even if not eating, the delightful upstairs restaurant should be viewed if possible it has an old sign giving licensing restrictions. The cellars and ground floor are reputed to go back to the 1400s. Unexplained happenings give rise to the thought the pub is haunted. The restaurant is open 6am to 9. The upstairs bar opens at 6pm is closed Sunday and Monday evenings. Open all permitted hours. Function room.

RISING SUN: 38 Cloth Fair. (C2/67) *Samuel Smith.*
OLD BREWERY BITTER, SAMUEL SMITH MUSEUM ALE. Grave-diggers used to meet here in the upper room to discuss sale of cadavers to doctors at nearby Barts. The building was for a few years used as offices until purchased by Sam Smiths a couple of years ago. It was previously a Courage house. The restaurant doubles as a function room in the evening. Cooked meals and cold snacks at all times. Darts. Open Monday to Friday 11.30-11. Saturday 12-3 and 5-11 plus normal Sunday hours.

THE ROSEBERRY: 59/61 Exmouth Market. (A1/68) *Free House.*
BODDINGTONS BITTER, ADNAMS BITTER, TETLEY BITTER, IND COOPE BURTON ALE, FULLERS LONDON PRIDE, ESB. The frontage is all folding doors, which give the pub a unique atmosphere when open. Hot and cold food is available at all times during the week with a restricted menu at weekends. On occasions selected beers will be a pound a pint. Open all permitted hours except Sunday evening when it is closed.

Royal Mail: 18 Myddleton Street. (A1/69) *Bass Charrington.*
No real ale!

ROYAL STAR: 220 City Road. (C1/70) *Grand Met-Watneys.*
WEBSTERS YORKSHIRE BITTER, RUDDLES BEST, RUDDLES COUNTY.
Darts and pool plus a disco at weekends. A
horseshoe-shaped bar gives the pub a two-bar style. This
wood-panelled pub has hot food lunchtimes and snacks at
all times. There is also an outside drinking area. Open
Monday to Thursday 11-3 and 5-11, Friday 11-11, Saturday
11-3.30 and 7-11 plus normal Sunday hours.

ST. JOHN OF JERUSALEM: 160 St. John Street. (B1/71) *Ind Coope*
Taylor Walker. *TETLEY BITTER, IND COOPE BURTON ALE.* Modern
one-bar pub on the site of the former Cannon Brewery.
Food orientated pub with a large eating area where
children can be accommodated at the discretion of the
management. A selection of musical instruments adorn the
walls. Unusually for central London there are car parking
facilities at the rear for patrons in the NCP park. Open
Monday to Wednesday 12-7 and Thursday to Friday 12-8.
Closed weekends.

ST. PAULS TAVERN: 56 Chiswell Street. (D2/72) *Whitbreads.*
FLOWERS IPA, BODDINGTONS BITTER, MARSTONS PEDIGREE.
Breakfasts from 8-10. Coffee available all day in this
four roomed pub with two bars. Collection of agricultural
implements on the wood-panelled walls. Open Monday to
Friday 11-11. Closed weekends but available for functions.

SEKFORDE ARMS: 34 Sekforde Street. (B1/73) *Young & Co.*
*YOUNGS BITTER, YOUNGS SPECIAL, WINTER WARMER (WINTER
ONLY).* Formerly a Charrington pub and latterly a free
house. The pub is built on land belonging to Thomas
Sekforde, who died in 1588. The Sekfordes came originally
from Suffolk and the pub still maintains its contacts
there in Woodbridge with inter-pub visits. Opens Monday to
Friday 11-11, Saturday 8pm-11pm and normal Sunday hours.
Excellent food at all times.

SHAKESPEARE: 2 Goswell Road. (C2/74) *Ind Coope Taylor Walker.*
TETLEY BITTER, YOUNGS SPECIAL, IND COOPE BURTON ALE. A
large pub with lots of nooks and crannies. One can check
on any weight loss in the gents, normally a facility of
train stations. Two bars, one L shaped, the other a small
one at the other end where the sofas are. Lively and
comfortable in an effortlessly smart style. Hot and cold
food at all times. A jukebox provides the music. Open
11-11 Moonay to Friday. Saturday 11-5 and 7.30-11. Sunday
12-3.

SHAKESPEARES HEAD: 1 Arlington Way. (A1/75) *Courage.*
COURAGE BEST BITTER, DIRECTORS BITTER. Small immaculate
theatre pub just behind Sadlers Wells. Food at all times.
Open Monday to Saturday 11-3 and 5.30-11. Normal Sunday
hours.

SHAKESPEARES HEAD: 46 Percival Street. (B1/76) *Bass Charrington.*

CHARRINGTON IPA. Another pub with an outside drinking area. Live music played here at weekends in this family pub. Cooked meals lunchtimes and snacks at all times. Darts and pool. Public and saloon bars with different prices. A bit of a gem. Open Monday to Friday 11-11 Saturday 11-4 and 7.30-11 and normal Sunday hours.

Sidney Arms: 9 Wakley Street. (B1/77) *Grand Met-Watneys. No real ale!*

SIMPSONS: 58 Hatton Garden. (A2/78) *Free House.*
GREENE KING IPA. This ex-Bass house was called the Rose. It is now a free house with a very swish bar-cafe style restaurant. The range of real ales may be extended at a future date. There is an outside drinking area. Private parties are catered for when the pub is closed at weekends. Cooked meals and snacks available at lunchtimes only. Open Monday to Friday 11-11.

SIR CHRISTOPHER HATTON: 4 Leather Lane. (A2/79) *Bass* Charrington. *CHARRINGTON IPA.* Large cellar bar with outside drinking area. Darts. Snacks and cooked meals are available at lunchtime only. A jukebox supplies the music. Open Monday to Friday 11-11. Closed weekends.

SMITHFIELDS FREE HOUSE: 334-338 Central Markets. (B2/80) *Free* House. *TETLEY BITTER, BODDINGTONS BITTER, ADNAMS BITTER, IND COOPE BURTON ALE.* The only changes from the last survey are that pool has replaced the darts and the Whitbread beers by Ind Coope beers and 'Past & Present' dropped from the name. Bars at ground and cellar level where there is also a restaurant. Lunchtime meals snacks other times. Early morning 5am to 8am licence. Function room. In the last guide this pub was placed in the EC4 section and while Farringdon Street is, Central Markets in that street isn't in EC4.

SMITHFIELD TAVERN: 105 Charterhouse Street. (B2/81) *Bass* Charrington. *CHARRINGTON IPA, BASS.* Breakfasts are served from 5am. The only bar billiards in EC1. Darts and function room. Food lunchtimes only (other than breakfasts). Open Monday to Friday 5am-3pm. Closed weekends.

SPORTSMAN: 315 City Road. (B1/82) *Whitbreads.*
WHITBREAD WETHERED. The frontage is shortly to be remodelled with an unusual condition applied, namely that planning permission would only be approved if facilities for the disabled were included. Outside drinking area. Darts and pool are very popular. Open all permitted hours.
STICK & WEASEL: 273 City Road. (B1/83) *Free House.*
ADNAMS BITTER FULLERS LONDON PRIDE RUDDLES COUNTY REAL

CIDER. Formerly the City Arms (Charrington). Completely remodelled since the last guide in 1986. It now has a septagonal island bar. Food continues to be a highlight of this pub and is available at all times. Live music and discos provide the entertainment Thurs, Fri and Sat. Outside drinking area and darts. Open all permitted hours.

SURPRISE: 32 Bowling Green Lane. (A2/84) *Free House.*
COURAGE BEST BITTER. This is as yet the only London outlet of Surrey Inns which has a number of pubs in that county and Hampshire. The pub was for many years the haunt of many well known jazz musicians who came by for a knock. Darts and pool are played here and a second bar can be used as a function room. Garden. Hot and cold food available lunchtimes. Open Monday – Wednesday 11-30-3 and 5.30-11 and till 2pm Thursday – Saturday.

SUTTON ARMS: 15 Great Sutton Street. (B1/85) *Whitbreads.*
WHITBREAD WETHERED, FLOWERS IPA, BODDINGTONS BITTER, BRAKSPEAR PA, MARSTONS PEDIGREE. This tenanted house has a range of Whitbread beer as well as beer from the breweries in which Whitbread have a substantial stake. The upstairs function room cum restaurant also has a bar with handpumps. Outside drinking area where it is unlikely you will hear the musak. Hot and cold food available at all times bar Saturday. Darts. Open Monday to Friday 11-11, Saturday 11-3. Closed saturday evening and all Sunday.

SUTTON ARMS: 6 Carthusian Street. (C2/86) *Bass Charrington.*
CHARRINGTON IPA, BASS, GREENE KING IPA. Guest beers. Recalls the name of the richest layman in England Sir Thomas Sutton, the founder of Charterhouse as a hospital chapel and school in 1611. Charterhouse was named from a monastery of Carthusian monks, Chartreuse which the locals corrupted to Charterhouse. A very interesting barrel-shaped frontage makes this a pub worth visiting. Function room. Food at all times. Open Mon-Fri 11.30-11. Sat 11.30-3. Closed Sundays.

THE THOMAS WETHERED: 33 Rosoman Street. (A1/87) *Whitbreads.*
WHITBREAD WETHERED, WHITBREAD FLOWERS ORIGINAL, FLOWERS IPA, CHISWICK, MARSTONS PEDIGREE. Pat Ferncombe won a landlady of the year competition. This is an extremely smart and comfortable selling food at all times. Formerly the Red Lion. Open all permitted hours.

THREE COMPASSES: 66 Cowcross Street. (B2/88) *Grand Met-Trumans.*
WEBSTERS YORKSHIRE BITTER, RUDDLES COUNTY, FULLERS LONDON PRIDE, REAL CIDER. The change in beers since the last guide in 1986 reflects the lack of brewing commitment by Grand Met. Live Jazz and Blues piano has continued at this smart pub. Cooked meals available lunchtime and cold snacks at all times. Open Monday to Friday 11-11. Saturday

11-3 and 5.30-11 with normal Sunday hours. Restaurant doubles as a function room.

THREE CROWNS: 8 Tysoe Street. (A1/89) *Whitbreads.*
WHITBREAD WETHERED. Small pub under new management offering live music at weekends. Outside drinking area and darts. Hot and cold food lunchtimes. Open all permitted hours.

THREE KINGS: 7 Clerkenwell Close. (B2/90) *Grand Met-Watneys.*
WEBSTERS YORKSHIRE BITTER, RUDDLES BEST, RUDDLES COUNTY. Sunday evenings finds the pub operating as a sports bar when there is a major sporting event via satelite television. Opens 12-3 and 5.30-11 Monday to Friday. Closed Saturday. Open Sunday should there be a sports event.

Turnmills: 63b Clerkenwell Road (B2/91) *Free House.*
No real ale!

TWO BREWERS: 121 Whitecross Street. (C1/92) *Whitbreads.*
WHITBREAD FLOWERS ORIGINAL, BODDINGTONS BITTER. This pub was one of the houses where Whitbread Gold Label Lager (a real lager served by handpumps) went on trial, it appears to have lost the case. One long bar with darts. Open all permitted hours.

VAULTS: 42 Chiswell Street. (D2/93) *Whitbreads.*
BODDINGTONS BITTER, MARSTONS PEDIGREE, GREENE KING ABBOT ALE. A very large vaulted cellar housing a wine bar large restaurant and several small conference rooms in addition to a large seating area. Lots of nooks and crannies; farm implements make this an interesting venue. Classical and jazz tapes are played. Open Monday to Friday 11-11. Closed weekends.

VIADUCT TAVERN: 126 Newgate Street. (C2/94) *Ind Coope Nicholsons* Free Hse. *TETLEY BITTER, MARSTONS PEDIGREE, YOUNGS BITTER, GREENE KING IPA.* Visit the Newgate Prison cellar by arrangement with Pub Walks (see Time Out for details). Cooked meals and snacks at all times. Open Monday to Friday 11.30-11 Saturday 11.30-3 and 7-11 Sunday 12-2 and 7-10.30.

WHITE BEAR: 57 St John Street. (B2/95) *Bass Charrington.*
CHARRINGTON IPA. Nice frontage well worth a visit to see a pub that has not suffered too much at the hands of the brewers. Many original features. The site of the Baptists Head is behind the White Bear in St Johns Lane. Across the road to the right can still be seen the sign in relief of the Cross Keys pub. Snacks at all times, hot food lunchtime. Darts. Function room. Open Monday to Friday 11-11, Saturday 11-3 and 6.30-11. Normal Sunday hours.

Victoria: 25 Charterhouse Street.

Ind Coope Taylor Walker. Pub demolished.

WHITE HART: 7 Giltspur Street. (C2/96) *Bass Charrington.*
CHARRINGTON IPA, BASS. Near Barts Hospital. Cooked meals
lunchtime. Restaurant and function room. Open Monday to
Friday 11-9.30 and 11-3 Saturday. Closed Sunday.

WHITE LION: 37 Central Street. (C1/97) *Whitbreads.*
WHITBREAD WETHERED, WHITBREAD FLOWERS ORIGINAL,
BODDINGTONS BITTER. It is a pleasure to find that nothing
has changed in this immaculate one-bar pub. Live piano
music is still a feature on Fri, Sat, Sun and Mon
evenings. Outside drinking area. Open Monday to Friday
11-11, Saturday 12-4 and 8-11 plus normal Sunday hours.

WILMINGTON ARMS: 69 Rosebery Avenue. (A1/98) *Grand Met-Watneys.*
WEBSTERS YORKSHIRE BITTER, RUDDLES BEST. This hugh
three-bar pub is open all permitted hours. Darts and pool
are played to the accompaniment of a jukebox. Wilmers as
it is known to its regulars does hot and cold food at all
times. Open all permitted hours.

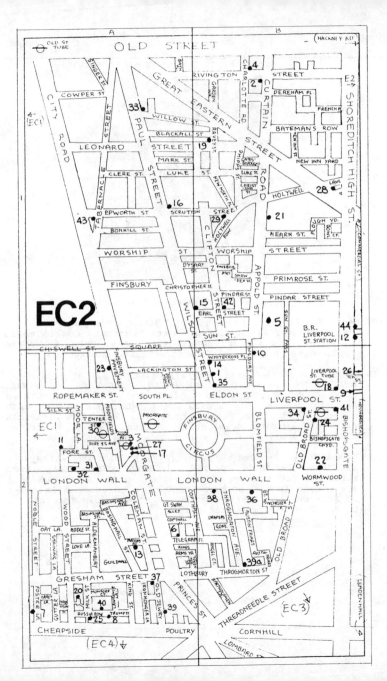

EC2

Stations - Liverpool Street (BR/Central/Circle/Metropolitan),
Moorgate (BR/Circle/Metropolitan/Northern), Bank
(Central/Northern/DLR).

Largely part of the city and dominated by banks and offices, this
area takes in Bank and Cheapside on the south and then extends up
to Old Street and Shoreditch taking in the Barbican and Liverpool
Street Station districts. As might be expected there are plenty
of places to drink in the afternoons but fewer and fewer stay
open as the evening goes on - unless you are in one of the
residential areas. A growing number of pubs require proper dress
at most times.

The new Broadgate complex around Liverpool Street Station has
seen the demise of three pubs in Bishopsgate. Keep a look out for
developments at the station itself as it is currently publess,
though the plans are there to have one. Elsewhere there seem to
be more of the larger brewers' pubs than in other parts of the
City - and particularly Whitbread houses around their former
brewery in Chiswell Street.

If you get lost in the Barbican complex follow the yellow line to
the exit.

Apples & Pears: Opp platforms 15-18 Liverpool Street Stn. *Free
House. Pub demolished.*

BANGERS: 2/12 Wilson Street. (B2/1) *Free House.*
DAVY'S OLD WALLOP. Called Bangers because they serve
traditional old English sausages. Downstairs beer is
served in pint pewter tankards or copper half gallon jugs.
Food at all times. Open Monday - Friday 11.30-3.30 and
5-30-8.30. Closed weekends.

Barbican Tavern: London Wall. *Pub demolished.*

BARLEY MOW: 127 Curtain Road. (B1/2) *Free House.*
*WEBSTERS YORKSHIRE BITTER, RUDDLES BEST, ADNAMS BITTER,
FULLERS LONDON PRIDE.* Free house on lease from Watney.
Outside seats. Restaurant. Function room. Open Monday -
Friday from 8am - 11 for breakfast, coffee etc then 11-11
but closed weekends except for private functions (licensed
till 1am).

BISHOP OF NORWICH: 91/3 Moorgate. (A2/3) *Free House.*
DAVY'S OLD WALLOP. Commissionaire on door. Beer served in
pewter tankards or in half gallon copper jugs for heavy
drinkers or those with bottomless pockets (beer has

increased by 65p in five years!). Food at all times. Open Monday – Friday 11.30-3.30 and 5-8.30.

BRICKLAYERS' ARMS: 63 Charlotte Road. (B1/4) *Free House.* *JOHN SMITH'S BITTER, DIRECTORS BITTER, BODDINGTONS BITTER, WADWORTH 6X, ARKELLS BB.* Basic pub with a couple of table outside. Beautiful Whitbread mirror behind bar. Darts. Restaurant. Function room. Two regular guest beers. Open Monday – Friday 11-11.

BROADGATE EXCHANGE: 2 Broadgate Place. (B1/5) *Grand Met-Watneys.*

WEBSTERS YORKSHIRE BITTER, RUDDLES COUNTY, GREENE KING IPA. New pub replacing one of three demolished three years back. Large outdoor drinking area. Lunchtime meals and snacks other times. Open Monday – Friday 11-9. Closed weekends. Toilets for the disabled.

BUTLERS HEAD: 11 Telegraph Street. (A2/6) *Ind Coope Nicholsons* Free Hse. *TETLEY BITTER, ADNAMS BITTER, BASS, MARSTONS PEDIGREE.* Also sells Nicholsons Bitter. Strong Bank of England and Stock Exchange clientele. Decorated with interesting brewery mirrors. Snacks at all times. Open Monday – Thursday 11.30-8.30, Friday 11.30-9.

CITY PIPE: Foster Lane (A2/7) *Free House.* *DAVY'S OLD WALLOP.* Famous for its port wine served from the wood. Next door to the City Vaults Wine Bar. Four separate drinking areas. Private parties can be catered for at weekends. Small function room. Don't turn the wrong way out of the toilets or you will end up in the wrong place. Open Monday – Friday 11.30-3.30 and 5-8.30.

CITY TAVERN: 29 Lawrence Lane. (A2/8) *Whitbreads.* *FLOWERS IPA, BODDINGTONS BITTER, WHITBREAD WETHERED.* Restaurant upstairs, function room downstairs. Three bars – one on each floor but real ale only at ground level. Refurbished internally in 1991. L shaped bar and more open drinking area replacing old snugs. Open Monday – Friday 11-11. Formerly the City Grill.

COLLINS: 4 Devonshire Row. (B2/9) *Grand Met-Watneys.* *WEBSTERS YORKSHIRE BITTER, RUDDLES COUNTY.* Whether this pub was trendy or not it now looks distinctly down at heel – faded modernism. Darts. Open Monday – Friday 11.30-11, Saturday 11-3 only. Formerly the Bull.

CRISPIN: 3 Finsbury Avenue. (B2/10) *Courage.* *COURAGE BEST BITTER, JOHN SMITH'S BITTER, DIRECTORS BITTER.* Modern one bar pub in redeveloped area. Lunchtime food. Open Monday – Friday 11-8.

CROWDERS WELL: Andrewes House – c/o Fore & Wood Streets. (A2/11) *Bass Charrington. CHARRINGTON IPA, BASS, PULLERS*

LONDON PRIDE. Restaurant downstairs. Private bar can be booked for functions (holds 36). Won the London District Wine Publican of the Year Award in 1989. Chef is a member of the Guild of Restauranteurs. Italian food a speciality. Also sells a genuine German lager. Open from 11.30 Monday - Friday.

DIRTY DICKS: 202/204 Bishopsgate. (B1/12) *Free House.*
GREENE KING IPA, RUDDLES BEST, RUDDLES COUNTY, WEBSTERS YORKSHIRE BITTER, WORTHINGTON BEST BITTER, BODDINGTONS BITTER, TETLEY BITTER. Minimum of six real ales at any one time. Expensive. Wines also a speciality. Ground floor and basement bars. Restaurant and function room. Open Monday - Friday 11-9 Closed Saturdays but open for the market trade on Sunday at lunchtime. Stop Press: Now owned by Youngs (August 1991)

YE OLDE DR BUTLERS HEAD: Mason's Avenue. (A2/13) *Free House.*
BRAKSPEAR PA, FULLERS LONDON PRIDE, FLOWERS IPA, BODDINGTONS BITTER, MARSTONS PEDIGREE. Split-level one-bar pub with seating area roped off. Two upstairs restaurants. Function room. Gas lit. Pub on the site since 1610. Building dates from 1666. Dr Butler was a specialist on nervous disorders whose miracle cures included holding consultations on London Bridge during which the unfortunate client would be dropped through a trapdoor into the torrent below. He was court physician to James I. Open Monday - Friday 11-11.

FLEETWOOD: 36 Wilson Street. (B2/14) *Fullers.*
CHISWICK, FULLERS LONDON PRIDE, ESB. Modern pub with light-wood fittings with outside drinking area. It has become a favourite CAMRA drinking place. Cooked food lunchtime and snacks at other times. Open Monday - Friday 11-9 and Saturday 11-3.

FLYING HORSE: 52 Wilson Street. (B1/15) *Courage.*
COURAGE BEST BITTER, DIRECTORS BITTER. Darts and pool in upstairs room which can be used as a function room. Lunchtime snacks. Open Monday - Friday 11-9.30.

FOX: 28 Paul Street. (A1/16) *Grand Met-Watneys.*
WEBSTERS YORKSHIRE BITTER, RUDDLES BEST, RUDDLES COUNTY, FULLERS LONDON PRIDE. Circular bar wooden floor prints on walls, with upstairs lounge (bookable for private functions). Cooked meals lunchtime snacks at all times. Open Monday - Friday 11.30-9.30.

GLOBE: 83 Moorgate. (A2/17) *Bass Charrington.*
CHARRINGTON IPA, BASS, FULLERS LONDON PRIDE. Completely refurbished pub. Open plan downstairs built mostly of light wood. Restaurant upstairs. Old adverts decorate the walls. Open Monday - Friday 11-9.30. Stop press: Now sells Stones.

GREAT EASTERN BAR: Great Eastern Hotel - Liverpool Street. (B2/18) *Free House. CHARRINGTON IPA.* Do not be put off by the hotel title as the management try to project a pub atmosphere in a hotel. Restaurant and function room. May have guest beers in the future. Open Monday - Friday 11-10.30, Saturday 11-3 and 5-10.30, Sunday 12-2 and 7-10.30. Formerly the City Gates.

GRIFFIN: 93 Leonard Street. (B1/19) *Free House.*
YOUNGS BITTER, YOUNGS SPECIAL, WORTHINGTON BEST BITTER, BASS, ADNAMS BITTER. Pool. Tables outside. Karaoke once a month (Friday night). Function room. Cooked food and doorstep sandwiches lunchtime with snacks at other times. Open Monday - Friday 11-11, closed weekends except for functions.

The Hand Pump: 185/7 Bishopsgate. *Whitbreads. Pub demolished.*

HOLE IN THE WALL: 1a Mitre Court. (A2/20) *Scottish & Newcastle.*
YOUNGERS IPA, THEAKSTON BEST BITTER. On edge of an old prison site. The name comes from a story that relatives used to feed prisoners through a hole in the prison wall cellars to dungeons. Believe that and you'll believe anything. Lunchtime food. Open Monday - Friday 11-9.30.

HORSE & GROOM: 28 Curtain Road. (B1/21) *Bass Charrington.*
CHARRINGTON IPA, BASS. Restaurant/function room has its
own bar. Near the site of Shakespeare's first theatre.
Guest ales are suggested by customers (currently Thomas
Hardy Country Bitter). Darts and bar billiards. Snacks at
all times. Open Monday – Friday 11-9.30.

Jazz Bar: Opp platforms 2-7 Liverpool Street Station. *Free
House. Pub demolished.*

KINGS ARMS: 27 Wormwood Street. (B2/22) *Grand Met-Trumans.*
WEBSTERS YORKSHIRE BITTER, RUDDLES BEST, RUDDLES COUNTY.
Busy two level modern pub. Lunches and snacks. Expensive.
Lunchtime food. Open Monday – Friday 11.30-9.30.

LONDON GENERAL: 127 Finsbury Pavement. (A2/23) *Bass Charrington.*

CHARRINGTON IPA, BASS, FULLERS LONDON PRIDE. Formerly the
Ship. Bus theme pub pass right down the bar please.
Cooked food lunchtime and snacks at other times. Darts.
Open Monday to Friday 11-9.30. Closed weekends.

LORD ABERCONWAY: 73 Old Broad Street. (B2/24) *Ind Coope Burton.*
*TAYLOR WALKER BEST BITTER, TETLEY BITTER, IND COOPE BURTON
ALE.* Formerly the Station Buffet. Unusual frontage makes
the upstairs drinking area seem very spacious. Cooked food
lunchtimes. Open Monday to Friday 11-8. Closed weekends.

MAGOGS: 8 Russia Row. (A2/25) *Grand Met – Chef & Brewer.*
*WEBSTERS YORKSHIRE BITTER, RUDDLES BEST, RUDDLES COUNTY,
GREENE KING IPA, ADNAMS BITTER.* Expensive one bar pub
where darts can be played by arrangement. The wine bar can
double as a function room. Cooked food and snacks at all
times. Open Monday to Friday 11-9. Closed weekends.

MAGPIE: 12 New Street. (B2/26) *Ind Coope Taylor Walker.*
TETLEY BITTER, IND COOPE BURTON ALE, YOUNGS SPECIAL.
Unimaginative restoration spoilt a pub that had a genuine
old fashioned feel to it. Yet another victim of the theme
pub syndrome. Ensure you read the John Thirkell write up
as a wealth of knowledge is revealed in these pub essays.
It may be found on the left hand side of the bar. Darts
and function room. Hot food and snacks lunchtime. Open
Monday to Friday 11.30-8.30. Closed weekends.

MOORGATE: 85 Moorgate. (A2/27) *Bass Charrington.*
CHARRINGTON IPA, BASS, FULLERS LONDON PRIDE. Unusually it
is next to another pub (the Globe). Bar food lunchtime
only. Open Monday to Friday 11-9.30 Saturday 11-3.

OLD BLUE LAST: 38 Great Eastern Street. (B1/28) *Grand-Met
Truman. WEBSTERS YORKSHIRE BITTER, RUDDLES BEST.* Large one
bar pub. It claims to have been the first pub to sell

Porter. Built 1700 rebuilt 1876. Lunchtime snacks. Open
Mon–Fri 11–11.
Olde Gresham: 54 Gresham Street. *Free House. No longer a pub.*

OLD KINGS HEAD: 28 Holywell Row. (B1/29) *Grand Met–Trumans.*
WEBSTERS YORKSHIRE BITTER, RUDDLES BEST, YOUNGS BITTER.
Two little girls, one of which was suffocated, are said to
haunt the cellars: it is said an appearance to a member of
staff resulted in his resignation. This small corner pub
boasts a pianist on Friday nights from 5–8.30. Rather
unusual hours but he has to get to another pub by 9. The
River Holywell runs beneath the pub. Hot food lunchtime
and on request in the evening. Open Monday to Friday 11–11
and Saturday and Sunday lunchtimes. Darts.

PENNY BLACK: Tenter House – Moorfields. (A2/30) *Free House.*
BRAKSPEAR SPECIAL, GREENE KING IPA, BODDINGTONS BITTER,
WORTHINGTON BEST BITTER. All beers at 150p a pint
including the newly launched Worthington Best Bitter. Best
to visit the pub when empty if you want to view the stamp
collection which appears to be unappreciated by most
drinkers. Patio. Hot and cold food lunchtime only. Open
Monday to Friday 11–9.30. Closed weekends.

PLOUGH: St. Alphage Highwalk – Fore Street. (A2/31) *Free House.*

WHITBREAD FLOWERS ORIGINAL, GREENE KING IPA, GREENE KING
ABBOT ALE, BODDINGTONS BITTER, MARSTONS PEDIGREE. It now
describes itself as a free house but with the beers listed
it takes some believing. Outside drinking area restaurant
and darts. Open Monday to Friday 11–11. Closed weekends.

PODIUM: St Alphage Highwalk – Fore Street. (A2/32) *Whitbreads.*
FLOWERS IPA, BODDINGTONS BITTER. One-bar pub in the
high-rise walkway in Barbican. Darts. Pizzas available
till 7.30 and Saturday lunchtime. Open Monday to Friday
11–11 and Saturday 12–3. Closed Sunday.

Primrose: 229 Bishopsgate.
Pub demolished.

PRINCESS ROYAL: 76/8 Paul Street. (A1/33) *Whitbreads.*
WHITBREAD WETHERED, FLOWERS IPA, WHITBREAD FLOWERS ORIGINAL, CASTLE EDEN. Large one-bar pub used as such for 120 years. The restaurant doubles as a function room. Snacks in the evening on request. Darts. Open Monday to Friday 11-11 and Saturday lunchtime 11-3.

RAILWAY TAVERN: 15 Liverpool Street. (B2/34) *Whitbreads.*
FLOWERS IPA, BODDINGTONS BITTER, BRAKSPEAR SPECIAL, MARSTONS PEDIGREE. The railway insignia are interesting and hard to miss. Darts can be played upstairs. A Pizza pub where they are available till 6pm. Function room. Open Monday to Friday 11-11. Closed weekends.

RED LION: 1 Eldon Street. (B2/35) *Grand Met-Watneys.*
WEBSTERS YORKSHIRE BITTER, RUDDLES BEST, RUDDLES COUNTY. A very busy expensive pub with an upstairs eating area. What appears to be original tongue-and-grove ceiling remains. Hot lunches and snacks at all times. Open Monday to Friday 11-9. Closed weekends.

SCOTTISH POUND: 50 London Wall. (B2/36) *Greene King.*
GREENE KING IPA, GREENE KING ABBOT ALE. Expatriate Scots might feel at home here as the walls are fitted with glass-fronted cases containing various clan regalia in appropriate tartans. A circular stairway leads to a downstairs bar. Cooked food lunchtime. Open Monday to Friday 11-8.30. Closed weekends.

SHORTS: 66 Gresham Street. (A2/37) *Grand Met - Chef & Brewer.*
WEBSTERS YORKSHIRE BITTER, RUDDLES BEST, RUDDLES COUNTY, BRAKSPEAR SPECIAL ADNAMS BITTER. Formerly called the Three Bucks. Expensive. Darts by arrangement. Cooked meals lunchtime and in the evenings by request. Open Monday to Friday 11-8.30.

Sir Paul Pindar:
213 Bishopsgate. *Bass.*
Pub demolished.

but see over

Stop press: New pub opened on same site (Aug 2 1991) selling
Bass IPA Worthington Best and Stones. Open 11-11 weekdays only

TALBOT: 64 London Wall. (B2/38) *Free House.*
WEBSTERS YORKSHIRE BITTER, RUDDLES BEST, RUDDLES COUNTY.
Expensive pub that doesn't seem to be much of a free
house. Pictures of ancient autos adorn the walls. Darts
may be played downstairs. Hot food lunchtime and snacks
other times. Open Monday to Friday 11.30-9. Closed
weekends.

THREE CROWNS: 5 Old Jewry. (A2/39) *Courage.*
COURAGE BEST BITTER, DIRECTORS BITTER. Wood panelled
cellar pub. Darts. Snacks at all times. Open Monday to
Friday 11.30-8.30. Closed weekends.

THROGMORTON RESTAURANT: 27a Throgmorton Street. (B2/39a) *Ind
Coope Burton. TETLEY BITTER, BASS, YOUNGS BITTER.* Easy to
imagine yourself back in the 1940s in what was probably a
Joe Lyons cafeteria. Two restaurants downstairs and three
- bars. Closes about 8pm.

UDDER PLACE: Russia Court - Russia Row - 1/6 Milk Street.
(A2/40) *Free House. DAVY'S OLD WALLOP.* Typical Davy's house
where the price of a pint has gone up by 65p in five
years! Cooked food at all times. Function room. Open
Monday to Friday 11.30-3.30 and 5-8.30. Closed weekends.

WHITE HART: 121 Bishopsgate. (B2/41) *Bass Charrington.*
CHARRINGTON IPA, BASS. Typical City pub in an area of Bass
houses. Wine Vaults is the name of the downstairs wine
bar. Cooked food lunchtimes and snacks other times. Open
Monday to Saturday 11-10 Sunday 12-3.

WHITE HART: 24 Clifton Street. (B1/42) *Bass Charrington.*
CHARRINGTON IPA, BASS. One or two original features of the
pub remain. The ceiling reveals the previous existence of
two bars. Small friendly pub with one bar and a function
room. Open Monday to Friday 11-9.30. Closed weekends.

WINDMILL: 27 Tabernacle Street. (A1/43) *Bass Charrington.*
CHARRINGTON IPA, BASS, FULLERS LONDON PRIDE. Former free
house now destroyed by the 'need' for office space. It is
festooned with memorabilia including some old beer bottles
of note above the bar. Noisy. Nice photos of windmills:
examples of post, smock and tower are represented but
their names and locations are not indicated for those of
you who are windmill fans. Hot food lunchtime. Darts. Open
Monday - Friday 11-9. Closed weekends.

WOODINS SHADES: 212 Bishopsgate. (B1/44) *Bass Charrington.*
CHARRINGTON IPA, BASS. Extremely popular pub with two bars
and a restaurant. Handy for the Petticoat Lane Market.
Cooked food lunchtime. Open Monday to Friday 11-8 closed
Saturday but open Sunday lunchtime.

EC3

Stations – Monument and Tower Hill (Circle/District), Aldgate (Circle/Metropolitan), Fenchurch Street (BR), Tower Gateway (DLR).

The south east part of the City, centred on the new Lloyds building and appropriately the home to many shipping and insurance businesses. This is the least residential part of the City and largely deserted at the weekend, away from the main tourist attractions such as the Tower and Monument. However, the visitor is as unlikely to find open pubs around there as anywhere else. In the evening the pubs begin shutting at 8pm, but at least most stay open during the afternoon.

The construction of large new office blocks in recent years has led to the demolition of many pubs, and their replacements are likely to be basement establishments. However, there are some good areas for finding more traditional drinking places and the visitor could do worse than have a look around the Leadenhall Market area the Fenchurch Street Station area, or the alleyways leading off Cornhill.

ANGEL: 14 Crosswall. **(A1/1)** *Bass Charrington.*
CHARRINGTON IPA, BASS. Smart lounge bar with interesting knick-knacks. Friendly staff offer home made cooked meals during lunchtime. Darts. Two function rooms for hire. It was called Mr Micawber until reverting to its former name.

Bulls Head: 80 Leadenhall Street. *Free House.*
Pub demolished.

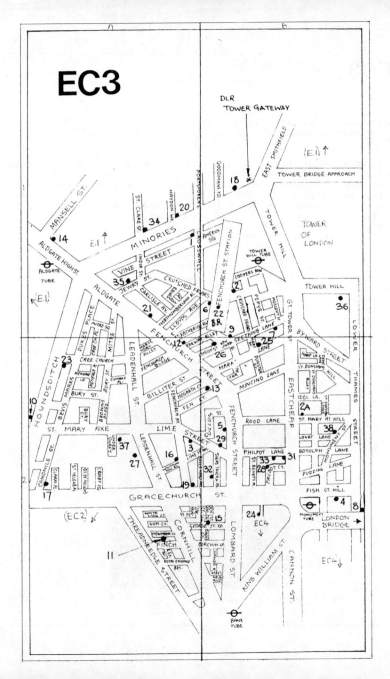

BANGERS TOO: 1 St Mary at Hill. (B2/2a) *Free House.*
DAVY'S OLD WALLOP. Stop press entry. Sells pints only in pewter tankards or by the half gallon.

BULLA: Crutched Friars. (B1/2) *Free House.*
GREENE KING ABBOT ALE. This year Greene King IPA masquerades as Monastery. Lunchtime food. Expensive. Open Monday to Friday 11-11. Formerly the Savage Grill.

BUNCH OF GRAPES: 14 Lime Street. (A2/3) *Bass Charrington.*
CHARRINGTON IPA, BASS, FULLERS LONDON PRIDE. One bar pub with a restaurant. The bow frontage has a preservation order. Open Monday to Friday 11-9.30. Closed weekends.

CANTERBURY ARMS: 20 Fish Street Hill. (B2/4) *Whitbreads.*
WHITBREAD WETHERED, BODDINGTONS BITTER. Darts and lunchtime snacks. Open Monday to Friday 11-9.

CHAPMANS WINE LODGE: 145 Fenchurch Street. (B2/5) *Young & Co.*
YOUNGS BITTER, YOUNGS SPECIAL, WINTER WARMER (WINTER ONLY). Named after a former landlord. Darts. Cooked food lunchtime and snacks other times. Open Monday to Friday 11-11.

CHESHIRE CHEESE: 48/50 Crutched Friars. (B1/6) *Bass* Charrington. *CHARRINGTON IPA, BASS.* Under a railway arch. Gaslights. Cooked food lunchtimes and snacks at other times. Open Monday to Friday 11-9.

CITY ALE & WINE HOUSE: Seething Lane. (B1/7) *Free House.*
FULLERS LONDON PRIDE, FLOWERS IPA, GREENE KING ABBOT ALE. Expensive bar with darts, restaurant and function room. Open Monday to Friday 11.30-11. Closed weekends except for parties.

CITY F.O.B.: Lower Thames Street - under London Bridge. (B2/8) *Free House. DAVY'S OLD WALLOP.* Food at all times. Open Monday to Friday 11.30-3.30 and 5-8.30.

CITY OF LONDON YEOMAN: 2 New London Street. (B1/9) *Ind Coope* Taylor Walker. *TAYLOR WALKER BEST BITTER, TETLEY BITTER, IND COOPE BURTON ALE.* Two dartboards. Restaurant. Licensee is a Burton Cellarmaster. Open Monday - Friday 11-9. Closed weekends.

CLANGER: 104 Hounsditch. (A2/10) *Bass Charrington.*
CHARRINGTON IPA BASS. Modern pub in 'parisenne' style on the site of an old fire station. Restaurant and function room. Open Monday to Friday 11am until quiet. Closed weekends.

COCK & WOOLPACK: 6 Finch Lane. (A2/11) *Bass Charrington.*
CHARRINGTON IPA, BASS. Snacks at all times. Open Monday to Friday 11-11.

Ye Olde Crutched Friars: 15A Crosswall. *Grand Met—Watneys.*

Pub demolished.

EAST INDIA ARMS: 67 Fenchurch Street. (A2/12) *Young & Co.*
YOUNGS BITTER, YOUNGS SPECIAL, WINTER WARMER (WINTER ONLY). Formerly a Charrington pub. Cooked meals lunchtimes and snacks. Open Monday to Friday 11-9 and Saturday 11-3. Closed weekends. Deservedly popular no frills pub in the heart of the City. Note the unusual handpumps. No jeans.

ELEPHANT: 119 Fenchurch Street. (B2/13) *Free House.*
BASS, YOUNGS BITTER. Hogarth used to live on the site. Locally called the Zoo. Snacks at all times. Open Mon to Fri 11-10.30. Stop press: Became a Youngs pub August 1991.

HOOP & GRAPES: 47 Aldgate High Street. **(A1/14)** *Bass Charrington.*

CHARRINGTON IPA, BASS, FULLERS LONDON PRIDE. Darts. Restaurant. Listed Building dating from the 11th century although it has been a pub for only the last 100 years. It missed the Great Fire of London by a few yards and is one of only a handful of timbered buildings still left in London. Open Monday - Friday 11-10.30 closed Saturday but open Sunday lunchtime for the Petticoat Market trade.

JAMAICA WINE HOUSE: St Michaels Alley - Cornhill. **(B2/15)** *Free* House. *FLOWERS IPA, BODDINGTONS BITTER, COURAGE BEST*

BITTER. Also a guest beer that changes every six weeks. Two bars with real ale in the basement only. Lunchtime snacks. Old business centre for the Jamaica trade. The original building was burnt down in the Great Fire of London. The present building dates from 1674. Open Monday - Friday 11.30-8. Closed weekends.

LAMB TAVERN: 10/12 Leadenhall Market. (A2/16) *Young & Co.*
YOUNGS BITTER, YOUNGS SPECIAL, WINTER WARMER (WINTER ONLY). It was a free house until 1985. Darts and function room. Cooked meals lunchtime, snacks other times. Open Monday to Friday 11-9.30. Multi-layered pub in a magnificent Victorian covered market. Crowded lunchtimes and early evenings.

MAILCOACH: 1 Camomile Street. (A2/17) *Scottish & Newcastle.*
YOUNGERS IPA, YOUNGERS SCOTCH THEAKSTON BEST BITTER. Basement bar with darts. Cooked food lunchtimes and snacks other times. Open Monday - Friday 11-11. Closed weekends.

MINORIES: 64/73 Minories. (B1/18) *Free House.*
BODDINGTONS BITTER, FULLERS LONDON PRIDE. New large pub in railway arches near Tower Gateway DLR station. Darts. Restaurant. Wall to wall yuppies. Disco Thursday and Friday (no jeans). No smoking area. Often queues on Friday. Open Monday - Tuesday 11.30-8.30, Wednesday - Thursday 11.30-10.30, Friday 11.30-11. Closed weekends.

NEW MOON: 88 Gracechurch Street. (A2/19) *Whitbreads.*
WHITBREAD WETHERED, FLOWERS IPA, WEBSTERS YORKSHIRE BITTER. Darts. Cooked meals lunchtime and snacks at other times. Split level pub. Lounge downstairs. Open Monday to Thursday 11-10, Friday 11-9, Saturday 11.30-3 and Sunday 12-2.

PEACOCK: 41 Minories. (A1/20) *Grand Met - Chef & Brewer.*
WEBSTERS YORKSHIRE BITTER, RUDDLES BEST, RUDDLES COUNTY. Darts and pool (upstairs). Function room. Cooked meals and snacks. Open 11-11 Monday to Friday. Expensive.

PUMPHOUSE: 82 Fenchurch Street. (A1/21) *Bass Charrington.*
CHARRINGTON IPA, BASS, FULLERS LONDON PRIDE. One-bar pub with piped musak. Basement bar with bare boards and masses of wooden beams (fake?). Open Monday - Friday 11-9.30. Stop Press: now selling Stones Bitter.

RAVEN: Fenchchurch Street Station Concourse. (B1/22) *Free House. BASS, ARKELLS BB.* Snacks at all times. Monday to Friday 11-10 and Saturday 11-9. Closed Sundays. Comfortable split-level bar with train departure indicator in one corner.

RED LION: 31 Hounsditch. *(A2/23)* *Bass Charrington.*
CHARRINGTON IPA, BASS, FULLERS LONDON PRIDE. Food at all times. Opens Monday to Friday 11-9.30. Closed weekends.

RED LION: 8 Lombard Court. *(B2/24)* *Ind Coope Nicholsons Free House.* *ADNAMS BITTER, TETLEY BITTER, WADWORTH 6X, GREENE KING IPA, BASS.* Ground and basement bars. Very popular. Food at all times. Open Monday to Friday 11.30-8 (9pm Friday).

SHIP: 3 Hart Street. *(B2/25)* *Scottish & Newcastle.*
YOUNGERS No3, YOUNGERS IPA, YOUNGERS SCOTCH, THEAKSTON BEST BITTER. Cooked meals lunchtime and snacks other times. Darts. Restaurant and function room. Open Monday to Friday 11-9.30. Closed weekends.

SHIP & COMPASS: 18 London Street. *(B2/26)* *Ind Coope Nicholsons Free Hse.* *TETLEY BITTER, GREENE KING IPA, MARSTONS PEDIGREE BASS.* Also sells Nicholsons Bitter. Expensive – not one beer under thirty bob. Darts. Cooked food lunchtime and snacks other times. Downstairs bar can be used as a function room. Open Monday – Thursday 11.30-8 Friday 11.30-9. Closed weekends.

SHIP & TURTLE: 122 Leadenhall Street – P&O Building. *(A2/27)* Courage. *COURAGE BEST BITTER, DIRECTORS BITTER.* One-bar pub with darts. Good range of imported bottled beers including the Czech Budweiser. Lunchtime food. Open Monday to Thursday 11.30-8 Friday till 9pm.

SHIP TAVERN: 11 Talbot Court *(B2/28)* *Ind Coope Nicholsons Free Hse.* *ADNAMS BITTER, TETLEY BITTER, GREENE KING IPA, MARSTONS PEDIGREE.* Cooked food lunchtime and snacks in the evenings. Function room. Open Monday to Friday 11-8.30.

SHIP TAVERN: 27 Lime Street. *(B2/29)* *Grand Met-Trumans.*
WEBSTERS YORKSHIRE BITTER, RUDDLES BEST, RUDDLES COUNTY. This was the cellar bar of the Ship and Shovel, so called because coal used to be carried by the shovel load as it was unloaded from Newcastle. Area available for use as a function room. Darts. Cooked meals lunchtime and snacks other times. Open Monday – Friday 11-9. Closed weekends.

SIMPSONS TAVERN: 38 Cornhill. *(B2/30)* *Free House.*
BASS. The only pub in the city serving Bass by electric pumps. Two bars, ground floor and basement. Lunchtime food. The pub was founded by Thomas Simpson in 1757 and is currently owned by E.J. Rose but is for sale as is the Jamaica Wine House. Open Monday- Friday 11.30-3.30. Closed weekends.

SIR JOHN FALSTAFF: 17 Eastcheap. *(B2/31)* *Free House.*
ADNAMS BITTER, BODDINGTONS BITTER, WHITBREAD WETHERED, FLOWERS IPA, BRAKSPEAR SPECIAL, GREENE KING ABBOT ALE.

Comfortable single-bar pub supposedly free but with a Whitbread range of beers. Snacks at all times. Open Monday - Friday 11-8.30.

SWAN: Ship Tavern Passage. (B2/32) *Whitbreads.*
WHITBREAD WETHERED, WHITBREAD FLOWERS ORIGINAL. Small ground floor bar with a larger bar upstairs that can be used as a function room. Darts. Lunchtime snacks. Open Monday- Friday 11-9 Saturday 11-3. To be tied to Fullers late 1991?.

TANNERS HALL: Philpot Lane. (B2/33) *Whitbreads.*
WHITBREAD FLOWERS ORIGINAL, BODDINGTONS BITTER, MARSTONS PEDIGREE. One-bar pub with a Pizza Hut. Open Monday to Friday 11-11.

THREE LORDS: 47 Minories. (A1/34) *Young & Co.*
YOUNGS BITTER, YOUNGS SPECIAL, WINTER WARMER (WINTER ONLY). Darts in the downstairs, bar where smoking is not permitted lunchtimes. Open Monday to Friday 11-11. Closed weekends. Built on the site of the old Franciscan nunnery - hence Minories. On dissolution the parish was granted the full privileges of the nunnery, including marriage without banns or licence and licensing their own publicans. The name Three Lords comes from three Jacobite Lords executed after the '45 rebellion.

THREE TUNS: 36 Jewry Street. (A1/35) *Bass Charrington.*
CHARRINGTON IPA, BASS, FULLERS LONDON PRIDE. Cooked meals lunchtime and snacks other times. Opens Monday to Friday 11am until quiet.

TIGER TAVERN: Bowring Building - Tower Place. (B1/36) *Bass* Charrington. **CHARRINGTON IPA.** Food at lunchtimes. Function room. Handy for the Tower of London which is why it is open Monday to Saturday 11-8 and Sunday lunchtime.

UNDERWRITER: 15 St. Mary Axe. (A2/37) *Scottish & Newcastle.*
YOUNGERS IPA, THEAKSTON BEST BITTER. Basement bar under Commercial Union Building. Snacks and lunchtime meals. Darts. Book-lined shelves. Open Monday to Friday 11-9.30.

WALRUS & CARPENTER: 45 Monument Street. (B2/38) *Bass* Charrington. **CHARRINGTON IPA, BASS.** Formerly called the Cock. Two lounges, a wine bar and function room as well as a restaurant. Open Monday to Friday 11.30-8. Occasionally Youngs Special. Stop press: One of the pubs sold to Youngs as part of their buy-up of Finchs.

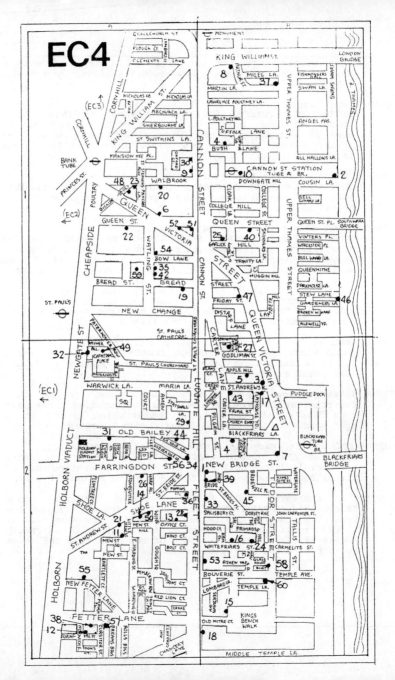

EC4

Stations – St Pauls (Central), St Pauls Thameslink (BR), Blackfriars (BR/District/Circle), Monument (District/Circle), Cannon Street (BR/District/Circle) Mansion House (District/Circle), Bank (Central/Northern/DLR).

The western part of the City running parallel to the river from Bank as far as the Law Courts and taking in St Pauls, Blackfriars and the Fleet Street area. There remains a variety of pubs here and the visitor will find some historical gems, although sadly many establishments have been demolished in recent years to make way for office developments.

The area around Fleet Street is well worth exploring, although since the newspapers moved out the character of the pubs has seemed to change and many close early in the evenings and at weekends. In the rest of the district things have been this way for some time – around Cannon Street station the commuter traffic is particularly important, although in this area you are more likely than elsewhere in the City to find places aiming at the younger market.

The larger brewers tend to have a large presence here but for a bit of variety try the area extending from Bank to St Pauls, especially around Watling Street.

Unless otherwise stated in the pub description all pubs close at weekends.

ALBION: 2 New Bridge Street. **(B2/1)** *Ind Coope Taylor Walker.*
TAYLOR WALKER BEST BITTER, TETLEY BITTER, IND COOPE BURTON ALE, YOUNGS SPECIAL. The circular entrance and door to this small pub may lead one to believe they are in a barrel. The prices here are probably the most competitive in the area. The restaurant becomes a function room in the evening. Food at the bar is cooked to order lunchtimes and snacks are available all times except weekends. Open Monday to Friday 11-11, Saturday 11-6 and Sunday 12-3.

BANKER: Cousin Lane. **(B1/2)** *Fullers.*
FULLERS LONDON PRIDE, CHISWICK, ESB. The pub is formed by an arch of Cannon Street BR Station bridge with two smaller arches forming a tunnel effect from which the river can be viewed. Interesting use of unpainted wood decorated in largely an Art Deco style. Patio. Cooked meals and snacks at all times. OK for the disabled. Open 11-3 and 5-9 Monday to Thursday, all day Friday but closed weekends.

BAYNARD CASTLE: 148 Queen Victoria Street. **(B2/3)** *Bass Charrington.* ***CHARRINGTON IPA, BASS.*** This pub has a medieval look with beams etc; the name commemorates a nearby castle; some of the remains can still be seen built by Baynard a mate of William the Conqueror. The pub has numerous levels and an upstairs games room (pool). A friendly place. Hot and cold meals and snacks at all times. Open 11-11 Monday to Friday and 11-3 on Saturday.

Bell: 6 Addle Hill.**(B2/4)** *Bass Charrington.* *No beer - closed.*

BELL: 29 Bush Lane. **(B1/5)** *Courage.* ***COURAGE BEST BITTER, DIRECTORS BITTER.*** At the time of surveying this old pub was surrounded by new building works for which extensive demolition was required; fortunately a preservation order prevented the Bell from becoming a casualty. Lunchtime food. Open Monday to Friday 11-10.

BENTLEYS (FORUM BAR): 2 Budge Row. **(B1/6)** *Whitbreads.* ***BODDINGTONS BITTER, MARSTONS PEDIGREE.*** Plenty of wood and central islands with high stools. A few plonkers drinking from bottles (a practice that should be banned as we do not in this country want to sink to the levels of Yanks and Aussies) can be seen. Restaurant (next door) can be hired for functions. Open Monday to Friday 11-10. Closed weekends.

BLACK FRIAR: 174 Queen Victoria Street. **(B2/7)** *Ind Coope* Nicholsons Free Hse. ***ADNAMS BITTER, TETLEY BITTER, BASS, MARSTONS PEDIGREE, NICHOLSONS BITTER.*** Built in 1875, this house was remodelled by H. Fuller Clark in 1905. Rich and elaborate marble alabaster and mosaic wall and ceiling designs, in art nouveau. It was restored by Larkin, May & Co. in 1983. Look for nursery rhymes in the Grotto bar. Outside drinking area. Food lunchtimes. Open Monday to Friday 11.30-9.30. Closed weekends.

BULL, BEAR & BROKER: 2 Arthur Street. **(B1/8)** *Bass Charrington.* ***CHARRINGTON IPA, BASS.*** Replaced the Square Rigger. There are two drinking establishments on this site the upstairs sports a champagne bar which host toilets for the disabled. Downstairs is the Bear Market. Some people might think that this should have been the Bull Market. Food lunchtimes. Open Monday to Friday 11-9. Closed weekends.

CANNON: 95 Cannon Street. **(A1/9)** *Bass Charrington.* ***CHARRINGTON IPA, BASS, FULLERS LONDON PRIDE.*** Modern long one bar pub with seating at either end drinking whilst standing is made easier by lots of tall tables. Electronic games. Hot food lunchtimes snacks at all times. Open Monday to Friday 11-9.30. Closed weekends.

CANNON STREET BUFFET BAR: Cannon Street Station. (B1/10) *Free* House. *BASS.* Cheapest pint of Bass in the area. Spartan facilities. No jukebox so listen to the train announcements instead (far more interesting). Open Monday to Friday 7-7 unless trains are on a divert. Closed weekends. Hot food at all times.

CARTOONIST: 76 Shoe Lane. (A2/11) *Grand Met-Watneys.* *WEBSTERS YORKSHIRE BITTER, RUDDLES COUNTY.* This pricey pub converts the restaurant into a function room in the evenings; a food counter is available at the bar. Outside drinking area. Open Monday to Friday 11-3 and 5-11.

CASTLE: 26 Furnival Street. (A2/12) *Ind Coope Friary Meux.* *FRIARY MEUX BEST BITTER, YOUNGS BITTER.* An ex-tenanted house, now managed. Upstairs bar which becomes a function room when required. Darts. Cooked food lunchtime and snacks other times. Open Monday - Friday 11-11.

YE OLDE CHESHIRE CHEESE: 145 Fleet Street. (A2/13) *Samuel Smith.*

OLD BREWERY BITTER, SAMUEL SMITH MUSEUM ALE. This pub rebuilt shortly after the Great Fire of London is to have a front extension, ie the present newspaper shop is to become part of the pub and the rear is due for one also. Sam Smiths have a good reputation on renovation but one has to ask whether the pub should not be left alone. Restaurant open 12-2.30 and 6-9 Monday to Saturday with the bar open from 11.30-11 Monday to Saturday. Stop Press: Pub now closed till August 1992 for the above extension.

CITY RETREAT: 74 Shoe Lane. (A2/14) *Bass Charrington.* *CHARRINGTON IPA, BASS.* Was Dizzys and Two Brewers. Nice light airy modern pub that replaces the Crown & Anchor? which was demolished 19 years ago. Open Monday to Friday 11-9.30. Stop press: Became a Youngs pub Sept 91.

CLACHAN: Old Mitre Court. (B2/15) *Scottish & Newcastle.* *YOUNGERS IPA, THEAKSTON BEST BITTER.* A large downstairs bar in addition to another upstairs. Home cooked food and positive guest beer policy (Youngs, Wadworth and Royal Oak). Mark this pub as one to be visited in an area of remarkable hostelries. Open Monday to Friday 11-9.30. Closed weekends.

COACH & HORSES: 35 Whitefriars Street. (B2/16) *Bass Charrington.*

CHARRINGTON IPA, BASS, WORTHINGTON BEST BITTER. Grade II listed building. Nicknamed Old Scotch Doors. Snacks lunchtime only. Darts. Function room.Open Monday to Friday 11-930. Closed weekends.

COCKPIT: 7 St Andrew's Hill. (B2/17) *Courage. COURAGE BEST BITTER, DIRECTORS BITTER.* Interesting galleried pub handy for cock fights in days gone by. Cooked meals and snacks at all times. Open Monday – Friday 11.30-9.30.

YE OLDE COCK TAVERN: 22 Fleet Street. (B2/18) *Grand Met-Trumans.*

WEBSTERS YORKSHIRE BITTER, RUDDLES BEST, RUDDLES COUNTY. Facilities include carvery and restaurant where children are welcome, two function rooms, a cocktail bar, and a compact disc jukebox from which silence can be obtained. The original Cock Tavern was located across the other side of Fleet Street. Open Monday to Thursday 11-9, Friday 11-10. Closed weekends.

DANDY ROLL: Gateway House – Bread Street. (A1/19) *Whitbreads.*
BODDINGTONS BITTER, WINTER ROYAL (WINTER ONLY), GREENE KING ABBOT ALE. A dandy roller is a wire gauze cylinder used in an early process of papermaking. The pub features a light modern decor and the restaurant is open from 12-2 but food is available at all times. Darts. Open Monday to Friday 11-9. Stop press: Pub closed and for sale.

DEACONS: 6 Walbrook. (A1/20) *Bass Charrington.*
CHARRINGTON IPA, BASS, FULLERS LONDON PRIDE. Nicely appointed large one bar pub with decoration based on a tea and coffee trading theme. Bar food lunchtimes and in the evenings by request. The restaurant doubles as a function room in the evenings. Open Monday to Friday 11-9.30. Closed weekends.

George: 25 Old Bailey. *Eldridge Pope.*
Pub demolished.

GLOBE: 66/67 Shoe Lane. (A2/21) *Grand Met-Watneys.*
WEBSTERS YORKSHIRE BITTER, RUDDLES BEST, RUDDLES COUNTY. Hanging baskets outside present a delightful appearance.

Unusually pool is played but no darts. There are two bars and the restaurant becomes a function room in the evenings on request. Cooked meal lunchtime with snacks at all times. Open Monday to Thursday 11-3 and 5-11 and on Friday 11-11. Closed weekends.

GOLDEN FLEECE: 9 Queen Street. **(A1/22)** *Greene King.*
GREENE KING IPA, GREENE KING ABBOT ALE. One of Greene King's growing estate in London, this delightful pub was the scene of the launching of Rayments Special. A downstairs restaurant doubles as a function room in the evenings. Children in restaurant only (roasted or fried?). Open Monday to Friday 11.30-8.30. Closed weekends.

GREEN MAN: 7/9 Bucklersbury. **(A1/23)** *Scottish & Newcastle.*
YOUNGERS No3, YOUNGERS SCOTCH, YOUNGERS IPA, THEAKSTON BEST BITTER, ELDRIDGE POPE ROYAL OAK. A lot of Victorian wood carving enhance the Marquetry portraits and scenes worked in rosewood. The downstairs restaurant is open 12-3. Darts can be private function. The pub prides itself on not having music (hurrah). Open Monday to Friday 11-9.30. Closed weekends. Another pub, like the Shades next door that is in danger of being demolished to produce another 20th century glass eyesore.

HARROW: 22 Whitefriars Street. **(B2/24)** *Bass Charrington.*
CHARRINGTON IPA, BASS, FULLERS LONDON PRIDE. Ask for the free handout on the pub history. A tastefully refurbished hostelry with three bars, one of which must be the smallest in the vicinity if not the whole of the East London & City area. The restaurant doubles as a function room with bar. Hot food lunchtimes and snacks at other times. Open Monday - Friday 11-11.

HATCHET: 28 Garlick Hill **(B1/25)** *Bass Charrington.*
CHARRINGTON IPA, BASS, FULLERS LONDON PRIDE. It seems that the name of this pub was derived from the Hatchet Trading Co. who were fur traders, and not as previously thought from a nearby timber yard. Food lunchtime. Darts. Open Monday to Friday 11-9. Closed weekends.

HOOP & GRAPES: 80 Farringdon Street. **(A2/26)** *Courage.*
To the rear there is a graveyard dating back to the 1600s now covered by a car park. The name supposedly originates from the inmates of the then nearby Fleet Debtors Prison who could secure their release by marriage to unwed mothers and were expected to pay a percentage of the outstanding debt. Certain nearby publicans were licensed to perform the ceremony. Hence the hoop and grapes? It will have been demolished by the time you read this!

HORN TAVERN: 29 Knightrider Street. **(B1/27)** *Eldridge Pope.* **THOMAS HARDY COUNTRY BITTER, ELDRIDGE POPE ROYAL OAK.** Guy Fawkes planned the destruction of the Houses of Parliament in the cellars of the original pub. One of the few Pope outlets in London. It has a dowwnstairs restaurant and two function rooms. Open Monday to Friday 11.30-7.30.

KING & KEYS: 142 Fleet Street. (A2/28) *Ind Coope Taylor Walker.* *FRIARY MEUX BEST BITTER, TETLEY BITTER, IND COOPE BURTON ALE.* A large one bar pub with jazz on the jukebox. Darts. Hot food lunchtime and snacks other times. Open Monday to Friday 11-9 and Saturday and Sunday lunchtimes.

YE OLDE LONDON: 42 Ludgate Hill (A2/29) *Scottish & Newcastle.* *YOUNGERS SCOTCH, YOUNGERS No3, YOUNGERS IPA, THEAKSTON OLD PECULIER.* City breakfast served from Monday to Friday from 7.45am - 9am. Open from 10.00am to 9pm Monday to Friday. Saturday 11-3 and Sunday 12-3. Snacks all times and cooked meals lunchtime. Bars upstairs and downstairs.

LONDON STONE: 105 Cannon Street. (A1/30) *Grand Met-Trumans.* *WEBSTERS YORKSHIRE BITTER, RUDDLES BEST, BEST BITTER.* Trumans Best was discontinued some time back so it's anyone's guess what it really is. Welcomig cellar pub with bar food lunchtimes. The actual London Stone from which the Romans measured mileage is now in a museum. Darts and pool. Open Monday to Friday 11-9. Closed weekends.

Ludgate Cellars: 1 Apothecary Street. *Whitbreads.*
Pub demolished.

MAGPIE & STUMP: 18 Old Bailey. (A2/31) *Bass Charrington.* *CHARRINGTON IPA, WORTHINGTON BEST BITTER, BASS, FULLERS*

LONDON PRIDE. The present pub is a replacement for a superb replication that was erected in the 1930s and was in the Tudor style. The present pub has been decorated in a quasi art deco style that appears to be taking over from the fake memorabilia syndrome. Very friendly staff in this three-bar pub that includes a restaurant. Function room. Facilities for the disabled. Open Monday – Friday 11–10 and Sunday lunchtime.

MASTER GUNNER: 37 Cathedral Place. (A2/32) *Free House.*
CHARRINGTON IPA, BASS, WEBSTERS YORKSHIRE BITTER, WADWORTH 6X, TETLEY BITTER, COURAGE BEST BITTER. A Finch's pub. Modern two-tiered pub with a military theme as the name suggests, with a display of sabres a point of interest. The downstairs bar can double as a function room and this is where the dartboards are located. Weekly discos and jukebox provide the music. Snacks at all times and hot food lunchtimes. Open 11–11 Monday to Friday but closed at weekends. Stop Press: Finch's taken over by Youngs August 1991.

Monument Tavern: 60 King William Street. *Fullers.*
Pub demolished.
OLD BELL: 95 Fleet Street. (B2/33) *Ind Coope Nicholsons Free Hse. TETLEY BITTER, GREENE KING IPA, MARSTONS PEDIGREE*

NICHOLSONS BITTER. The Nicholsons Bitter has the dubious distinction of being the only beer under 30/-. Until a few years ago there was a large brass knife and fork embedded in the pavement outside the pub. This served to indicate that food and lodgings were available. Hot bar snacks available at all times. Function room. Open Monday to Friday 11-10. Closed weekends. Darts by appointment.

Old King Lud: Ludgate Circus **(A2/34)** *Whitbreads.*
No beer – closed.

PAVILION END: 23 Watling Street. **(A1/35)** *Free House.*
BASS, YOUNGS SPECIAL. Live sport coverage every day via satellite TV. Pricey yuppies' pub. A downstairs bar, garden and function room complete this rambling pub. Snacks at lunchtime. Open Monday to Friday 11.30-8.30. Closed weekends.

POPPINJAY: 119 Fleet Street. **(A2/35)** *Bass Charrington.*
CHARRINGTON IPA, BASS. Yet another pub to be demolished and replaced by a wine bar behind the present site. Appears to be living a month-to-month existence and could close any time. Hot food lunchtime and snacks other times. Open Monday to Friday 11-9. Closed weekends.

PORTERS LODGE: Arthur Street. **(B1/36)** *Bass Charrington.*
CHARRINGTON IPA, BASS. Comfortable wood panelled Regency styled pricey one par pub. Lunchtime food, but only on request in the evenings. Function room. Open Monday to Friday 11-9.30. Closed weekends.

PRINTERS DEVIL: 98 Fetter Lane. **(A2/38)** *Whitbreads.*
FLOWERS IPA, BODDINGTONS BITTER, MARSTONS PEDIGREE. Formerly the Vintner's Arms. The 'devil' is the urchin-like errand boy of tradition. Very friendly nicely renovated pub not overdone with memorabilia. The Pizza Hut becomes a function room in the evenings. Darts. Open Monday – Friday 11-11 and Saturday 11-3.

PUNCH TAVERN: 99 Fleet Street. **(B2/39)** *Ind Coope Nicholsons Free Hse. TETLEY BITTER, GREENE KING IPA, MARSTONS PEDIGREE, WADWORTH 6X, NICHOLSONS BITTER.* Nicholsons Bitter is the only beer under thirty bob a pint – just. Immaculate restoration, for which Nicholsons have become noted. Linger in the entrance and note the pictures and decoration when it's not crowded that is. Hot food lunchtimes and snacks at all times. Darts. Open all permitted hours.

Queens Arms: 30/1 Queen Street. **(B1/40)** *Courage.*
No beer – closed.

QUEENS HEAD: 31 Blackfriars Lane. **(B2/41)** *Ind Coope Taylor Walker. ADNAMS BITTER, TETLEY BITTER, YOUNGS BITTER.* Rare basic City pub with semi-circular bar, unique in the City. This one-time backstreet pub is a totally detached building (the rest had been dealt with by the Adolf Hitler Demolition Co Ltd. Modern developers have not quite yet finished the job). Darts. Snacks at all times. Open Monday to Friday 11-11.

RED LION: 17 Watling Street. (A1/42) *Bass Charrington.*
CHARRINGTON IPA, FULLERS LONDON PRIDE. Modern pub with function room and darts. Snacks at all times. Open Monday to Friday 11-9. Closed weekends.

RISING SUN: 61 Carter Lane. (B2/43) *Grand Met-Trumans.*
RUDDLES COUNTY, FULLERS LONDON PRIDE. Cathedral Bitter is possibly Websters. The pub is the rendezvous of college youths who ring the bells of St. Pauls. More aptly they should meet in the Bell around the corner but it is closed. Darts. Upstairs restaurant doubles as a function room. Cooked meals lunchtime snacks other times. Open Monday to Friday 11-11, Saturday 12-2.30. Closed Sunday.

Riverside Inn: Queen Street Place. *Free House.*
Pub demolished.

RUMBOE: 27 Old Bailey. (A2/44) *Ind Coope Taylor Walker.*
TAYLOR WALKER BEST BITTER, TETLEY BITTER, IND COOPE BURTON ALE. Smart City pub opened by Mick Jagger in 1973. Some jazz greats played here in the late 70s and early 80s. One-bar pub with darts and food at all times. Open 11-11 Monday to Friday only.

ST. BRIDES TAVERN: 5 Bridewell Place. (B2/45) *Grand Met-Watneys.*

WEBSTERS YORKSHIRE BITTER, RUDDLES BEST. Window boxes are an outside feature of this pub and a plaque designates them as belonging to the Worshipful Company of Gardeners. Two bars of which the upstairs becomes a function room in the evening. Darts are played in this wood panelled room. Food available lunchtimes only. Open Monday to Friday 11.30-11.

Samuel Pepys: Brooks Wharf - 48 Upper Thames Street. (B1/46) *Bass Charrington. No beer - closed.*

SEA HORSE: 92 Queen Victoria Street. (B1/47) *Courage.*
COURAGE BEST BITTER, DIRECTORS BITTER, WEBSTERS YORKSHIRE BITTER. Good choice of jazz tapes in this small one bar pub. Snacks at all times. Darts. Open open for functions at the weekends but normal times are from Monday to Friday 11-11. Closed weekends.

SHADES: 5/6 Bucklersbury. (A1/48) *Greene King.*
GREENE KING IPA, RAYMENTS SPECIAL BITTER, GREENE KING ABBOT ALE. Bought from Sam Smiths in February 1989. Large pub where darts are played downstairs. Extensive range of hot food lunchtime with something hot or cold available on request in the evening. Open Monday to Friday 11.30-9. Closed weekends. Expected to be replaced by a building more suitable to downtown Chicago. We are right behind you your Highness.

SIR CHRISTOPHER WREN: 17/19 Paternoster Square. (A2/49) *Grand* Met - Clifton Inn FH. *WEBSTERS YORKSHIRE BITTER, RUDDLES BEST, RUDDLES COUNTY.* Plaques around the walls of this multi-roomed pub commemorate many of Wren's achievements. Basically an ancient pub recently built but in danger of being demolished in the near future. Settles feature prominently in the seating arrangements. Open Monday to Friday 8am (for breakfasts) to 10pm and 8am to 2.30 Saturday. Closed Sunday but the function room is bookable seven days a week. Darts by arrangement. Restaurant. Patio in summer.

Spatz: Hill House - Shoe Lane. (A2/50) *Courage.*
No real ale!

Square Rigger: 2 Arthur Street. *Bass Charrington.*
Pub demolished and replaced by Bull, Bear & Broker.

Sugar Loaf: 65 Cannon Street. (A1/51) *Bass Charrington.*
No real ale!

SWEETINGS: 39 Queen Victoria Street. (A1/52) *Free House.*
ARKELLS BB. A restaurant selling an expensive pint of real ale. Open Monday to Friday 11-3. Closed weekends.

TIPPERARY: 66 Fleet Street. (B2/53) *Greene King.*
GREENE KING IPA, GREENE KING ABBOT ALE. This pub has been closed the majority of the past five years whilst a new building has surrounded it. Very well preserved, a credit to all those concerned in keeping the pub as it was and an object lesson for those who wish to destroy everything in their path. Upstairs bar and food lunchtime. No jeans, makes you woder what sort of clientele they wish to encourage. The biggest crooks in the world do not own jeans! Open Monday to Friday 11.30-9.

YE OLDE WATLING: 29 Bow Lane. (A1/54) *Bass Charrington.*
CHARRINGTON IPA, BASS, FULLERS LONDON PRIDE. Bar billiards as well as darts can be played here in this largely unspoilt pub reputedly built by Sir Christropher Wren. The upstairs restaurant doubles as a function room in the evening. Open Monday to Friday 11-9.

WHITE HART: 3 New Fetter Lane. (A2/55) *Courage.*
COURAGE BEST BITTER, JOHN SMITH'S BITTER, DIRECTORS BITTER. Known locally as the 'Stab in the Back'. Outside drinking area which will be unaffected by recent legislation banning drinking in public places. One of the few newspaper pubs left worth a visit if only for the photos on the walls. Usually there is a car park available during the evenings. Hot food lunchtimes and snacks other times. Open Monday to Saturday 11-11.

White Horse: 90 Fetter Lane. *Ind Coope Taylor Walker.*
Pub demolished.

WHITE SWAN: 18 Farringdon Street. (A2/56) *Grand Met - Chef &* Brewer. *WEBSTERS YORKSHIRE BITTER, RUDDLES BEST, RUDDLES COUNTY, SHEPHERD NEAME MASTER BREW, CHARLES WELLS BOMBARDIER.* This modern building replaces another Mucky Duck demolished some six years back. The wood panelled walls sport memorabilia of a country life. Restaurant downstairs can be used as a function room. Open Monday to Thursday 11-9 Friday 11-11. Closed weekends.

WHITE SWAN: 108 Fetter Lane. (A2/57) *Bass Charrington.* *CHARRINGTON IPA BASS.* A pub whose tenants have had a very personal involvement with the area for over 25 years. A collection of Fleet Street memorabilia and plates from many sources make it worth a visit. Two bars, one of which can be used as a function room if required. Open Monday to Friday 11-11, Saturday 11-3 and 5-11 and normal Sunday hours.

WHITE SWAN: 28/30 Tudor Street. (B2/58) *Grand Met-Trumans.* *WEBSTERS YORKSHIRE BITTER, RUDDLES BEST, RUDDLES COUNTY.* At last a pub with some real authentic pub memorabilia ie a water pump which was used to extract well water when it was known as the White Swan Hotel. The restaurant becomes a function room in the evenings if required. Occasional live music. Darts and pool. Open Monday - Wednesday 11-9 and till 11pm Thursday and Friday.

WILLIAMSONS TAVERN: 1 Groveland Court. (A1/59) *Ind Coope* Nicholsons Free Hse. *TETLEY BITTER, ADNAMS BITTER, WADWORTH 6X.* The library bar has a lighted reading alcove where the Illustrated London News circa March 1849 is available. Downstairs wine bar. One of London's oldest hotels, it was used by 18th century drapers doing business at Wood Street. Cooked meals lunchtimes snacks at all times. Function room. Open Monday to Friday 11-9. Closed weekends.

WITNESS BOX: 36 Tudor Street. (B2/60) *Grand Met-Watneys.* *WEBSTERS YORKSHIRE BITTER, RUDDLES COUNTY.* One of an increasing number of City pubs that are content to host dart competitions by arrangement but don't make a board available at all times. There is also a wine bar cum restaurant. Function room. Musak. Snacks at all times. Open Monday - Friday 11-11.

Stations – Aldgate East & Stepney Green (District), Whitechapel
(District/East London), Tower Gateway & Shadwell (DLR), Shadwell
Wapping & Shoreditch (East London).

This large area extends from the City boundaries and Brick Lane
in the west out as far as Stepney, and from the river in the
south to Whitechapel in the north. It is probably the most
diverse of the districts in the Guide, following the effects of
the wholesale replacement of housing stock with flats in many
areas after wartime bombing, the development of Docklands along
the river, and the creation of communities such as the
Bangladeshi concentration along Brick Lane – which has become
gastronomically famous for its wide range of Indian restaurants.
Of course, the flats are now crumbling and in recent years there
has been more of a trend to restoration of the remaining terraced
houses, whilst growth in the Docklands has largely stopped.

1989 saw the closure of Trumans Brewery (founded 1666) in Brick
Lane and the end of the rich brewing tradition which had endured
since brewers moved outside the City boundary in the seventeenth
century. Much of Trumans remains, and along Whitechapel Road one
can also see what is left of the Anchor (Charrington founded
1738 and closed in 1975) and Albion (Manns – bought by Watney in
1958) Breweries. Another notable local firm although now long
gone was Tilney, whose Alma Brewery in Spelman Street fell to
Charrington in 1927. The pub, the Alma remains on the site.
The pubs of the area are also a mixture but the majority are
'local' in nature, with many being notable examples of either the
great rebuilding period of the 1890's or later estate pub
developments. However, they are often small and have suffered
more than most in recent closure – especially around the
Docklands which used to be famous for their concentration of
licensed houses. Near the City and along the river more upmarket
establishments have sprung up, although surprisingly few are
graced with river views.

ALMA: 41 Spelman Street. (A1/1) *Free House.*
       HOOK NORTON BITTER, YOUNGS BITTER, FULLERS LONDON PRIDE.
       Formerly the Ed Tilney brewery, which used the same source
       of water as Trumans. The site of the pump and well are
       still in existence in the garden. Cooked meals at
       lunchtime and snacks at other times The price of beer and
       food are probably the most reasonable for the area. Darts.
       Rumour has it that the landlord is a former Leyton Orient
       supporter. Open all permitted hours.

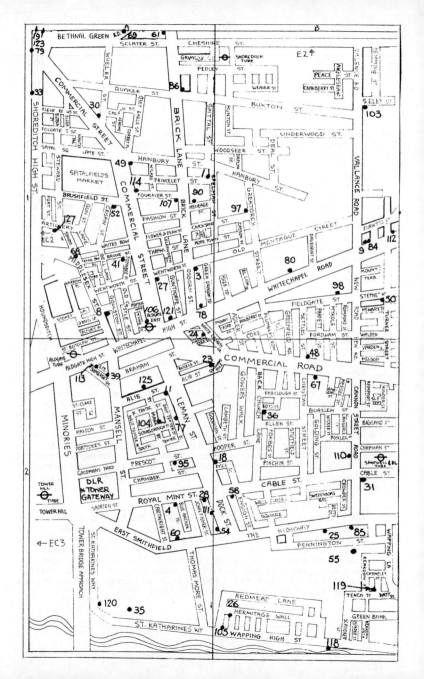

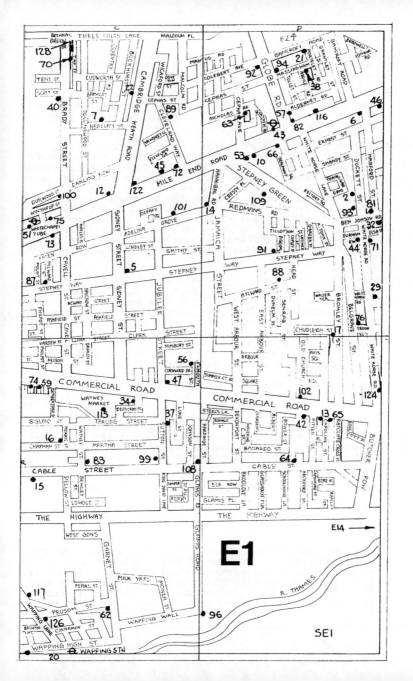

Anchor & Hope: 90 Duckett Street. (D1/2) *Grand Met-Watneys.*
No real ale!

ARCHERS: 42 Osborn Street. (A1/3) *Whitbreads.*
WHITBREAD FLOWERS ORIGINAL. Real ale not always available.
Typical one-bar locals pub. Lunchtime snacks. Open all
permitted hours.

ARTFUL DODGER: 47 Royal Mint Street. (A2/4) *Free House.*
*WEBSTERS YORKSHIRE BITTER, YOUNGS BITTER, FULLERS LONDON
PRIDE, WHITBREAD FLOWERS ORIGINAL, FLOWERS IPA, RUDDLES
COUNTY CHARRINGTON IPA.* Ex Ind Coope pub called the Crown
& Seven Stars, it is a Grade II listed building. It
originally got its licence in 1904 and was closed for four
years before finally being re-opened in September 1985.
Upstairs is a wine bar while downstairs the bar is smartly
decorated and plans to serve 12 real ales eventually. Home
cooked food lunchtimes. Darts and shove halfpenny.
Function room. Open Monday - Friday 11-11, Saturday 11-4,
Sunday 11-3.

ARTICHOKE: 91 Stepney Way. (C1/5) *Grand Met-Watneys.*
WEBSTERS YORKSHIRE BITTER, RUDDLES COUNTY FLOWERS IPA.
Large and welcoming modern pub. Darts and pool. Restaurant
and function room. Open all permitted hours. Displays of
photos and information on the famous siege of Sidney
Street (3/1/1911) which took place near here. This was
where Peter Piatkov (affectionately known by the locals as
Peter the Painter) and two other comrades made a stand
against the capitalist system and the authorities, afraid
of this act of revolt, sent armed police, troops with
machine guns and field artillery against them. Peter
Piatkov escaped and later in his life did a sterling job
as head of the International Security Service of the first
peoples state, the Soviet Union. One of the photos also
shows the Home Secretary of the time, a certain Winston
Churchill, who later became famous for planning a military
adventure, so as to advannce his political career, this
was at Gallipoli. Darts and pool. Restaurant and function
room. Open all permitted hours.

Bancroft Arms: 410 Mile End Road. (D1/6) *Grand Met-Trumans.*
No real ale!

Barley Mow: 42 Headlam Street. (C1/7) *Grand Met-Watneys.*
No real ale!

BELL: 50 Middlesex Street. **(A1/8)** *Grand Met-Trumans.* *WEBSTERS
YORKSHIRE BITTER, RUDDLES COUNTY, FLOWERS IPA.* Ideal
watering hole for Petticoat Lane Sunday Market. Downstairs
snug bar and ground floor bar which is comfortably
decorated and has a collection of Guinness (satirical)
brewing pictures. Restaurant. Function room. Open Mon -
Fri 11-11, closed Saturday. Sunday 12-3 only.

Australian Arms: 18 Bigland Street. *Courage.*
No longer a pub.

Black Bull: 199 Whitechapel Road. **(B1/9)** *Free House.*
No real ale!

Black Horse: 168 Mile End Road. **(D1/10)** *Bass Charrington.*
No real ale!

BLACK HORSE: 40 Leman Street. **(A2/11)** *Courage.*
COURAGE BEST BITTER, DIRECTORS BITTER. Smartly furnished
pub with brick fireplace and bar. Decorated with a
collection of old warming pans. Selection of electronic
and video games. Darts and function room. Lunchtime food.
Open Monday – Friday 11-11, Saturday 11-3 only Sunday
12-3 only.

BLIND BEGGAR: 337 Whitechapel Road. **(C1/12)** *Grand Met-Watneys.*
WEBSTERS YORKSHIRE BITTER, RUDDLES BEST, RUDDLES COUNTY.
Large and well decorated one bar pub popular with the
young and old. It supposedly gets its name from the
'Ballad of the Blind Beggar of Bethnal Green' which is 60
verses long. General Booth gave one of his first sermons
from around here in 1865. The pub was the scene of a Kray
gangland killing in the 1960s. The pub itself was built in
1895. Lunchtime food. Open all permitted hours. Garden.

Brewery Tap: 500 Commercial Road. **(D2/13)** *Grand Met-Watneys.*
No real ale!

BRICKLAYERS ARMS: 71 Redmans Road. (D1/14) *Grand Met-Watneys. WEBSTERS YORKSHIRE BITTER, RUDDLES COUNTY.* One-bar corner locals' pub with wood panelled walls with photographs and prints. Lunchtime food. Facilities for the disabled. Garden. Darts. Open Monday – Thursday 11-3 and 5-11, Friday – Saturday 11-11.

Britannia: 232 Cable Street. (C2/15) *Ind Coope Taylor Walker. No real ale!*

Britannia: 44 Morris Street. (C2/16) *Belhaven. No real ale!*

British Prince: 49 Bromley Street. (D1/17) *Ind Coope Taylor Taylor Walker. No real ale!*

BROWN BEAR: 139 Leman Street. (B2/18) *Ind Coope Taylor Walker. TETLEY BITTER, TAYLOR WALKER BEST BITTER, IND COOPE BURTON ALE, YOUNGS SPECIAL.* A Grade II Listed Building because part of original glass remains with brass letters on sills and brass rails inside. An excellent Edwardian decorated pub, superb facilities and very comfortable. Menu combines beer with food. Lunchtime cooked food and snacks at other times. Open at 8.30 for breakfasts (not for beer), then Monday – Friday 11-11, Saturday 11-3 only, closed Sunday. Darts and bar billiards.

BULL & PUMP: 72 Shoreditch High Street. (A1/19) *Ind Coope Taylor Taylor Walker. TETLEY BITTER, IND COOPE BURTON ALE.* Basically furnished with food at lunchtime only and pool. On the site of a former pub used by Sir Isaac Newton. The name refers to Shoreditch being a favourite stop for cattle drovers on the way to Smithfield Market and to the nearby Shoreditch parish pump. Local office workers at lunchtime, a gay pub in the evening. Open Monday to Saturday 12-3 and 5-1am, Sunday 12-4 and 7-12.

CAPTAIN KIDD: 108 Wapping High Street. (C2/20) *Samuel Smith. OLD BREWERY BITTER, SAMUEL SMITH MUSEUM ALE.* A new pub converted from a warehouse and decorated in a style that befits the new clientele of the area. Views overlooking the river. Darts. Restaurant and childrens room. Garden. Open all permitted hours.

Carlton Arms: 238 Bancroft Road. (D1/21) *Bass Charrington. No real ale!*

Carpenters Arms: 135 Cambridge Heath Road. (C1/22) *Bass Charrington. No real ale!*

CASTLE: 44 Commercial Road. (A2/23) *Courage. COURAGE BEST BITTER, DIRECTORS BITTER, JOHN SMITH'S BITTER.* Friendly two bar pub which had boxing connections. The brewery originally planned to demolish this pub but have now offered the publican a 20 year lease. Darts restaurant and function room. Open Monday - Friday 11-11. Closed weekends.

CAUTHENS: 21 White Church Lane **(A1/24)** *Grand Met-Trumans.*
WEBSTERS YORKSHIRE BITTER, RUDDLES BEST, YOUNGS BITTER.
Renamed in September 1989, was the Horse & Groom. Former 19th century coaching inn, now revamped as a modern split-level bar decorated mainly decorated with sporting pictures. Darts. Restaurant. Function room. Open Monday - Friday 11-11, Saturday 11-3 only and Sunday 12-3 only.

CAXTON: 50/2 The Highway. **(B2/25)** *Grand Met-Watneys.*
WEBSTERS YORKSHIRE BITTER, YOUNGS BITTER. Formerly the Artichoke. The publican refused to answr questions and instructed staff to do so also.

China Ship: 4 Orton Street. **(B2/26)** *Bass Charrington.* No real ale!

CITY DARTS: 40 Commercial Street. **(A1/27)** *Grand Met-Trumans.*
WEBSTERS YORKSHIRE BITTER, RUDDLES COUNTY, YOUNGS BITTER.
On the Local List of Listed Buildings. Busy darts orientated pub formerly called the Princess Alice after the Thames river boat which sunk last century with heavy loss of life. Pool. Function room. Cooked meals lunchtime and snacks other times. Open Monday - Friday 11-11, Saturday 11-3 and 7-11, normal Sunday hours.

City of Carlisle: 61 Royal Mint Street. **(A2/28)** *Grand* Met-Trumans. *No real ale!*

COLET ARMS: 94 White Horse Road. **(C1/29)** *Bass Charrington.*
CHARRINGTON IPA. A building on the 'Local List'. Traditional semi-island bar surrounded with mirrors and red walls with gilded ornamentation. Comfortable, quiet, very much a locals pub. Named after founder of St Pauls School (1509), Dean of St Pauls Cathedral, John Colet who lived in White Horse Road. Darts. Function room. Snacks at all times. Open 11-11 Monday to Friday. 11 - 4 and 7.30 -11 Saturday.

COMMERCIAL TAVERN: 142 Commercial Road. **(A1/30)** *Bass* Charrington. *CHARRINGTON IPA.* Poems about famous race horses on the walls. Darts and pool. Lunchtime food. A Grade II Listed Building. Function room. Open Monday to Friday 11-11, Saturday 11-5 only Sunday 12-3 only.

Crown & Dolphin: 56 Cannon Street Road. **(B2/31)** *Bass* Charrington. *No real ale!*

CROWN & SCEPTRE: 84 Ben Jonson Road. (D1/32) *Shepherd Neame.*
SHEPHERD NEAME MASTER BREW. Comfortable locals' pub, also known as the Jug House. Darts. Snacks lunchtime. Open permitted hours.

Crown & Leek: 11 Deal Street. *Grand Met-Trumans.*

No longer a pub.

Crown & Shuttle: 226 Shoreditch High Street. (A1/33) *Grand Met-Trumans. No real ale!*

DEAN SWIFT: 2 Deancross Street. (C2/34) *Grand Met-Watneys.*
RUDDLES BEST. Expensive side street pub with a mixed clientele of locals and young drinkers. Pool and shove halfpenny. Outside drinking area and car park. Open all permitted hours.

DICKENS INN: St Katherines Dock. (A2/35) *Courage.*
COURAGE BEST BITTER, DIRECTORS BITTER, REAL CIDER. Larkins Bitter (og 1035) is also available if you want to pay 180p a pint. Expensive tourist attraction in style of beams, benches and sawdust. Behind an 18th century warehouse stood the present structure made of European redwood. The building was moved 75 yards to its present site. Two restaurants and a function room. Handy for visitors to the Tower and St Katherines Dock. Opens Monday - Saturday 11-11.

DOG & TRUCK: 72 Back Church Lane. (B2/36) *Grand Met-Watneys.*
WEBSTERS YORKSHIRE BITTER, RUDDLES BEST, RUDDLES COUNTY. Smart and comfortable local with a collection of chamberpots and plates. Darts. Garden. Snacks at all times. Open Monday to Friday 11-11 Saturday 11.30-2.30 and 8-11.

DOVER CASTLE: 55 Sutton Street. (C2/37) *Ind Coope Taylor Walker.*

TETLEY BITTER. Back street local with black and white interior. Darts and pool. Snacks at all times. Open all permitted hours.

DUKE OF NORFOLK: 30 Massingham Street. (D1/38) *Ind Coope Taylor Walker. GREENE KING IPA.* Friendly and homely back street local that seems not to have changed since the early sixties. Darts and pool. Shove halfpenny. Lunchtime snacks. Open Monday – Saturday 12-3 and 5-11.

DUKE OF SOMERSET: 14 Little Somerset Street. (A2/39) *Bass* Charrington. *CHARRINGTON IPA, BASS, YOUNGS BITTER.* Busy modern one bar pub named after a former Duke of Somerset who used: to own property nearby. Darts. Cooked food lunchtime. Facilities for the disabled. Outside drinking area. Open Monday – Friday 12-9.30 Saturday 12-3 only plus normal Sunday hours.

Duke of Wellington: 63 Brady Street. (C1/40) *Free House.*
No real ale!

DUKE OF WELLINGTON: 12 Toynbee Street. (A1/41) *Bass Charrington.*

CHARRINGTON IPA, BASS, FULLERS LONDON PRIDE. Well lit two-bar locals' pub with basic public bar and comfortable lounge. Cooked food lunchtime. Darts. Garden. Facilities for the disabled. Open Monday – Friday 11-1 Saturday 11-3 and Sunday 11-3 only.

Dukes: 474 Commercial Road. (D2/42) *Grand Met-Trumans.*
No real ale!

Fifth Avenue: 169 Mile End Road. (D1/43) *Courage.*
No real ale! Stop press: For sale as free house.

FISH & RING: 141a White Horse Road. (D1/44) *Free House.*
FULLERS LONDON PRIDE, ESB, TETLEY BITTER. Name derives from a cry for help to St Mungo, Patron St of Glasgow, from Queen Langouteth. Her husband suspected her of dallying with a knight. As the knight slept the King stole his ring (which the Queen had given to the knight, having had it given to her by the King) and threw it in the river. The Queen was asked to produce it and turned to St Mungo for help; he sent a man to the river with orders to bring back the first fish he caught. The man caught a salmom and in its mouth was the ring. A comfortable and friendly locals' pub. Open all permitted hours. Darts, public bar and snacks at lunchtime.

FORTY FIVE: 45 Mile End Road. (C1/45) *Ind Coope Taylor Walker.*
TETLEY BITTER, IND COOPE BURTON ALE. Wood panelled one-bar

pub with old photos of Billingsgate Fish Market. Darts and pool. Lunchtime food. Open all permitted hours.

FOUNTAIN: 438 Mile End Road. (D1/46) *Bass Charrington*.
CHARRINGTON IPA. Modern two-bar pub with chandelier style lights in the saloon. Near St Mary College. Darts and pool. Lunchtime meals and snacks. Garden. Open all permitted hours.

Frying Pan: 13 Brick Lane. *Grand Met-Trumans*.

No longer a pub.

George Tavern: 373 Commercial Road. (C2/47) *Free House*.
No real ale!

Gloster Arms: 93/95 Commercial Road. (B2/48) *Grand Met-Watneys*.

No beer – closed.

GOLDEN HEART: 110 Commercial Street. (A1/49) *Grand Met-Trumans*.
WEBSTERS YORKSHIRE BITTER, YOUNGS BITTER. Pleasant wood panelled pub with engraved names of old Truman beers. Frequented by locals and Spitalfields Market workers (until it closed they took advantage of the early morning licensing hours) Open Monday to Friday 6am-9am and 11-11, Saturday 6-9 and 11-5. Cooked meals at lunchtime and snacks at all times. Restaurant and wine bar.

GOOD SAMS: 87 Turner Street. (B1/50) *Grand Met-Trumans*.
WEBSTERS YORKSHIRE BITTER, RUDDLES COUNTY. Formerly the

Good Samaritan and locally known as Sammys to generations of staff and students from the London Hospital. Lively pub with a young clientele and a dubious choice of wallpaper. Patients from the hospital have been known to nip in for a quick drink. Cooked food lunchtime. Open Monday - Saturday 11-11 Sunday 7-10.30 only.

GRAVE MAURICE: 269 Whitechapel Road. (C1/51) *Grand Met-Trumans.* *WEBSTERS YORKSHIRE BITTER, RUDDLES COUNTY.* Smart and pricey one-bar pub named after Count Maurice of Nassau, prominent soldier of late 16th and early 17th centuries. Food at all times. Open Monday - Saturday 11-2.30 and 5-11.

GUN: 54 Brushfield Street. (A1/52) *Grand Met-Trumans.* *WEBSTERS YORKSHIRE BITTER, RUDDLES COUNTY, FLOWERS IPA.* On its 3rd site in 300 years. The first site was in Artillery Lane, the second site is now part of Spitalfield Market. It has been on the present site since 1926. This comfortable pub no longer uses its early licence since Spitalfelds Market moved. Pool, restaurant and function room. Open all permitted hours except Sunday when it is closed.

HAYFIELD TAVERN: 158 Mile End Road. (D1/53) *Bass Charrington.* *FULLERS LONDON PRIDE.* Now a bright cocktail style (at one time called the Pearly Queen) bar but formerly the brewery tap of Charrington: the brewery opposite closed in 1975. The site is now offices of the brewery but it is rumoured that Charrington is to move from the area. The upstairs room used to be the brewery directors dinning room used by the Charrington family owners. Restaurant and function room. Open Monday to Saturday 11-3 and 5-11.

Hearts of Oak: 36 Dock Street. (B2/54) *Courage.* *No real ale!*

Henrys Cafe & Bar: 8 Balkan Walk-Tobacco Dock Shopping Centre. (B2/55) *Free House. No real ale!*

HOLLANDS: Brayford Square (ex 9 Exmouth Street). (C3/56) *Free* House. *WHITBREAD WETHERED.* A Grade II Listed Building because of 'Original interior with boarded ceiling, pine panelling and settles. Engraved and painted glasswork. Elaborate fireplaces and overmantles. Listed for Interior'. Treasure house of Victoriania, breweriania and old photos and press cuttings. In the hands of the Holland family since the 19th century. Rumour has it that Youngs may buy it. Lunchtime food. Outside drinking area. Open all permitted hours. Darts.

Horn of Plenty: 36 Globe Road. (D1/57) *Grand Met-Trumans.* *No beer - closed.*

Horns & Horseshoe: 10 Cable Street. **(B2/58)** *Bass Charrington.*
No real ale!

HUNGERFORD ARMS: 240 Commercial Road. **(C2/59)** *Grand Met-Watneys.*

WEBSTERS YORKSHIRE BITTER. One long bar with wood
panelling and a red and pink decor. Collection of pots
jugs plates and other bric-a-brac. Darts. Snacks at all
times. Open all permitted hours.

IVORIES: 43 East Smithfield. **(A2/60)** *Bass Charrington.*
CHARRINGTON IPA. A cocktail style bar (formerly the
Moorings) which is now suited for the new office clientele
of the area. Cooked food lunchtime. Live music. Open
Monday – Thursday 11.30–11, Friday 11–midnight, Saturday
7–midnight. Closed Sunday.

Jolly Butchers: 157 Brick Lane. **(A1/61)** *Grand Met-Trumans.*
No beer – closed.

Jolly Sailor: 8 Garnet Street. **(C2/62)** *Bass Charrington.*
No real ale!

KATHERINE WHEEL: 50a Cephas Avenue **(D1/63)** *Wiltshire Brewery.*
Stonehenge Best Bitter. First Wiltshire Brewery pub in the
East End. Real ales may vary. Smart comfortable one bar
pub decorated in the style of a Victorian dinning room
with a grey and pink colour scheme. Ex Charrington.
Lunchtime snacks. Open all permitted hours, though it may
close afternoons if there is no custom.

KINGS ARMS: 513 Cable Street. **(D2/64)** *Grand Met-Watneys.*
WEBSTERS YORKSHIRE BITTER, RUDDLES BEST. Lively
comfortable locals' pub with pleasant atmosphere to suit
most tastes. Darts and pool. Food at lunchtimes only. Open
Monday to Friday 11–3 and 5–11, Saturday 11.30–4.00 and
7.30–11.

Kings Arms: 514 Commercial Road. **(D2/65)** *Bass Charrington.*
No real ale!

KINGS ARMS: 230 Mile End Road. **(D1/66)** *Ind Coope Taylor Walker.*
TETLEY BITTER, IND COOPE BURTON ALE. Horseshoe bar with
old copies of childrens comics and comical pictures on the
wall along with a fine engraved mirror depicting a horse
race scene. For many years the upstairs rooms were the
first offices of the Doctor Barnardo organisation. Darts.
Food lunchtime. Open Monday to Friday 11–11, Saturday 11–3
and 7–11.

KINGS HEAD: 128 Commercial Road. **(B2/67)** *Bass Charrington.*
CHARRINGTON IPA, BASS. Lively pub with a cosmopolitan
clientele. Pool. Outside drinking area. Snacks at all

times. Open Monday to Friday 11-3.30 and 5-11 Saturday from 7.

KINGS STORES: 14 Widegate Street. **(A1/68)** *Whitbreads.* *WHITBREAD WETHERED, BODDINGTONS BITTER, WHITBREAD FLOWERS ORIGINAL, MARSTONS PEDIGREE, GREENE KING ABBOT ALE.* Well decorated pub popular with local office workers. It has its own Pizza Hut. Darts (3 boards). Function room. Open Monday - Friday 11-11, closed Saturday, Sunday 12-3 only. Facilities for the disabled.

Knave of Clubs: 25 Bethnal Green Road. **(A1/69)** *Ind Coope Taylor Walker. No real ale!*

Lion: 8 Tapp Street. **(C1/70)** *Grand Met-Trumans. No real ale!*

LITTLE STAR: 164 White Horse Road. **(D1/71)** *Grand Met-Watneys. RUDDLES BEST, YOUNGERS IPA.* Two bar local community pub with pictures of ships and churches. Darts pool and shove halfpenny. Snacks lunchtime only. Open all permitted hours.

Location: 67 Mile End Road. **(C1/72)** *Free House. No real ale!*

LONDON HOSPITAL TAVERN: 176 Whitechapel Road. **(C1/73)** *Ind Coope Taylor Walker. TETLEY BITTER, YOUNGS SPECIAL.* A very popular pub which has always offered music and real beer. Popular with young people and the staff of the London Hospital which is just next door. Prints on the ceiling, Video jukebox. A bit loud. Darts. Function room. Cooked food lunchtime. Open all permitted hours.

LORD NELSON: 230 Commercial Road. **(C2/74)** *Bass Charrington. CHARRINGTON IPA.* Wood panelled bar with enclosed clock. Lounge bar wall has a smart collection of mirrors. Pictures of Napoleonic sea battles adorn the walls as would be expected with a pub of this name. Pool and shove halfpenny. Snacks at all times. Open all permitted hours.

LORD RODNEYS HEAD: 285 Whitechapel Road. **(C1/75)** *Banks & Taylor.*

SHEFFORD MILD, SHEFFORD BITTER, SHEFFORD OLD STRONG, BLACK BAT. Banks and Taylor flagship pub in East London offering a full range of beers and welcoming atmosphere. Sometimes crowded when popular bands are on. Name comes from Admiral George Brydges Rodney, head of the late 18th century wars against France. Victor of the moonlight battle against Spain in 1750, he conceived the strategy of breaking the line. Visit this pub and 'splice the mainbrace' to him, a victor before Nelson. Next to Whitechapel Tube with a good selection of wines. Open all permitted hours.

MERCERS ARMS: 34 Belgrave Road. (D1/76) *Bass Charrington.*
CHARRINGTON IPA. A Grade II Listed Building. Darts and
facilities for the disabled. Snacks at lunchtime. Opens 11
- 2.30 and 5 - 11 Monday to Saturday. Live music at the
weekends.

MR PICKWICKS: 70 Leman Street. (A2/77) *Grand Met-Trumans.*
WEBSTERS YORKSHIRE BITTER, RUDDLES COUNTY, YOUNGS BITTER.
Formerly the Garrick Tavern. A Grade II Listed Building
now with a Dickensian theme. Pictures of novel characters
around the wood panelled walls. Darts and function room.
Cooked food lunchtimes. Open Monday - Friday 11-11,
Saturday 11-2.30 and 7-11.

Nags Head: 15 Whitechapel Road. (A1/78) *Courage.*
No real ale!

NORFOLK VILLAGE: 199 Shoreditch High Street. (A1/79) *Bass*
Charrington. *CHARRINGTON IPA, BASS.* On the site of the
former Cambridge Theatre of which this pub was the bar.
During World War II the pub was taken over by the US Army.
The upstairs rooms were used as a brothel. Lunchtime meals
and evening snacks, live music, Friday disco. Garden.
Other than the lack of a dartboard nothing has changed at
this pub during the last five years - not even the
landlord! Open Monday to Wednesday 11-9.30, Thursday &
Friday 11-11, Sat 7-11, Sun 12-3 only.

Old Blue Anchor: 133 Whitechapel Road. (B1/80) *Bass Charrington.*

No real ale!

Old Carpenters Arms: 78b Ben Jonson Road. (D1/81) *Grand*
Met-Watneys. *No real ale!*

Old Globe: 191 Mile End Road. (D1/82) *Charles Wells.*
No real ale!

Old House at Home: 87 Watney Street. (C2/83) *Grand Met-Watneys.*
No real ale!

Old Red Lion: 217 Whitechapel Road. (B1/84) *Free House.*
No beer - closed. Pub signs taken down, future not known
but outside local drunks gather waiting hopefully for its
imminent re-opening.

OLD ROSE: 128 The Highway. (B2/85) *Grand Met-Trumans.*
WEBSTERS YORKSHIRE BITTER, RUDDLES BEST. Locals' one bar
pub with lunchtime snacks. Open Monday to Friday 11-3
(3.30 Fri and Sat) and 5 (7 on Saturday)-11.

Old Two Brewers: 154 Brick Lane. (A1/86) *Grand Met-Trumans.*
No beer - closed. Stop press: No longer a pub.

OXFORD ARMS: 43 Stepney Way. (C1/87) *Grand Met-Watneys.*
WEBSTERS YORKSHIRE BITTER. Very small comfortable pub
behind London Hospital which has been run by the same
publican for the last 15 years. Lunchtime snacks. Open
Monday – Friday 11-11, Saturday 11-3 and 7-11.

Peacock: 145 Aylward Street. (D1/88) *Grand Met-Watneys.*
No real ale!

Peasants Revolt: 56 Cleveland Way. (C1/89) *Grand Met-Watneys.*
No real ale!

PRIDE OF SPITALFIELDS: 3 Heneage Street. (A1/90) *Free House.*
FULLERS LONDON PRIDE, ESB, THEAKSTON OLD PECULIER.
Formerly the Romford Arms. A single bar pub with photos of
old East End street scenes on the walls. Appealing to
visitors and locals alike. Good value pints and handy for
the curry houses of Brick Lane.

Pride of Stepney: 269 Stepney Way. (D1/91) *Grand Met-Trumans.*
No real ale!

Prince Regent: 105 Globe Road. (D1/92) *Grand Met-Trumans.*
No real ale!

Prince of Wales: 14 Waley Street. (D1/93) *Grand Met-Watneys.*
No real ale!

Prince of Wales: 124 Globe Road. (D1/94) *Grand Met-Watneys.*
No real ale!

PRINCESS OF PRUSSIA: 15 Prescot Street. (A2/95) *Grand
Met-Trumans. WEBSTERS YORKSHIRE BITTER, RUDDLES BEST,
RUDDLES COUNTY.* Expansive pub with many drinking areas.
Walls filled with prints and paintings. Friendly and easy
to relax in. Good facilities and well worth a visit.
Darts, pool and shove halfpenny. Garden. Function room.
Open Monday – Tuesday 11-9, Wednesday – Friday 11-11,
closed weekends.

PROSPECT OF WHITBY: 57 Wapping Wall. (D2/96) *Grand Met-Watneys.*
WEBSTERS YORKSHIRE BITTER, RUDDLES BEST, RUDDLES COUNTY.
Very famous pub. Grade II Listed Building originally built
550 years ago. 18th century panelling on first floor.
Restaurant upstairs, childrens room. Snacks and cooked
meals at all times. Riverside balcony. Outside drinking
area. Opening hours: Monday to Wednesday 11.30 – 3 and
5.30 to 11. Thursday – Saturday 11.30 – 11.00.

Queens Head: 57 Greatorex Street. (B1/97) *Grand Met-Watneys.*
No real ale!

Queens Head: 83 Fieldgate Street. (B1/98) *Grand Met-Trumans.* *No real ale!*

Railway Arms: 60 Sutton Street. (C2/99) *Grand Met-Watneys.* *No real ale!*

Roebuck: 27 Brady Street. (C1/100) *Grand Met-Watneys.* *No real ale!*

Rose & Punchbowl: 7 Redmans Road. (C1/101) *Belhaven.* *No real ale!*

Royal Duchess: 543/547 Commercial Road. (D2/102) *Bass* Charrington. *No real ale!*

Royal George: 7 Selby Street. (B1/103) *Grand Met-Trumans.* *No real ale!*

Royal Oak: 120 Whitechapel Road. *Grand Met-Watneys.*

No longer a pub.

SCARBOROUGH ARMS: 35 St. Marks Street. (A2/104) *Bass* Charrington. *CHARRINGTON IPA. BASS.* Named after one of James II's henchmen who was made Earl of Scarborough for his success in smashing the rebels at the Battle of Sedgemoor in 1685, the last battle on English soil. Darts. Function room. Cooked meals lunchtime and snacks at all times. Open Monday - Friday 11-9.30. Closed weekends.

SCOTS ARMS: 1 Wapping High Street. (A2/105) *Grand Met-Trumans.*
FLOWERS IPA. Comfortable two bar pub with pool and garden.
Hot meals and snacks to 19.30. Opens 11-11 Friday and
Saturday.

SEVEN STARS: 112 Whitechapel High Street. (A1/106) *Ind Coope*
Taylor Walker. *TETLEY BITTER, IND COOPE BURTON ALE.*
Modern, spacious, lock-up pub with two bars. Darts and
pool. Function room. Cooked food lunchtime and snacks at
other times. Open Monday - Friday 11-11, closed Saturday,
Sunday 12-3 only.

SEVEN STARS: 49 Brick Lane. (A1/107) *Grand Met-Watneys.*
WEBSTERS YORKSHIRE BITTER. The ony pub currently open in
Brick Lane. A down to earth place, it is one of the few
with an Asian landlord. Darts and pool. Open all permitted
hours.

Ship: 387 Cable Street. (C2/108) *Ind Coope Taylor Walker.*
No real ale!

SHIP ON THE GREEN: 60 Stepney Green. (D1/109) *Free House.*
TOLLY COBBOLD BITTER, TOLLY COBBOLD ORIGINAL. Formerly the
Ace of Hearts and Astric Lodge. Intimate atmosphere.
Comfortable pub with pictures on the walls and motor horns
on the ceiling. Darts and pool. Outside drinking area.
Open Monday to Saturday 12-3.30 and 6-11. Brent Walker.

Sir John Falstaff: 111 Cannon Street Road. (B2/110) *Grand*
Met-Watneys. *No real ale!*

SIR SIDNEY SMITH: 22 Dock Street. (A2/111) *Grand Met-Trumans.*
WEBSTERS YORKSHIRE BITTER, RUDDLES BEST, RUDDLES COUNTY,
BODDINGTONS BITTER. Formerly the Pepperpot. A two-bar pub
with a very comfortable lounge and basic public bar. The
pub has not changed for years one of the few. Very much a
locals pub with the publican shunning publicity. Cooked
food lunchtime. Facilities for the disabled. Open Monday -
Friday 11-4 and 5-9, closed weekends.

STAR & GARTER: 233 Whitechapel Road. (B1/112) *Charles Wells.*
CHARLES WELLS EAGLE, CHARLES WELLS BOMBARDIER. Small
corner pub which had changed hands (was Charrington) on
the day surveyed so decor and facilities are expected to
improve. One wall lined with mirrors, which makes the pub
seem larger than it is. The building adjacent,
Grodzinskys was also a pub as can be seen by the sign -
the Lord Napier. Cooked food lunchtimes. Open all
permitted hours.

STILL & STAR: 1 Little Somerset Street. (A2/113) *Bass*
Charrington. *CHARRINGTON IPA.* Small one-bar pub dispensing
beer through one of four handpumps. Snacks at all times.
Probably the only pub in the country so named. It may
derive from the combination of distillation apparatus

(still) and the symbol of an early licensees' association
(star). Open Monday – Friday 11-3 and 5-9. Closed w/ends.

TEN BELLS: 84 Commercial Street. **(A1/114)** *Grand Met-Trumans.*
WEBSTERS YORKSHIRE BITTER, YOUNGS BITTER. 19th century
tiling which depicts a 18th century street scene gave this
pub a Grade II Listing. One of the unfortunate victims
during the murderous reign of Jack the Ripper (a former
name) was last seen live leaving this pub. Lunchtime food.
Open Monday to Friday 11-11, Saturday 11-5 and Sunday
lunchtime only.

THOMAS NEALE: 39a Watney Market. **(C2/115)** *Free House.*
*ADNAMS BITTER, OLD BREWERY BITTER, DIRECTORS BITTER,
FLOWERS IPA, WADWORTH 6X.* One-bar pub in a shopping
precinct/market. Darts. Snacks at all times. Open all
permitted hours.

THREE CROWNS: 237 Mile End Road. **(D1/116)** *Bass Charrington.*
CHARRINGTON IPA. Two-bar pub with unusual brick beam and
Elizabethan style interior. Darts. Lunchtime food. Nice
tiling inside the front door depicts three monarchs and is
entitled 'The field of cloth and gold'. Open Monday to
Thursday 11-3 and 5-11, Friday and Saturday 11-11.

Three Suns: 61 Garnet Street. *Grand Met-Trumans.*
No longer a pub.

Three Swedish Crowns: 83 Wapping Lane. **(C2/117)** *Grand
Met-Watneys. No real ale!*

TOWN OF RAMSGATE: 62 Wapping High Street. **(/B2 118)** *Bass*
Charrington. *CHARRINGTON IPA, BASS.* A Grade II Listed
Building because of 'Inside beamed ceiling. benches plank
panelling and engraved glass screen'. Judge Jeffreys was
reputedly captured at this Inn. Grade II for 'interior
group value and historical association'. The cellars were
dungeons for those awaiting deportation to Australia. Near
to site of Execution Dock. Has gallow on river terrace.
Food at all times. Open Monday – Friday 12-3 and 5.30-11,
Saturday 12-3 and 7-11.

TURNERS OLD STAR: 14 Watts Street. **(B2/119)** *Ind Coope Taylor*
Walker. *TETLEY BITTER, YOUNGS BITTER, IND COOPE BURTON
ALE.* Formerly the Old Star. Named after the great British
painter Joseph Turner 1775-1851. Corner locals' pub, once
very basic, but now renovated to reflect the upward trend
of the area. Darts. Garden. Snacks and cooked meals at all
times. Open Monday – Wednesday 11-3.30 and 5.30-11,
Thursday – Saturday 11-11.

VINEYARD: St Katherines Way. **(A2/120)** *Free House.*
DAVY'S OLD WALLOP. Commissionaire on the door. Real ale in
downstairs bar only. A 'basic style' ale bar with sawdust
on the floor with interesting signs and collections of old

wine barrels. Quite expensive (a till receipt given with every purchase). Pints only - from pewter tankards. Restaurant and function room. Open Monday - Friday 11-3 and 5-8.30, clsoed weekends. No Jeans.

WHITE **HART:** 89 Whitechapel High Street. **(A1/121)** *Ind Coope* Taylor Walker. *TAYLOR WALKER BEST BITTER, IND COOPE BURTON ALE, YOUNGS BITTER.* Pleasantly decorated one-bar pub. Not too loud or intrusive. Old photos of local area and collection of china plates around the walls. Has a long bar running back through the pub which makes its size deceptive. Cheap pint. Cooked food lunchtime. Open all permitted hours.

WHITE **HART:** 1 Mile End Road. **(C1/122)** *Free House.*
YOUNGS BITTER, YOUNGS SPECIAL, FULLERS LONDON PRIDE, REAL CIDER. Basic and clean boozers pub with a superb glass partition and mirrors. Known as Murphys. No food. Pool. Open all permitted hours.

WHITE **HORSE:** 48 White Horse Road. **(D2/124)** *Bass Charrington.*
CHARRINGTON IPA. Small old-fashioned and friendly one-bar pub just off Commercial Road. Snacks lunchtime only. Darts and pool. Outside drinking area. Opens all permitted hours. Rumour has it that the pub is for sale.

WHITE **HORSE:** 64 Shoreditch High Street. **(A1/123)** *Grand* Met-Trumans. *WEBSTERS YORKSHIRE BITTER, RUDDLES BEST.* There has been a pub on the site since 1462, its history is shown in the bar. Has an eight foot TV screen which can receive 43 channels. Striptease acts are performed on Thursday and Friday 6.30-9.30 and Sunday lunchtimes. Open Monday - Friday 11-3 and 5-11. Closed Saturday and Sunday evenings. Cooked meals lunchtime and snacks at all times. Snooker, darts and pool.

WHITE **SWAN & CUCKOO:** 97 Wapping Lane. **(C2/126)** *Grand* Met-Trumans. *WEBSTERS YORKSHIRE BITTER, RUDDLES COUNTY, RUDDLES BEST, THEAKSTON BEST BITTER.* Comfortable locals pub previously called the White Swan but now gone cuckoo. Wood panelling with old photos and beer names long since gone. Also ships' badges. Darts. Snacks and meals lunchtime only.

WHITE SWAN: 21 Alie Street. (A2/125) *Shepherd Neame.*
SHEPHERD NEAME MASTER BREW, SHEPHERD NEAME BEST BITTER. Former free house that re-opened in 1989 after a fire. Grade II listed building with wood fronted bar and half wood wall panelling. Display of old photographs and news sheet editions. Shepherd Neame makes a welcome addition to the beers available in this area. Restaurant and function room. Open Monday - Friday 11-11. Might open on Saturdays in the future but currently closed weekends. Shame about the rather loud music, no doubt for the barstaff.

WILLIAMS: 22/24 Artillery Lane. **(A1/127)** *Whitbreads.*
FLOWERS IPA, BODDINGTONS BITTER, GREENE KING ABBOT ALE.
Formerly the Ship. Recreated Georgian style wine and ale
pub with beamed ceiling and wall curios. Darts. Cooked
food lunchtime. Open Monday – Friday 11-11 but closed
weekends.

YORKSHIRE GREY: 180 Brady Street. **(C1/128)** *Free House.*
*CHARLES WELLS BOMBARDIER, MARSTONS PEDIGREE, COURAGE BEST
BITTER.* Formerly JJ's Free House. Friendly comfortable pub
at the back of Bethnal Green BR Station with a nicely
engraved mirror behind the bar and old photos of the area
around the walls. Darts and pool. Garden. Cooked food at
all times. Open Monday – Thursday 11-3 and 5-11, Friday
11-11, Saturday 11-3 and 7-11.

Jolly Butchers: 157 Brick Lane. *Grand Met-Trumans.*
No beer – closed.

E2

Stations – Bethnal Green (Central), Bethnal Green & London Fields (BR Liverpool Street).

At the heart of the East End, this is where people expect all those grimy 1950s and 60s films have been set, with the pubs full of tough (but fair) villains discussing their latest jobs "out west". Reality is more prosaic, but the local pubs here are still amongst the friendliest in the area covered by this Guide. However, the bad news is that whilst there has been a trend for forty years or so to turn perfectly respectable pubs into discos with strange names (perhaps aided by the relatively easy availability of late music licences), not only is it getting worse but the loss of the 'locals' has been accelerated by the large brewers' programmes of closures of their smaller establishments in recent years. Many of these are good examples of pub architecture of a hundred years ago and worth a look.

Unfortunately the area is one of our worst for real ale and that which is available has historically been dominated by Charrington and Watney/Truman (due to their large breweries in the East End), but watch out for the enterprising free houses and smaller brewers' pubs, a recently expanding sector and one which is deserving of support. The only notable local brewery in this century was Wests, whose Three Crowns Brewery (with 60 pubs) was taken over by Hoare (itself then bought by Charrington) in 1929 and closed. One or two pubs still have relics of the company.

Acorn: 149 Queensbridge Road. **(A2/1)** *Belhaven.*
No real ale!

Angel & Crown: 170 Roman Road. **(B1/2)** *Bass Charrington.*
No real ale!

APPROACH TAVERN: 47 Approach Road. **(A1/3)** *Free House.*
ADNAMS BITTER, KING & BARNES SUSSEX BITTER, DIRECTORS BITTER, EVERARDS OLD ORIGINAL. Friendly two bar pub with a varying range of beers. Darts and pool. Function rooms. Lunchtime snacks. Possibly what in the minds of outsiders is what all East End pubs are like, we should be so lucky! Open all permitted hours.

Beehive: 230 Roman Road. **(B1/4)** *Grand Met-Watneys.*
No real ale!

Birdcage: 80 Columbia Road. **(B2/5)** *Grand Met-Trumans.*
No real ale!

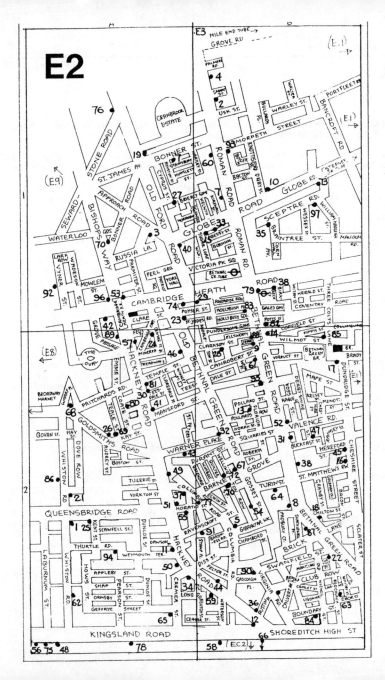

Bishop Bonner: 21 Bonner Street. **(A1/6)** *Ind Coope Taylor Walker.*

No real ale!

Black Horse: 67 Roman Road. **(B1/7)** *Belhaven.*
No real ale!

Blade Bone: 185 Bethnal Green Road. **(B2/8)** *Bass Charrington.*
No real ale!

Bohola House: 423 Bethnal Green Road. **(B2/9)** *Free House.*
No real ale!

Britannia: 206 Globe Road. **(B1/10)** *Grand Met-Watneys.*
No real ale!

British Lion: 193 Hackney Road. **(A2/11)** *Whitbreads.*
No real ale!

BROWNS: 1 Hackney Road. **(B2/12)** *Grand Met-Watneys.*
WEBSTERS YORKSHIRE BITTER. Formerly the Horns. Large cafe style pub with large pool area at rear. Working clothes allowed, but no dirty boots/overalls. Cooked meals lunchtime and 5.30-8 Thurs/Fri. Open Monday – Saturday 11-3 and 5.30-11.

Buskers Free House: 2 Pollard Row. **(B2/13)** *Free House.*
No beer – closed.

Camdens Head: 456 Bethnal Green Road. **(B1/14)** *Bass Charrington.*
No beer – closed.

Camel: 277 Globe Road. **(B1/15)** *Free House.*
No real ale!

Carpenters Arms: 73 Cheshire Street. **(B2/16)** *Free House.*
No real ale!

Cavalier: 89 Dunbridge Street. **(B2/17)** *Free House.*
No real ale!

Chiltons: 12 Chilton Street. **(B2/18)** *Grand Met-Trumans.*
No real ale! Formerly the Britannia

City of Paris: 178 Old Ford Road. **(A1/19)** *Grand Met-Trumans.*
No real ale!

CONQUEROR: 2/4 Austin Street. **(B2/20)** *Free House.*
FULLERS LONDON PRIDE. Plus currently Adnams Broadside. Small wood-panelled two bar pub with a collection of bric-a-brac. Ex Charrington pub with darts and pool. Cooked food lunchtime with snacks at other times. Open Monday – Saturday 11-2.30 and 5-11.

Crown: 144 Whiston Road. **(A2/21)** *Belhaven.* ***No real ale!***
Dolphin: 85 Redchurch Street. **(B2/22)** *Grand Met-Trumans.*
    Stop press: Now sells Boddingtons.

Dover Castle: 118 Old Bethnal Green Road. **(A1/23)** *Grand
    Met-Trumans.* ***No real ale!***

Duke of **Cambridge:** 25 Cambridge Crescent (formerly Felix St).
    (A2/24) *Belhaven.* ***No real ale!***

Duke   of   **Cambridge:**   101   Queensbridge   Road.   **(A2/25)**   *Bass
Charrington.* ***No real ale!***

DUKE OF SUSSEX: 94 Goldsmith's Row. **(A2/26)** *Shepherd Neame.
SHEPHERD NEAME MASTER BREW.* Tiny two bar pub – friendly.
Real fire. Open Monday – Thursday 11–3 and 5.30–11   Friday
– Saturday 11–11.

DUKE OF **WELLINGTON:** 52 Cyprus Street. **(A1/27)** *Grand Met-Watneys.*

    WEBSTERS   YORKSHIRE   BITTER.   Comfortably   furnished
    wood-panelled central bar pub. Darts and pool. Snacks at
    lunchtime and early evening. Open all permitted hours if
    sufficient trade. Grade II Listed Building.

Duke of York: 65 Ellsworth Street. **(B2/28)** *Grand Met-Trumans.*
    No real ale!

DUNDEE **ARMS:** 339 Cambridge Heath Road. **(B1/29)** *Ind Coope Taylor
Walker. **TETLEY BITTER, IND COOPE BURTON ALE, GREENE KING
IPA.*** Note the sunken hook on the right hand side of the
entrance to facilitate the handling of barrels to and from
the cellar. Unusual curved glass frontage. Locals' pub
opposite the York Hall where the Pigs Ear Beer Festival
was founded. Handy for the fisticuffs held there. The
Greene King IPA at 99p was the cheapest pint to be had by
any pub in this area. Food at all times. Hot toddies with
lemon ancloves etc. Open all permitted hours.

Durham **Arms:** 408 Hackney Road. **(A2/30)** *Grand Met-Trumans.*
    No real ale!

Earl Grey: 272 Bethnal Green Road. **(B2/31)** *Grand Met-Watneys.*
    No real ale!

Flamingos: 163 Gossett Street. **(B2/32)** *Free House.*
    No real ale!

FLORISTS: 255 Globe Road. **(B1/33)** *Grand Met-Watneys.
RUDDLES BEST, RUDDLES COUNTY.* No real ale available at
time of survey. Open all permitted hours.

Flying Scud: 137 Hackney Road. **(A2/34)** *Grand Met-Trumans.*
    No real ale!

Fountain: 123 Sceptre Road. (B1/35) *Grand Met-Watneys.*
No real ale!

George & Dragon: 2/4 Hackney Road. (B2/36) *Grand Met-Watneys.*
No beer - closed.

Globe: 109 Columbia Road. (A2/37) *Belhaven.*
No real ale!

Green Gate: 228/230 Bethnal Green Road. (B2/38) *Ind Coope*
Taylor Walker. *No real ale!*

GREEN MAN: 287 Cambridge Heath Road. (B1/39) *Grand Met-Trumans.*
RUDDLES BEST. Expensive one bar pub very busy at
lunchtimes when cooked meals are available. Pool, but not
weekday lunchtimes. Open all permitted hours.

GREYHOUND: 32 Old Ford Road. (A1/40) *Courage.*
COURAGE BEST BITTER, DIRECTORS BITTER. One bar pub
refurbished in 'cafe' style separate pool room. Garden.
Cooked meals lunchtime and snacks at other times. Open all
permitted hours.

Halfway House: 388 Hackney Road. (A2/41) *Ind Coope Taylor* Taylor
Walker. *No real ale!*

HARE: 505 Cambridge Heath Road. (A1/42) *Grand Met-Trumans.*
WEBSTERS YORKSHIRE BITTER, RUDDLES BEST. Horseshoe shaped
bar now under new management so expect facilities to
change. Darts. TV. Open all permitted hours. Snacks at all
times.

Jeremiah Bullfrog: 68 Warner Place. (A2/43) *Grand Met-Watneys.*
No real ale!

JOINERS ARMS: 116/8 Hackney Road. (B2/44) *Belhaven.*
IND COOPE BURTON ALE. One roomed pub with central bar.
Darts and pool. Open Monday to Saturday 11.30-5 and 7-11.

King & Queen: 89 Cheshire Street. (B2/45) *Belhaven.*
No real ale!

Kings Arms: 67 Old Bethnal Green Road. (B2/46) *Grand*
Met-Watneys. *No real ale!*

Kings Arms: 11a Buckfast Street. (B2/47) *Courage.*
No real ale!

KINGS HEAD: 257 Kingsland Road. (A2/48) *Ind Coope Taylor Walker.*

IND COOPE BURTON ALE. Beer not on when surveyed. Island
bar with plastic beams. Darts and pool. Cooked meals
lunchtime and snacks other times. Open all permitted
hours.

Limes: 324 Hackney Road. **(A2/49)** *Free House.*
No beer – closed. Stop press: No longer a pub.

The Little Wonder: 155 Hackney Road. **(A2/50)** *Free House.*
No real ale!

Lyons Corner: 121 Bethnal Green Road. *Free House.*

No longer a pub.

MARKSMAN: 254 Hackney Road. **(A2/51)** *Free House.*
PITFIELD HOXTON HEAVY, EVERARDS OLD ORIGINAL, WADWORTH 6X.
Former West Brewery (was near the Childrens Hospital) pub
and only one of 3 pubs out of a dozen to sell real ale in
Hackney Road. Cooked meals at lunchtime and snacks other
times. Pool. Opens all permitted hours if custom warrants.

MARQUIS OF CORNWALLIS: 304 Bethnal Green Road. **(B2/52)** *Grand*
Met–Trumans. *RUDDLES COUNTY.* Comfortable island bar pub.
Darts. Cooked meals lunchtime and snacks other times.

Metropolis: 234 Cambridge Heath Road. **(A1/53)** *Grand Met–Watneys.*

No real ale! Formerly Martins and Arabian Arms.

Montys: 111 Gosset Street. **(B2/54)** *Free House.*
No beer – closed.

NELSONS HEAD: 32 Horatio Street. **(A2/55)** *Batemans.*
BATEMANS DARK MILD, BATEMANS XB, BATEMANS XXXB. Small dim
pub often with loud music. Darts and pool. Open Monday –
Friday 12-3 and 5-11. Currently for sale. Ex Charrington
and Gibbs Mew.

Nice Little Earner: 281 Kingsland Road. (A2/56) *Free House.*
No real ale!

Norfolk Arms (Pickles): 460 Hackney Road. (A2/57) *Free House.*
No real ale!

Old Basing House: 25/7 Kingsland Road. (A2/58) *Courage.*
No real ale!

YE OLDE AXE: 69 Hackney Road. (B2/59) *Free House.*
TETLEY BITTER, FRIARY MEUX BEST BITTER. Victorian pub that
for a long time was a warehouse. Has wood panelling and
secluded alcoves. Snacks lunchtime. Open all permitted
hours.

Old Friends: 129 Roman Road. (B1/60) *Grand Met-Watneys.*
No real ale!

OLD GEORGE: 379 Bethnal Green Road. (B2/61) *Grand Met-Trumans.*
RUDDLES BEST. Large plush pub with interesting prints on
walls and separate pool area. Cooked meals lunchtime and
snacks at other times. Open all permitted hours.

Old King Johns Head: 90 Whiston Road. (A2/62) *Bass Charrington.*
No real ale!

THE OWL & PUSSYCAT: 34 Redchurch Street. (B2/63) *Free House.*
*CASTLE EDEN, WHITBREAD FLOWERS ORIGINAL, YOUNGS SPECIAL,
WADWORTH 6X, THOMAS HARDY COUNTRY BITTER.* Formerly
Taylors, Alternative and the Crown. Also sells Owl and
Pussycat Bitter. Roomy pub with open fireplace and garden
area at back, upstairs bar/function room. Cooked food at
all times. Open Monday – Friday 11-11 Saturday 11-3 and
5-11. Grade II Listed Building. Ex Charrington.

Panther: 15 Turin Street. (B2/64) *Whitbreads.*
No real ale!

PARTNERS: 32 Cremer Street. (A2/65) *Free House.*
WHITBREAD FLOWERS ORIGINAL. Formerly the Marquis of
Lansdowne. Small comfortable back-street local with happy
hour 5-6pm Mon-Fri (20p off a pint). Darts. Cooked food
lunchtime and snacks at other times. Open all permitted
hours.

Penny Farthing: 3 Kingsland Road. (B2/66) *Free House.*
No real ale!

Perseverance: 125 Gosset Street. (B2/67) *Grand Met-Watneys.*
No real ale!

Perseverance: 112 Pritchards Road. (A2/68) *Grand Met-Watneys.*
No real ale!

Prince of Wales: 1 Teale Street. **(A2/69)** *Grand Met-Watneys.*
No real ale!

Prince of Wales: 59 Barnet Grove. **(B2/70)** *Free House.*
No beer - closed.

PRINCE OF WALES: 76 Bishops Way. **(A1/71)** *Charles Wells.*
CHARLES WELLS EAGLE. Long lounge with separate darts area.
TV. Comfortable pub. Occasional live music. Open all
permitted hours. Former Charrington pub.

Queen Victoria: 72 Barnet Grove. **(B2/72)** *Belhaven.*
No real ale!

Railway Tavern: 131 Globe Road. **(B1/73)** *Bass Charrington.*
No real ale!

RED DEER: 393 Cambridge Heath Road. **(A1/74)** *Grand Met-Watneys.*
YOUNGS BITTER. Friendly comfortable split level pub with
darts and pool. Cooked meals lunchtime and snacks at other
times.

Royal Alfred: 267 Kingsland Road. **(A2/75)** *Belhaven.*
No real ale!

ROYAL CRICKETERS: 211 Old Ford Road. **(A1/76)** *Whitbreads.*
WHITBREAD WETHERED, GREENE KING ABBOT ALE. On the local
List of Listed buildings. Probably the most picturesque
setting for any pub in E2. Two level pub with canal-side
patio and bar (open evenings only with Bar B Q in
spring/summer). Close to Victoria Park. Snacks at all
times. Open Monday - Saturday 11-3 and 5.30-11.

Royal Oak: 73 Columbia Road. **(B2/77)** *Belhaven.*
No real ale!

ROYAL STANDARD: 165 Kingsland Road. **(A2/78)** *Whitbreads.*
FLOWERS IPA, WHITBREAD FLOWERS ORIGINAL, PITFIELD BITTER.
Comfortable two bar pub that is now back in the hands of
Whitbread having been leased to Youngs these past 20
years. Whitbread beers were not available when surveyed.
Darts, pool and an outside drinking area. Snacks at all
times.

SALMON & BALL: 502 Bethnal Green Road. **(B1/79)** *Grand
Met-Watneys. WEBSTERS YORKSHIRE BITTER, RUDDLES BEST.* No
real ale available when surveyed. Cafe-style one-bar pub.
A Listed Building. Cooked food lunchtimes and snacks at
other times. Formerly Tipples. Open all permitted hours.

SEBRIGHT ARMS: 31/5 Coate Street. **(A2/80)** *Free House.*
OLD BREWERY BITTER. Formerly Sollys (ex Gibbs Mew). Guest
beers include Castle Eden and Ruddles Best. Restaurant.
Large comfortable smart wood-panelled pub off Hackney Road

E2

down Sebright Passage. Live music wed-Sun evenings and jazz Sunday lunchtime. Open all permitted hours.

Septembers: 428 Hackney Road. (A2/81) *Bass Charrington.*
No real ale!

Shakespeare: 460 Bethnal Green Road. (B1/82) *Grand Met-Trumans.*
No real ale!

Ship: 473 Bethnal Green Road. (B1/83) *Grand Met-Watneys.*
No real ale!

SHIP & BLUE BALL: 13 Boundary Street. (B2/84) *Pitfield.*
PITFIELD BITTER, HOXTON HEAVY, DARK STAR, OLD MERLIN KNIGHTLY BREW. Friendly pub with old-fashioned stove in the centre of the room. Posters of Reids Stout and Whitbread London Stout also display case of tin hats, respirators and shell dressings and old bullets. Quite a bit of old breweriana. piano. Pizzas a speciality. Function room. Open Monday - Saturday 11.30-3 and 5.30-11. Rumour has it that it may revert back to Watney.

SPORTING LIFE: 36 Wilmot Street. (B2/85) *Free House.*
CHARRINGTON IPA, ADNAMS BITTER. Large two-bar pub opposite Bethnal Green BR Station. Separate pool area. Darts. Snacks at all times, cooked meals lunchtime. Former Charrington pub called the Lamb and dates back to 1860 at least. Open all permitted hours.

Sportsman: 42 Whiston Road. (A2/86) *Free House.*
No real ale!

Stick of Rock: 143 Bethnal Green Road. (B2/87) *Grand Met-Trumans. No real ale!*

Sun: 441 Bethnal Green Road. (B2/88) *Whitbreads.*
No real ale!

Tantrums: 481 Hackney Road. (A2/89) *Free House.*
No real ale! Was Hop Picker and Keeleys.

Turtles: 57 Virginia Road. (B1/90) *Grand Met-Watneys.*
No real ale! Formerly the Three Loggerheads.

VICTORIA: 4 Ravenscroft Street. (B2/91) *Grand Met-Watneys.*
WEBSTERS YORKSHIRE BITTER. Beer not available when surveyed. Darts and pool. Garden. Snacks at lunchtime.

Victory: 27 Vyner Street. (A1/92) *Free House.*
No real ale!

WEAVERS ARMS: 100 Roman Road. (B1/93) *Ind Coope Taylor Walker.*
TETLEY BITTER, YOUNGS BITTER. Large one bar pub with

occasional live music. Darts. Snacks at all times. Open all permitted hours.

Weymouth Arms: 80 Weymouth Terrace. **(A2/94)** *Grand Met–Watneys.*
No real ale!

White Hart: 359 Bethnal Green Road. **(B2/95)** *Grand Met–Trumans.*
No real ale!

White Horse: 236 Cambridge Heath Road. **(A1/96)** *Whitbreads.*
No real ale!

Woolpack: 89 Sceptre Road. **(B1/97)** *Grand Met–Watneys.*
No real ale!

Old Two Brewers E1. *No longer a pub.*

E3

Stations - Mile End (Central/District), Bow Road and Bromley by Bow (District), Bow Church and Devons Road (DLR).

The original Bow was a village around the ford over the River Lea, now replaced by Bow flyover, and in this area there still remains something of a village atmosphere, despite sufferings from bombing and road building. The large Tesco is far from anyone's image of the village shop, although many of the pubs still have a traditional atmosphere. For this guide the Bow area extends rather further, to Stepney in the west Poplar in the south and Victoria Park in the north.

The railway and canal network shows its importance as the one-time gateway to London from the east, and amongst the Victorian terraces (and a few squares) the visitor will find a good range of 'corner locals' remaining. To an extent, the pubs have not suffered as much as other parts of the East End although this may reflect the greater mix of ownership, including a sprinkling of regional brewers houses. In other parts substantial development of flats has taken place with associated estate pubs mixed in with older survivors.

Taylor Walker have a strong influence here, much derived from their purchase of Smith Garrett in 1927 - which they then closed.

Albert: 74 St Stephens Road. **(A1/1)** *Belhaven.*
      No real ale!

Albion: 25 St. Pauls Way. **(A2/2)** *Belhaven.*
      No beer - closed.

Ancient Briton: 44a Glaucus Street. **(B2/3)** *Bass Charrington.*
      No real ale!

BEEHIVE: 104 Empson Street. **(B2/4)** *Free House.*
      MORLAND SPECKLED HEN, BRAINS SA. Beer range vairies; Adnams Mild and Mansfield Old Bailey were on when surveyed. Lively backstreet local behind St Andrews Hospital. It has an unusual collection of ties and over 200 key rings. Darts and pool. Childrens room. Cooked meals at all times. Open Monday - Saturday 11-3 and 5-11.

Bird in Hand: 126 Bow Road. *Grand Met - Trumans.*
      Pub demolished.

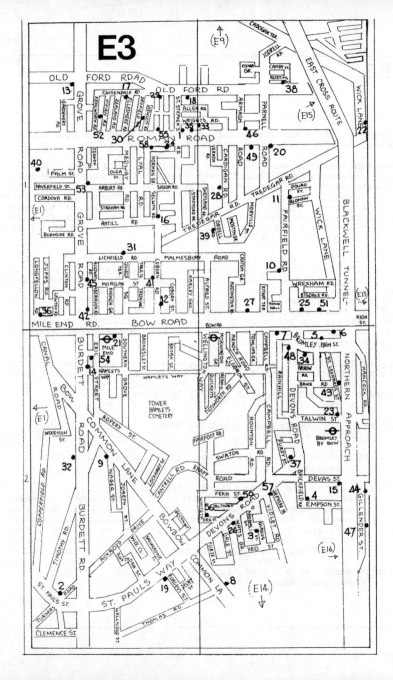

BLUE ANCHOR: 67 Bromley High Street. (B2/5) *Belhaven.*
WEBSTERS YORKSHIRE BITTER. Traditional East End local with
darts and shove halfpenny. Lunchtime snacks. Originally
owned by the Kings Arms Brewery, part of the London &
Burton Brewery Co. who were taken over by Watney Combe
Reid in 1929. The freehold was sold to the LCC in 1950.
Open Monday - Saturday 11-3 and 5-11.

Bombay Grab: 246 Bow Road. (B2/6) *Free House.*
No real ale!

BOW BELLS: 116 Bow Road. (B2/7) *Ind Coope Taylor Walker.*
TETLEY BITTER, IND COOPE BURTON ALE. Large comfortable pub
with interesting collection of toby jugs prints and, as
you might expect considering its name, a collection of
bells. The only pub in Bow with a genuine guest beer
policy, it could be anthing! Fives dartboard. Live music
at lunchtime on Sunday. Lunchtime cooked food. Open Monday
- Friday 11-11, Saturday 11-4 and 7-11

Bridge House: 14 Bow Common Lane. (B2/8) *Belhaven.*
No real ale!

BRITANNIA: 185 Bow Common Lane. (A2/9) *Courage.*
DIRECTORS BITTER. Large backstreet local with darts and
snacks at lunchtime. Open all permitted hours.

BROMLEY ARMS: 51 Fairfield Road. (B1/10) *Shepherd Neame.*
SHEPHERD NEAME MASTER BREW, SHEPHERD NEAME SPITFIRE ALE.
Small pub opposite Bow Bus Garage. Darts and pool.
Lunchtime snacks. It has some nice stained glass windows.
Garden. Open Monday - Wednesday 11-3 and 5.30-11 Thursday
- Saturday 11-11.

CALEDONIAN ARMS: 62 Fairfield Road. (B1/11) *Shepherd Neame.*
SHEPHERD NEAME MASTER BREW. Basic backstreet local near
the old Bryant & May match factory that has been yuppified
to form the 'Little Apple'. But not before one
construction company went bust in the attempt. Darts and
pool. Lunchtme snacks. Open all permitted hours.

COBORN ARMS: 8 Coborn Road. (A1/12) *Young & Co.*
*YOUNGS BITTER, YOUNGS SPECIAL, WINTER WARMER (WINTER
ONLY).* Until 1984 was a Whitbread pub. Dartboards in
constant use. Former Lacon Brewery pub. Outside drinking
area. Cooked food lunchtime. Open Monday - Saturday
11-2.30 and 5-11 except Friday (11-11).

Crown Hotel: 223 Grove Road. (A1/13) *Belhaven.*
No real ale!

Crystal Tavern: 25 Burdett Road. (A2/14) *Ind Coope Taylor
Walker. No real ale!*

Duke of Wellington: 16a Newmill House – Devas Street.
(B2/15) *Grand Met-Watneys.*
No real ale!

DUKE OF YORK: 129 Antill Road. (A1/16) *Ind Coope Taylor Walker.*
YOUNGS SPECIAL. Former Smith Garrett (Bow Brewery) pub as
can be seen by the original tiling. Darts. Open Monday –
Saturday 11-3 and 5-11.

EARL OF ELLESMERE: 19 Chisenhale Road. (A1/17) *Ind Coope Taylor*
Walker. *TETLEY BITTER, IND COOPE BURTON ALE.* Popular
backstreet local opposite the former Godson Brewery.
Darts pool and shove halfpenny. Garden. Open Monday –
Saturday 11-2.30 and 5-11.

Eleanor Arms: 460 Old Ford Road. (A1/18) *Shepherd Neame.*
No real ale!

George & Dragon: 92 St Pauls Way. (A2/19) *Belhaven.*
No real ale!

HAND & FLOWER: 72 Parnell Road. (B1/20) *Whitbreads.*
WHITBREAD WETHERED, WHITBREAD FLOWERS ORIGINAL. At the end
of Roman Road Market. Snacks at lunchtime. Live music
Friday and Saturday nights until midnight. Open all
permitted hours.

Horn of Plenty: 588 Mile End Road. (A2/21) *Ind Coope Taylor*
Walker. *No real ale!*

ICELAND: 421 Wick Lane. (B1/22) *Grand Met-Watneys.*
WEBSTERS YORKSHIRE BITTER. Basic mock Tudor pub just off
the motorway. Pool and shove halfpenny. Lunchtime snacks.
Open all permitted hours.

Imperial Crown: 50 St Leonard's Street. (B2/23) *Ind Coope Taylor*
Walker. No real ale!

John Bull: 490 Roman Road. (A1/24) *Ind Coope Taylor Walker.*
Stop press: Re-opened but still keg.

Kings Arms: 167 Bow Road. (B1/25) *Ind Coope Taylor Walker.*
No real ale!

Kitsons: 171 Devons Road. (B2/26) *Grand Met-Watneys.*
No real ale!

LITTLE DRIVER: 125 Bow Road. (B1/27) *Bass Charrington.*
CHARRINGTON IPA, BASS. Enormous 50 year old Hoare & Co
Celebrated Stout mirror on the wall near the dartboard. A
Finch's pub. Cooked food lunchtime. Garden. Open Monday –
Thursday 11-3 and 5-11, Friday and Saturday 11-11.

LORD CARDIGAN: 12 Anglo Road. **(B1/28)** *Ind Coope Burton.*
TETLEY BITTER, IND COOPE BURTON ALE, ADNAMS BITTER. Sells Youngs beers occasionally. Lively pub just off Roman Road market. Live music Saturday nights. Darts pool and shove halfpenny. Garden. Open Monday – Saturday 11-3 and 5-11.

Lord Morpeth: 402 Old Ford Road. **(A1/29)** *Whitbreads.*
No real ale!

Lord Palmerston: 45 Hewlett Road. **(A1/30)** *Free House.*
No real ale!

LORD TREDEGAR: 50 Lichfield Road. **(A1/31)** *Ind Coope Taylor* Walker. *TETLEY BITTER, IND COOPE BURTON ALE, ADNAMS BITTER.* Friendly and comfortable one bar pub on the fringe of a conservation area. Darts and pool. A Grade II Listed Building. Garden. Open all permitted hours.

Melody Park Inn: 2 Midlothian Road. **(A2/32)** *Grand Met-Watneys.*
No beer – closed. Stop press: Re-opened still keg.

Milton Arms: 28 Wright's Road. **(B1/33)** *Free House.*
No real ale!

MOULDERS ARMS: 50/2 Bromley High Street. **(B2/34)** *Grand* Met-Watneys. *WEBSTERS YORKSHIRE BITTER, RUDDLES BEST.* The pub looks out of place amongst the high rise flats. Pictures of film stars decorate the lounge bar walls. Cooked food at all times. Pool. Open all permitted hours except Saturday when the hours are 11-4 and 7-11.

Needle Gun: 527 Roman Road. **(A1/35)** *Ind Coope Taylor Walker.*
No real ale!

NEW GLOBE: 359 Mile End Road. **(A1/36)** *Whitbreads.*
FULLERS LONDON PRIDE, MARSTONS PEDIGREE. Parissene style cafe-bar with good range of food. Open all permitted hours plus till 2am on Thurs, Fri and Sat nights. On the local list of Listed Buildings.

Old Duke of Cambridge: 158 Devons Road. **(B2/37)** *Belhaven.*
No real ale!

Old Ford Tavern: 393 Old Ford Road. **(B1/38)** *Free House.*
No real ale!

Ordell Arms: 22 Ordell Road. **(B1/39)** *Free House.*
No real ale!

PALM TREE: 24/6 Palm Street. **(A1/40)** *Free House.*
TOLLY COBBOLD BITTER, TOLLY COBBOLD MILD. Canalside pub that has been isolated by what is known as Mile End Park. Darts. Well worth finding (if you can). Brent Walker owned. Garden.

E3

Playwrights: 43 Morgan Street. **(A1/41)** *Grand Met–Watneys.*
No real ale! Formerly Morgan Arms.

Prince of Wales: 2 Grove Road. **(A1/42)** *Grand Met–Watneys.*
No real ale!

Pearly King: 94 Bromley High Street. *Free House.*

No longer a pub.

Priory Tavern: 37 St Leonard Street. **(B2/43)** *Grand Met–Trumans.*
No real ale!

Queen Victoria: 1 Gillender Street. **(B2/44)** *Free House.*
No real ale!

Railway Tavern: 30 Grove Road. **(A1/45)** *Free House.*
No real ale!

Ranelagh Arms: 599 Roman Road. **(B1/46)** *Courage.*
No real ale!

Rising Sun: 14 Gillender Street. **(B2/47)** *Belhaven.*
No real ale!

ROSE & CROWN: 8 Stroudley Walk – Devons Road. **(B2/48)** *Ind Coope*
Taylor Walker. *IND COOPE BURTON ALE.* One-bar pub near Bow
Church. Darts and shove halfpenny. Cooked food lunchtime.
Garden. Open all permitted hours. A Grade II Listed
Building.

Rose of Denmark: 612 Roman Road. (B1/49) *Belhaven.*
No real ale!

TENTERDEN ARMS: 224 Devons Road. (B2/50) *Grand Met-Trumans.*
RUDDLES BEST. Large one bar pub with darts. Mural tiles inside. Lunchtime snacks. Open all pemitted hours.

YE OLDE THREE TUNS: 185 Bow Road. (B1/51) *Whitbreads.*
FLOWERS IPA. Friendly, mock Tudor style one-bar pub. Three Tuns appear on the arms of the Company of Vintners and the Brewers Company. The pub was enlarged in 1985. Darts. Lunchtime snacks. Open all permitted hours.

Unicorn: 27 Vivian Road. (A1/52) *Whitbreads.*
No real ale!

VICTORIA: 110 Grove Road. (A1/53) *Charles Wells.*
CHARLES WELLS EAGLE. Former Charrington pub acquired by Charles Wells in March 1991. Pool. Garden. Lunchtime food. Open all permitted hours.

WENTWORTH ARMS: 97 Eric Street. (A2/54) *Charles Wells.*
CHARLES WELLS EAGLE. Recently (1991) acquired from Charrington. Expensive. Lunchtime food. Open all permitted hours. Situated behind Mile End Station.

White Horse: 473 Roman Road. (A1/55) *Grand Met-Watneys.*
No real ale!

Whitethorn: 30 Whitethorn Street. (B1/56) *Grand Met-Trumans.*
No real ale!

WIDOWS SON: 75 Devons Road. (B2/57) *Ind Coope Taylor Walker.*
TETLEY BITTER, IND COOPE BURTON ALE. Shove h'p and darts in this single bar pub. Live music at weekends. A Grade II Listed Building because: 'Interior retains almost completely its circa 1870s fittings, including engraved mirrors, decorated panels to pilastersgilt capitals and glass, fronted cabinets containing assorted china. Ornamental lettered panels states: 'Importer and bonder of choice Foreign cigars: The Widow's Son. Family Wine Spirit and Malt Liquor Establishment'. Lunchtime snacks. Every Easter a sailor places a hot cross bun amongst others in memory of a mothers sailor son who was lost at sea. Open Mon - Wed 11-11, Thurs 11-midnight, Fri 11-1am Saturday 11-4 and 8-1am.

Young Prince: 448 Roman Road. (A1/58) *Free House.*
No real ale!

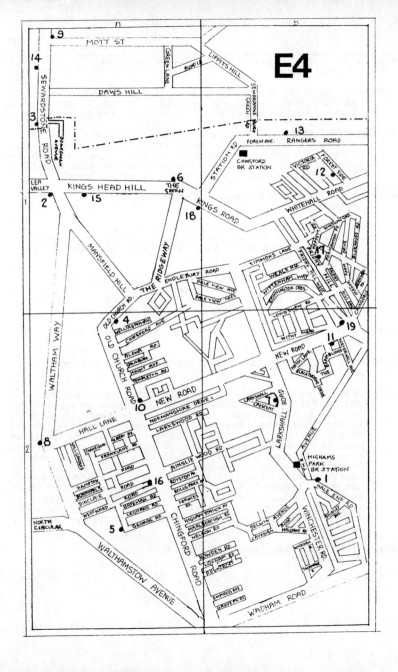

E4

Station - Chingford and Highams Park (BR Liverpool Street).

Although having its attractions, such as the area around the Church much of Chingford is suburban sprawl dating from the 1920s and 1930s and encouraged by the railway. Look out for the occasional remains of older hamlets, and also rural parts where the area gives way to Epping Forest in the north. Because of the Forest, this was a popular destination for excursions from the 1860s until this century, when people were able to venture further afield. Most of the pubs date from the twentieth century and are further spread out than in most of the districts in this guide.

In the north of the area the Guide covers the Essex hamlet of Sewardstone.

THE COUNTY ARMS: 420 Hale End Road. (B2/1) *Grand Met-Trumans. WEBSTERS YORKSHIRE BITTER, RUDDLES COUNTY.* Big and busy corner pub strong on pub team games (pool, darts, quizzes etc). Decorated with dray horses and knick-knacks. Function room. Disabled welcome. Snacks at all times. Opens 11-3 and 5.30 to 11 Monday to Thursday and 11-11 on Friday and 11-3 and 7-11 on Saturday.

Crooked Billet: Chingford Road. *Ind Coope Taylor Walker. Pub demolished.*

FOUNTAIN: 51 Sewardstone Road. (A1/2) *Ind Coope Taylor Walker. TETLEY BITTER.* Large comfortable pub at busy junction. Plenty of seating, strong on local charities, barbecues in summer. Quiet at lunchtimes but disco in the evening. Pin table. Garden. Open Monday to Thursday 12-3 and 5.30-11, Friday 12-11, Saturday 11-3 and 6-11.

FOX & HOUNDS: Sewardstone Road (A1/3) *Grand Met-Watneys. ADNAMS BITTER.* Large two-bar pub that is actually in Essex whilst being in London the postal district of E4. Live music Saturdays. Snacks. Darts and pool. Garden. Open all permitted hours.

The Green Man: 195 Old Church Road. (A2/4) *Grand Met-Watneys. No real ale!*

The Greyhound: 2 Silver Birch Avenue. (A2/5) *Bass Charrington. No real ale!*

THE LARKSHALL: Larkshall Road. (B2/7) *Courage.*
COURAGE BEST BITTER, JOHN SMITH'S BITTER, DIRECTORS BITTER. Superb old looking pub with various little rooms and large ornate eating section. The only thing against it are the artificial fires. Larkshall Farm was on this site from 1890 till the pub was built. Disabled welcome. Food at lunchtime only. Darts. Open Monday to Friday 11-3 and 5.30 to 11. Saturday 12-4 and 7-11.

KINGS HEAD: Kings Head Hill. (A1/6) *Ind Coope Taylor Walker.*
TETLEY BITTER, IND COOPE BURTON ALE. Busy one-bar pub just off main shopping area of North Chingford. Guest beer currently Youngs Bitter. Darts garden and function room. Food at lunchtime only. Open Monday to Thursday 11-3 and 5.30-11. Friday from 11-11 and Saturday 11-3 and 7-11.

OLD HALL TAVERN: Hall Lane. (A2/8) *Grand Met-Watneys.*
WEBSTERS YORKSHIRE BITTER, RUDDLES COUNTY. Large pub between Chingford and the North Circular Road. Restaurant and garden gone since last survey but food lunchtimes. Darts and pool. Open all permitted hours.

PLOUGH: Mott Street. (A1/9) *McMullens.*
McMULLENS AK, McMULLENS COUNTRY BITTER, STRONGHART. Surrounded by superb walking countryside but when visiting the pub check the frequency of the bus service as it is 2 hourly after 6 with the last bus to un-civilisation at 9.30. The previous Plough can be seen around the corner. Darts, pool and shove halfpenny as well as bar billiards. Garden. Food at all times except Monday evening. At 108p the AK is the cheapest regular pint in this guide. Open Mon to Sat 11-2.30 (3.30 Sat) and 6(7 Sat)-11.

PRINCE ALBERT: 1 Old Church Road. (A2/10) *Whitbreads.*
WHITBREAD WETHERED, WHITBREAD FLOWERS ORIGINAL. Comfortable one bar pub under shopping centre that used to be at ground level before it became the Iceland store. Food at lunchtime based on Pizza Hut menu. Open all permitted hours.

PRINCE OF WALES: 71 Hatch Lane. (B2/11) *Bass Charrington.*
CHARRINGTON IPA, BASS. Busy friendly locals' pub with plenty of wood panelling. Disabled welcome. Darts and snooker. Children's room and garden. Snacks at lunchtime only. Open Monday to Thursdays 11-3 and 5.30-11. Friday 11-4 and 5.30-11. Saturday 11-11.

QUEEN ELIZABETH: 95 Forest Side. (B1/12) *Grand Met-Trumans.*
WEBSTERS YORKSHIRE BITTER, RUDDLES BEST RUDDLES COUNTY. Barnaby's Carvery opposite Epping Forest. Main bar with real ale is decorated with old beams. In our last guide this pub sold the Truman range of Bitter, Best and Sampson. Facilities: Darts, pool, restaurant, function and

childrens rooms. Piped musiic in the loos. Open Monday to
Saturday 11-3 and 5.30-11. Restaurant open all day Sunday.

Royal Forest Hotel: Rangers Road. (B1/13) *Free House.*
No real ale!

ROYAL OAK (VENNERS):   Sewardstone Road. (A1/14) *Free House.*
DIRECTORS BITTER. Darts and function room. Snacks at all
times. Open Monday to Saturday 11-2.30 and 6-11. Garden.
At 122p a cheap pint!

ROYAL OAK: 219 Kings Head Hill. (A1/15) *McMullens.*
McMULLENS AK, McMULLENS COUNTRY BITTER, STRONGHART. Meals
in separate lounge area at lunchtime and evenings (7-9).
Two distinctive bars - public clean and comfortable
lounge quiet and plush. Darts shove halfpenny and bar
billiards. Garden. Car park. Open Monday to Friday 11-3
and 5.30 to 11, public bar open all day Saturday.

ROYSTON ARMS: 101   Chingford   Mount   Road.   (A2/16)   *Bass*
Charrington. *CHARRINGTON IPA, BASS.* Huge two-bar local
tastefully decorated with prints and paintings etc. Darts
and shove halfpenny with six pool tables. Garden. Opens
Monday to Wednesday 12-3 and 5.30-11. Thursday 11-3 and
5.30-11. Friday 11-11. Saturday 11-4 and 7-11.

THE SIRLOIN: Friday Hill. (B1/17) *Grand Met-Watneys.*
WEBSTERS YORKSHIRE BITTER, RUDDLES BEST, RUDDLES COUNTY.
Large pub with conservatory and over 21's policy. Two bars
in differnt styles one for eating. Darts, garden and
childrens room. Food at lunchtime only. Open Monday to
Saturday 11-3 and 5.30-11.

SLUG & LETTUCE: The Green. (A1/18) *Ind Coope Burton.*
TETLEY BITTER. Large pub now made into one bar. Formerly
the Bull & Crown. Snacks lunchtime only. Darts. Open
Monday to Saturday 12-11.

WHEELWRIGHTS: 94 Hatch Lane. (B2/19) *Whitbreads.*
WHITBREAD WETHERED, WHITBREAD FLOWERS ORIGINAL. Large
Beefeater Inn decorated with large wheels and photos of
old Chingford Hatch and wheelwrights at work on the walls.
Restaurant and garden. Open Monday to Saturday 11-3 and
5.30-11.

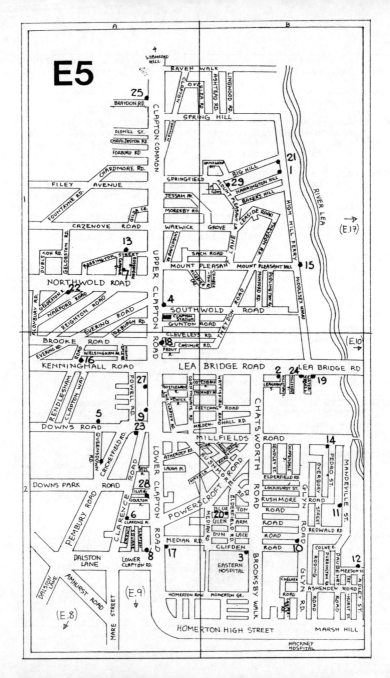

E5

Station - Clapton (BR Liverpool Street).

Clapton is part of northern Hackney, sloping down to the River Lea through an extensive mixture of many of the residential building styles of the past hundred and fifty years or so - although few of the pubs seem to display the earlier styles. The railway cuts through the area and leaps the Lea besides the only real riverside stretch in this guide, from which a string of pubs benefits from some tranquil views over the Hackney Marshes. The river is part of our canal network, and the intrepid can sail to Manchester and even beyond from here. There is still some commercial traffic although not as much as when local Victorian canal poet Cosmo Pilkington came over to pen a few lines - "I sail my barge down the Lea/and see a pub - It's ale for me!/Off the barge and in the bar/Soon I'm getting down a jar". Truly the local answer to McGonagall.

The Lea Valley Regional Park extends from here right up to Ware in Hertfordshire.

ANCHOR & HOPE: 15 High Hill Ferry. (B1/1) *Fullers.*
FULLERS LONDON PRIDE ESB. No food just good beer. One-bar pub on the waterfront. Darts. Opens at 6pm Saturday evenings.

British Oak: 130 Lea Bridge Road. (B2/2) *Grand Met-Watneys.*
No real ale!

Clapton Park Tavern: 9 Chatsworth Road. (B2/3) *Bass Charrington.*

No real ale!

CROOKED BILLET: 84 Upper Clapton Road. (A1/4) *Grand Met-Watneys.*

WEBSTERS YORKSHIRE BITTER. Large one bar pub with restaurant in the old saloon bar. Darts. Open all permitted hours.

The Downs: 75 Downs Road. (A2/5) *Ind Coope Taylor Walker.*
No real ale!

Duke of Clarence: 78 Clarence Road. (A2/6) *Grand Met-Trumans.*
No real ale!

Duke of York (Pudlocks): 2 Charnwood Street. **(A1/7)** *Grand* Met-Watneys. *No real ale!*

ELEPHANTS HEAD: 43 Lower Clapton Road. (A2/8) *Courage.*
COURAGE BEST BITTER, DIRECTORS BITTER. Live Irish music weekends. Darts pool and TV. Open Monday to Friday 11-11 11-3 and 7.30-11 Saturday.

Fountain: 211 Lower Clapton Road. (A2/9) *Grand Met-Watneys.*
No real ale!

George: 171 Glyn Road. (B2/10) *Courage.*
No real ale!

Glyn Arms: 1 Mandeville Street. (B2/11) *Ind Coope Taylor Walker.*

No real ale!

Golden Shoe: 47 Meeson Street. (B2/12) *Grand Met-Watneys.*
No real ale!

Hope & Anchor: 30 Rossington Street. (A1/13) *Belhaven.*
No real ale!

Jubilee: 278 Millfields Road. (B2/14) *Belhaven.*
No real ale!

Kings Head: 44 Middlesex Wharf. (B1/15) *Grand Met-Watneys.*
No real ale!

London Tavern: 92 Rendlesham Road. (A2/16) *Bass Charrington.*
No real ale!

LORD CECIL: 42 Lower Clapton Road. (A2/17) *Courage.*
COURAGE BEST BITTER, DIRECTORS BITTER YOUNGS SPECIAL. Darts pool and a garden. Live music Thursday Friday and Saturday evenings. Food lunchtimes. Open all permitted hours with extensions till midnight.

Old Kings Head: 28 Upper Clapton Road. **(A2/18)** *Grand* Met-Trumans. *No real ale!*

PRINCE OF WALES: 146 Lea Bridge Road. (B2/19) *Young & Co.*
YOUNGS BITTER, YOUNGS SPECIAL, WINTER WARMER (WINTER ONLY). The one Youngs pub in the East End that did not revert to Whitbread. Darts. Food at all times. Open all permitted hours if custom allows.

PRIORY TAVERN: 57 Elderfield Road. (B2/20) *Bass Charrington.*
BASS. Darts, pool and garden. Opens Monday to Friday 11-3 and 5-11 Saturday 11-11.

ROBIN HOOD: High Hill Ferry. (B1/21) *Courage.*
COURAGE BEST BITTER, DIRECTORS BITTER RUDDLES BEST. One-bar pub with rowing paraphernalia on the ceiling. Darts. Food lunchtimes.

ROYAL SOVEREIGN: 64 Northwold Road. (A1/22) *Bass Charrington.*
CHARRINGTON IPA. One-bar pub with collection of regulars'
ties cut whilst being worn. Open brickwork on most walls.
Darts and pool. Children's outdoor area and garden with
fish pond and aviary. Snacks at all times. Open all
permitted hours.

Shamps: 181 Clarence Road. (A2/23) *Grand Met-Watneys.*
No real ale!

SHIP AGROUND: 144 Lea Bridge Road. (B2/24) *Bass Charrington.*
BASS. Large pub with darts and pool and outside drinking
area. Cooked meals lunchtime and snacks at other times.
Open all permitted hours.

SWAN: 73 Clapton Common. (A1/25) *Bass Charrington.*
CHARRINGTON IPA, BASS, FULLERS LONDON PRIDE. Large one-bar
pub with loud music/TV. Darts and pool. Pinball. Food at
lunchtime only. Open all permitted hours.

Three Sisters: 35 Queensdown Road. (A2/26) *Belhaven.*
No real ale!

White Hart: 231 Lower Clapton Road. (A2/27) *Bass Charrington.*
No real ale!

WINDSOR CASTLE: 135 Lower Clapton Road. (A2/28) *Grand
Met-Watneys. WEBSTERS YORKSHIRE BITTER.* Darts pool and
garden. Cooked meals till 10pm. Disco. Opens Monday to
Thursday 11-3 and 5-11 Friday 11am-2am Saturday 11-5 and
8-2am.

WOODMAN: 199 Mount Pleasant Lane. (B1/29) *Grand Met-Watneys.*
RUDDLES BEST, RUDDLES COUNTY. Darts and pool. Garden.
Cooked food lunchtimes and snacks other times. Open all
permitted hours.

This guide on your PC?

Profits from our Pig's Ear Beer Festivals have enabled us to
purchase a 'small business' Amstrad PCW computer. A database with
80 fields was designed and assembled on Datastar and currently
accounts for 450k of memory. The ASCII files produced were then
'mailmerged' with Locoscript II (a word processing package) to
create the style.

We plan to convert data currently on 3" discs to 5¼" and 3½"
discs. If you would like a copy of our database design and data
send £5 plus three blank discs to: Keith Emmerson, 111 Ordell
Road, Bow, London E3 2EQ.

We would welcome other database designs mirroring our own.
Currently the only other design we have is for Dataease. Again if
you would like a copy (not of the database, that is illegal) send
a disc to the above address.

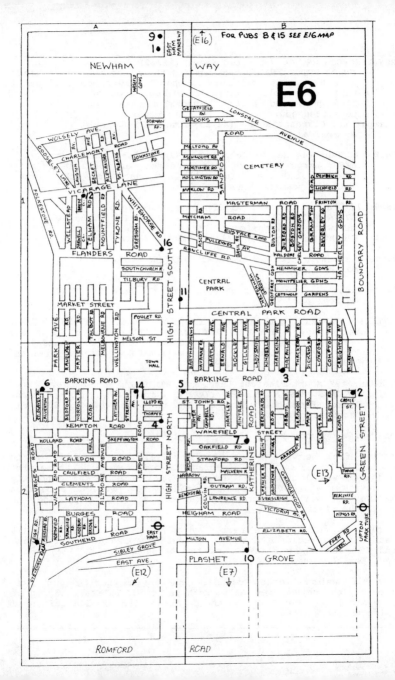

Stations – none. East Ham and Upton Park (District) are just outside the area and Beckton (DLR) is expected to open during the currency of this guide.

Spreading along the Barking Road forming part of the sprawling mass of Victorian urban development between Stratford and Barking or Ilford East Ham also extends downwards to Beckton and the edges of the Docklands developments. The two parts are divided by the A12 bypass south of which there used to be mainly derelict land extending as far as Beckton Gas Works – once famed since its owners refused to allow any electricity on the premises, even for lighting.

Now, a mushrooming growth of hypermarkets extends from the Ski Slope (near the A12) as far as the little community of Cyprus just north of the Docks. Pubs here are few and the best range in the area is back on the Barking Road near the station, where a good selection of Victorian town pubs near the well restored Town Hall gives some relief from the more suburban types elsewhere. However, domination of the pubs by the Big Four breweries is general – although guest beers are starting to creep in.

West Ham United (a lesser known club than Leyton Orient) ·have their football ground near Upton Park station.

Alpine Bar: Mountain Top Dri Ski Slope – Alpine Way. **(A1/1)**
Free House. No real ale!

BOLEYN TAVERN: 1 Barking Road. **(B2/2)** *Ind Coope Taylor Walker.*
TAYLOR WALKER BEST BITTER TETLEY BITTER. Large three-bar Victorian pub close to West Ham FC. Darts in public bar, pool in the saloon. History lesson now starts: Anne Boleyn married Henry VIII secretly in 1533 and was the mother of Elizabeth I. Three years later she died of a sore neck. Lunchtime snacks. Open all permitted hours.

CENTRAL HOTEL: 150 Barking Road. **(B2/3)** *Ind Coope Taylor Walker.*

TETLEY BITTER, IND COOPE BURTON ALE. Three-bar Victorian pub. Darts and pool in basic public bar. Live music and talent nights Thursday to Sunday in the saloon. Lounge bar entrance in Macaulay Road. Snacks lunchtime. Function room and garden. Open Monday to Wednesday 11-11 and till midnight Thursday to Saturday.

Cock: 56 High Street North. **(B2/4)** *Bass Charrington.*
No real ale!

DENMARK ARMS: 381 Barking Road. **(A2/5)** *Ind Coope Taylor Walker.*
TETLEY BITTER, IND COOPE BURTON ALE. Large Victorian
corner pub recently refurbished into one bar. Darts and
function room. Cooked food lunchtime and snacks at other
times. Open all permitted hours.

DUKES HEAD: 593 Barking Road. **(A2/6)** *Bass Charrington.*
CHARRINGTON IPA. Real ale not always available. Large
basic Victorian pub with East London fives dartboard and a
fish tank in the public bar. Two pool tables in cavernous
saloon. Occasional disco. Garden. Open Monday to Friday
12-11, Saturday 12-4 and 7-11.

EARL OF WAKEFIELD: 72 Katherine Road. **(B2/7)** *Bass Charrington.*
CHARRINGTON IPA, BASS. Comfortable two-bar side street pub
with mainly local clientele but still welcoming. Darts and
pool. Snacks and meals at lunchtime.Garden. Live music at
weekends. Open Monday to Thursday 12-11, Friday 11-11,
Saturday 11-4 and 7-11.

FERNDALE HOTEL: 40 Cyprus Place. **(A1/8)** *Bass Charrington.*
CHARRINGTON IPA. A pub whose fortunes have been revived by
a new housing estate. Recently renovated with pictures of
Old Beckton and local docks. Large variety of live music,
discos and karaoke on Wed Fri to Sun nights. Darts and
pool. Lunchtime snacks. Restaurant/function room. Open all
permitted hours unless there is no custom.

Golfer: East Ham Manor Way. **(A1/9)** *Free House.*
No real ale!

GREEN MAN: 190 Plashet Grove. **(B2/10)** *Ind Coope Taylor Walker.*
TETLEY BITTER, IND COOPE BURTON ALE. Large pub recently
converted to one bar. Separate pool room with three
tables. Darts. Function room for over 200 people. Garden
and car park. Cooked meals lunchtime and snacks at other
times. Open Monday to Friday 11-11, Saturday 11-4 and
7-11.

HAMMERS: 80 High Street South. **(A1/11)** *Grand Met-Watneys.*
WEBSTERS YORKSHIRE BITTER, RUDDLES COUNTY. In 1959 it was
called the Red Lion. Small friendly one-bar pub with
numerous pictures of West Ham FC decorating the walls.
Darts, lunchtime meals. Occasional barbecues in the
garden. Open all permitted hours.

PERSEVERANCE: 33 Vicarage Lane. **(A1/12)** *Free House.*
TETLEY BITTER FULLERS LONDON PRIDE. Friendly one-bar
locals' pub. At the time of survey (May 91) the landlord
had just bought the pub from Charrington and it was in the
middle of renovation. Beer range may increase when this is
finished. Darts (fives board), snacks at lunchtime,
occasional discos and beer garden with monthly barbecues.
Known as the Drum and Monkey, after the previous landlord

who kept a monkey and barrel organ. Open Monday – Friday 11-11   Saturday 11-4 and 7-11.

RODING: Southend Road. (A2/13) *Ind Coope Taylor Walker.*
TETLEY BITTER, IND COOPE BURTON ALE. Large corner pub with one rambling bar. Stuffed annimals and assorted nick-nacks on the walls. Occasional discos and barbecues in the garden. Darts and pool. Open Monday to Thursday 11-3 and 5.30-11, Friday to Saturday 11-11. The pub name relates to the nearby tributary of the Thames.

Spirit Bar: 419/429 Barking Road. (A2/14) *Free House.*
No beer – closed. Formerly Biancos.

TOLLGATE TAVERN: 16 Mary Rose Mall – Frobisher Road. (B1/15) *Whitbreads.* *FLOWERS IPA, WHITBREAD FLOWERS ORIGINAL, GREENE KING ABBOT ALE.* Large comfortable one-bar pub opened in December 1984. Extension promised to include a restaurant and childrens room. Darts. Live music Saturday night and Sunday lunchtime. Toilets for the disabled. Open all permitted hours. Garden.

WHITE HORSE: 125 High Street South. (A1/16) *Bass Charrington.*
BASS, FULLERS LONDON PRIDE. Modern one-bar pub recently renovated with numerous portraits of horses. Darts and pool. Cooked meals lunchtime. Outside drinking area. Open all permitted hours.

Follies   ex Empress of India E9.
No longer a pub.

Stations – Forest Gate (BR Liverpool Street), Wanstead Park and Woodgrange Park (BR Barking line). Upton Park (District) is just outside the area.

Forest Gate forms an almost entirely residential district between Stratford and Manor Park, extending along the line of the Romford Road. Once it was so rural that the first railway station in the area was soon closed through lack of custom but those days can now only be imagined at its northern boundary where it is bordered by the parklands of Wanstead Flats. The area was largely built up in the second half of the nineteenth century and the pubs reflect that period.

Much of the Taylor Walker influence in this and adjoining districts derives from Holt's, who operated the Marine Brewery in Ratcliff Road from 1837 until it was taken over by the Cannon Brewery in 1912 with 27 pubs. Cannon were themselves acquired by Taylor Walker in 1930.

Albion Hotel: 141 Boleyn Road. (A2/1) *Grand Met-Watneys.*
No real ale!

CAMDEN ARMS: 70 Field Road. (A1/2) *Grand Met-Watneys.*
WEBSTERS YORKSHIRE BITTER, RUDDLES COUNTY. Public bar contains darts and pool table. Cosy saloon. Snacks at all times. Open Monday – Friday 11-3 and 5.30-11 and all day Saturday.

Duke of Fife: 350 Katherine Road. (B2/3) *Courage.*
No real ale!

Eagle & Child: 112 Woodgrange Road. (A1/4) *Ind Coope Burton.*
No real ale!

EARL OF DERBY: 16 Station Road. (A1/5) *Courage.*
COURAGE BEST BITTER, DIRECTORS BITTER. One-bar pub with darts and pool. Food to order at all times. Open all permitted hours.

FOREST GATE HOTEL: 105 Godwin Road. (B1/6) *Ind Coope Taylor Walker. TETLEY BITTER, IND COOPE BURTON ALE.* One-bar pub with lunchtime snacks. Darts and pool. Function room for 150 people. Garden. Entertainment Friday and Saturday night and Sunday lunchtime. Open Monday – Friday 11-3 and 5-11, Saturday 11-11.

FOREST GLEN: 39 Dames Road. (A1/7) *Bass Charrington.*
CHARRINGTON IPA. Large pub with a colonial atmosphere and Irish slant. Darts and two pool tables. Garden. Cooked food lunchtimes and snacks other times. Open all permitted hours.

FOX & HOUNDS: 178 Forest Lane. (A2/8) *Grand Met-Watneys.*
WEBSTERS YORKSHIRE BITTER, RUDDLES BEST, RUDDLES COUNTY. Unusual array of army buttons and cap badges. Darts. Snacks at all times. Open all permitted hours.

HOLLY TREE: 129 Dames Road. (A1/9) *Bass Charrington.*
CHARRINGTON IPA, BASS. Large public house with a restaurant. Darts. Garden. Open Monday - Friday 11-3 and 5-11, Saturday 11-4 and 7-11.

LIVE & LET LIVE: 264 Romford Road. (A2/10) *Bass Charrington.*
CHARRINGTON IPA, BASS. Pub with plastic plants that look dead and great lumps missing from the ceiling. About time Charrington dug into their pockets and shelled out a few bob on redecorating. Darts and bar billiards. Lunchtime snacks. Open Monday - Thursday 11-3.30 and 5.30-11, Friday 11-11, Saturday 11-5 and 7-11.

MICKEY FINNS: 76 Woodgrange Road. (A2/11a) *Free House.*
GREENE KING IPA. Stop Press entry. Wine bar/Bistro with garden opposite Forest Gate BR Station. Snacks all day. Open Monday 6-11, Tues - Sat 12-11, normal Sunday hours.

Odessa Arms: 53 Odessa Road. (A1/11) *Courage.*
No real ale!

OLD SPOTTED DOG: 212 Upton Lane. (A2/12) *Grand Met-Watneys.*
RUDDLES COUNTY, CHARRINGTON IPA. This pub is well worth a visit for the food as well as the drink. Public bar. Childrens room. Jazz on Friday night. Open Monday - Friday 11-3 and 5.30-11, Saturday 11-3 and 7-11.

PRINCESS ALICE: 329 Romford Road. (A2/13) *Ind Coope Taylor Walker. TETLEY BITTER, IND COOPE BURTON ALE.* This consists of three bars, four pool tables and pin ball machine. Upstairs night club open till 1am. Piped music. Food at all times. Open all permitted hours.

RAILWAY TAVERN: 173 Forest Lane. (A2/14) *Ind Coope Taylor Walker. TETLEY BITTER.* One-bar pub with darts and pool. Snacks at all times. Open Monday to Wednesday 11-3 and 5-11, Thursday to Saturday 11-11.

Rising Sun: 528 Romford Road. (B2/15) *Bass Charrington.*
No real ale!

Simpsons: 342 Romford Road. (A2/16) *Grand Met-Trumans.*
No real ale!

Towers: 83 Tower Hamlets Road. (B2/17) *Grand Met-Watneys.*
No real ale!

Travellers Rest: 12 Cemetery Road. (A1/18) *Free House.*
No real ale!

WAGON & HORSES: 392 Romford Road. (B2/19) *Grand Met-Watneys.*
WEBSTERS YORKSHIRE BITTER, RUDDLES BEST, RUDDLES COUNTY.
Two-bar pub with darts and pool. Cooked food lunchtime and
snacks other times. The 'London & Burton Brewery Sparkling
Ales' sign outside refers to the brewery that was in
Medland Street, Stepney.

WHITE HART: 249/251 Green Street. (B2/20) *Bass Charrington.*
CHARRINGTON IPA, FULLERS LONDON PRIDE. Predominantly
cosmopolitan pub with music at weekends. Snacks at all
times. Cheapest pint of London Pride in this guide. Open
all permitted hours.

Falcon E14. *Demolished.*

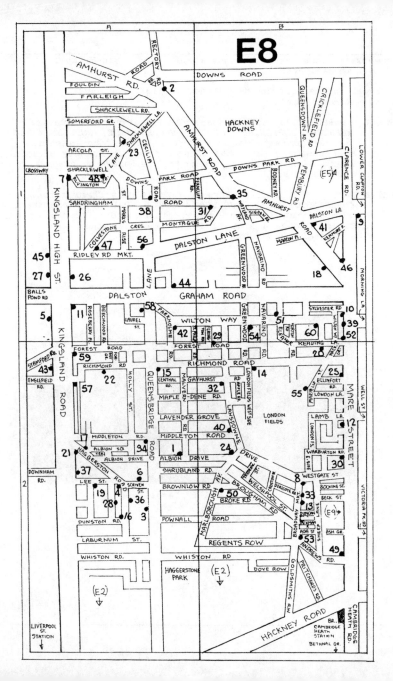

E8

Stations - London Fields and Hackney Downs (BR Liverpool Street),
Hackney Central and Dalston Kingsland Road (BR North London).

This guide covers the central part of Hackney, from Kingsland
Road to Mare Street and including those parts around the Town
Hall and church. Other parts of the borough fall into Clapton and
Homerton and the western end is covered by CAMRA's North London
Guide. Much of the borough is covered by waves of terraced
housing, punctuated (especially in the south towards the Regents
Canal) by some more modern estates and the inevitable blocks of
flats.

The E8 district has retained many of its original pubs and a good
number still display an interesting range of late Victorian
styles. There are some concentrations around the local markets,
such as Ridley Road or Broadway Markets. Many have an Irish
clientele and music is a popular feature, although sadly real ale
is not as widely available as we would like and the beer range is
dominated by the Big Four.

ALBION TAVERN: 33 Albion Drive. (A2/1) *Shepherd Neame.*
SHEPHERD NEAME MASTER BREW. One cocktail-style bar with
darts and pool. Open Monday - Saturday 11-3 and 5.30-11.

Amhurst Arms: 240 Amhurst Road. (A1/2) *Grand Met-Watneys.*
No real ale!

Belgrave Arms: 217 Queensbridge Road. (A2/3) *Bass Charrington.*
No real ale!

Black Bull: 217 Haggerston Road. (A2/4) *Belhaven.*
No beer - closed.

Brewery Tap: 525 Kingsland Road. (A1/5) *Belhaven.*
No real ale!

Brownlow Arms: 10 Scriven Street. (A2/6) *Bass Charrington.*
No real ale!

Castle: 148 Kingsland High Street. (A1/7) *Courage.*
No real ale!

CAT & MUTTON: 76 Broadway Market. (B2/8) *Bass Charrington.*
CHARRINGTON IPA, BASS. Loud music pub overlooking London
Fields. Nice handpumps. Snacks at all times. Darts and
pool. Open all permitted hours.

Cock Tavern: 315 Mare Street (B1/9) *Grand Met–Trumans.*
No real ale!

CROWN: 418 Mare Street. (B1/10) *Grand Met–Trumans.*
WEBSTERS YORKSHIRE BITTER. One-bar pub with darts and pool. Garden. Facilities for the disabled. Lunchtime snacks. Open all permitted hours.

Crown & Castle: 600 Kingsland Road. (A1/11) *Grand Met–Watneys.*
No real ale!

Dolphin: 165 Mare Street. (B2/12) *Grand Met–Trumans.*
No real ale!

DOVE: 24 Broadway Market. (B2/13) *Free House.*
FULLERS LONDON PRIDE, BODDINGTONS BITTER, MARSTONS PEDIGREE, FLOWERS IPA. One-bar brought back to original Victorian look, (wood bar walls and window frames). Very well decorated. Yucca trees and plants in windows. Only one number on the clock – 11. Jazz on Sunday at lunchtime. Garden. Former Taylor Walker pub named the Goring Arms. Cooked food and snacks 11–10. Open all permitted hours.

DUKE OF MARLBOROUGH: 212 Richmond Road. (B2/14) *Shepherd Neame.*
SHEPHERD NEAME MASTER BREW. Large one-room pub with rectangular bar. Darts, pool and shove halfpenny. Garden. Cooked meals and snacks at all times. Open Monday – Saturday 12–11. Facilities for the disabled. Ex Watney.

Duke of Richmond: 316 Queensbridge Road. (A2/15) *Whitbreads.*
No beer – closed.

Duke of Sussex: 151 Haggerston Road. (A2/16) *Whitbreads.*
No real ale!

DUKE OF WELLINGTON: 260 Haggerston Road. (A2/17) *Courage.*
DIRECTORS BITTER. The pub took its present name to celebrate the adoption of the Duke as Prime Minister. Haggerston appears in the Doomsday Book as Hergodstone after Hergod a local Saxon leader who erected a stone memorial in the area. Darts and pool. Lunchtime meals and snack at other times. Open Monday – Friday 11–2.30 and 5–11, Saturday 11–4 and 7–11.

EARL AMHURST: 19 Amhurst Road. (B1/18) *Bass Charrington.*
CHARRINGTON IPA, BASS. Medium sized one-bar town centre pub near Hackney Central BR Station. Collection of washing jugs and basins and poes over the bar. Pool. Snacks and limited meals at all times. Open all permitted hours.

Earl of Zetland: 50 Lee Street. (A2/19) *Whitbreads.*
No real ale!

FLORFIELD ARMS: 40 Florfield Road. (B2/20) *Belhaven.*
JOHN SMITHS BITTER. Brightly lit family pub with a collection of mirrors. Darts. Lunchtime food. Open all permitted hours.

Fox: 372 Kingsland Road. (A2/21) *Grand Met-Watneys.*
No real ale!

Grange Tavern: 6 Richmond Road. (A2/22) *Bass Charrington.*
No real ale!

Green Man: 71 Shacklewell Lane. (A1/23) *Grand Met-Watneys.*
No real ale!

Havelock Arms: 113 Albion Drive. (B2/24) *Whitbreads.*
No real ale!

HOBSONS CHOICE (Horse & Groom): 255 Mare Street. (B2/25)
Free House. *BODDINGTONS, ADNAMS, GREENE KING ABBOT, FLOWERS IPA.* The Hobbson Nobbler Bitter is no doubt another name for Wethereds. Has various guest beers. All day food bar. Garden. Children welcome. Late licence to midnight Mon-Thurs and 1am Fri and Sat.

Kings Arms: 18 Kingsland High Street. (A1/26) *Bass Charrington.*
No real ale!

The Kingsland: 37 Kingsland High Street. **(A1/27)** *Ind Coope* Taylor Walker. *No real ale!* Formerly the Young Prince

L.A.: 64 Clarissa Street. (A2/28) *Free House.*
No beer - closed.

LADY DIANA: 95 Forest Road. (B2/29) *Free House.*
FULLERS LONDON PRIDE, CHISWICK, ADNAMS BITTER, GREENE KING ABBOT ALE, MARSTONS PEDIGREE. Formerly the Prince Arthur. Reasonably priced comfortable relaxed pub in fashionable part of Hackney. Photographs of the area c1900. Attractive lettering above the bar. Cooked meals and snacks at all times. Open Monday - Friday 11.30-3 and 5.30-11, Saturday 11-3 and 7-11.

THE LONDON FIELDS: 137 Mare Street. (B2/30) *Ind Coope Taylor* Walker. *TETLEY BITTER TAYLOR WALKER BEST BITTER GREENE KING IPA.* Formerly the Warburton Arms. Modernised in tasteful style with pictures of early Hackney and cricket scenes. Darts. Cooked food lunchtimes and snacks till 7pm. Open all permitted hours.

Lord Stanley: 136 Sandringham Road. (B1/31) *Courage.*
No real ale!

Lord Truro: 180 Dalston Lane. *Grand Met-Trumans.*
No longer a pub.

MARION ARMS: 46 Lansdowne Drive. (B2/32) *Bass Charrington.*
BASS. Friendly horseshoe-shaped bar with Wenlock Brewery
mirrors. Insults guaranteed until November when the pub
will belong to the Wiltshire Brewing Co. Darts, pool and
shove halfpenny. Live music Saturdays. Open all permitted
hours.

Market House: 30/2 Broadway Market. (B2/33) *Belhaven.*
No real ale!

Middleton Arms: 303 Queensbridge Road. (A2/34) *Bass Charrington.*

No real ale!

MITFORD TAVERN: 133 Amhurst Road. (B1/35) *Ind Coope Taylor*
*IND COOPE BURTON ALE.*Two-bar pub with a Smith & Garrett
(Bow Brewery) facade. Darts, pool and shove halfpenny.
Snacks. Open Monday - Friday 11-3 and 5-11, Saturday
11-11. Closed Wednesday lunchtime.

Nineteenth Hole: 216 Haggerston Road. (A2/36) *Belhaven.*
No real ale! Formerly the Young Prince

Nolans Bar: 296 Kingsland Road. (A2/37) *Free House.*
No real ale! Formerly the Acton Arms

NORFOLK ARMS: 49 Cecilia Road. (A1/38) *Free House.*
*WEBSTERS YORKSHIRE BITTER, MARSTONS PEDIGREE, GREENE KING
IPA, GREENE KING ABBOT ALE.* Former Youngs pub now owned by
Inn Leisure. Darts and pool. Cooked food at all times.
Live music most Fridays. Open all permitted hours.

OLD SHIP: 2 Sylvester Path. (B1/39) *Courage.*
DIRECTORS BITTER. One-bar pub with darts and pool. Basic
town pub. Also has an entrance in Mare St up a tiled
corridor. Lunchtime food. Open all permitted hours.

Paget Arms: 197 Middleton Road. (B2/40) *Courage.*
No real ale!

PEMBURY TAVERN: 90 Amhurst Road. (B1/41) *Grand Met-Trumans.*
RUDDLES BEST, RUDDLES COUNTY, FULLERS LONDON PRIDE.
Expensive and large one public bar pub with mixed
clientele. For a while was tied to Banks & Taylor. Pool.
Cooked meals lunchtime including Sundays. Live music most
nights. Open Monday - Thursday 12-12, Friday - Saturday
12-1am.

PRINCE GEORGE: 40 Parkholme Road. (A1/42) *Whitbreads.*
WHITBREAD FLOWERS ORIGINAL, BRAKSPEAR PA, GREENE KING
ABBOT ALE, WINTER ROYAL (WINTER ONLY), BODDINGTONS BITTER.
Large one bar pub. Sparsely furnished with interesting
prints of Brighton and pub sign of Prince Regent in
flagrante. Decorated with bust of Brunel and stuffed birds
in glass cages. Pool. Food at all times with monthly theme
dinners. 10'x8' map of the world. Mercator protection and
ionisers. Two real fires and function room. Currently
guest beer is London Pride. Open 12-3 and 5-11 Monday to
Friday and 11-11 on Saturdays and Bank Holidays.

PRINCE GEORGE:

Prince of Wales: 447 Kingsland Road. (A2/43) *Grand Met-Trumans.*
No real ale!

QUEEN ELIZABETH: 9 Graham Road. (A1/44) *Free House.*
TETLEY BITTER. Real ale may not always be available. Darts
and pool. Open Monday - Friday 12-11 Saturday 11-11.

Railway Tavern: 59 Kingsland High Street. **(A1/45)** *Bass*
Charrington. *No real ale!*

Railway Tavern: 339 Mare Street. (B1/46) *Bass Charrington.*
No real ale!

Ridley **Arms**: 17 Ridley Road. (A1/47) *Free House.*
No real ale!

ROBIN HOOD: 42 Shacklewell Lane. (A1/48) *Free House.*
CHARLES WELLS BOMBARDIER, COURAGE BEST BITTER. Fullers
London Pride and Everards Tiger are the alternating guest
beers. Ex Ind Coope and formerly called Taylors. Live
music on Wednesdays. Upstairs pool room and darts on
raised platform at back. Discos on Friday with quiz. Food
till 9pm. Open all permitted hours.

ROSE & CROWN: 13/15 Mare Street. (B2/49) *Whitbreads.*
*BODDINGTONS BITTER, CASTLE EDEN, FLOWERS IPA, WHITBREAD
FLOWERS ORIGINAL, MARSTONS PEDIGREE, BRAKSPEAR PA, YOUNGS
SPECIAL.* Former Youngs pub. Single bar with three-piece
suites and large Guinness toucan keeping an eye on
customers from above the bar. Darts pool and function
room. Garden. No food. Open all permitted hours.

Rosie O'Gradys: 27 Marlborough Avenue. (B2/50) *Belhaven.*
No real ale! Formerly the Lee Arms.

Royal Oak: 83 Wilton Way. (B1/51) *Belhaven.*
No real ale!

Samuel Pepys: 289 Mare Street. (B1/52) *Ind Coope Taylor Walker.*
No real ale! Formerly Mr Pepys.

Sir Walter Scott: 2 Broadway Market. (B2/53) *Whitbreads.*
No real ale!

SPURSTOWE ARMS: 68 Greenwood Road. (B1/54) *Free House.*
BASS. Two long narrow bars with striped blue decor. Big
Bass and Wenlock mirrors. Restaurant due to open towards
the end of 1991. Darts. TV in lounge. Currently tied to
Bass but will become a free house in June 1991. Function
room. Food at all times. Outside drinking area. Facilities
for the disabled. Open Monday – Thursday 11-4 and 7-11
(all day if busy), Friday – Saturday 11-11.

Taylors: 19 Martello Street. (B2/55) *Free House.*
No beer – closed. Formerly the Queen Eleanor.

THREE COMPASSES: 99 Dalston Lane. (A1/56) *Bass Charrington.*
CHARRINGTON IPA. Friendly locals' pub with plants and TV
in the lounge, basic public bar and spartan private bar.
Lunchtime snacks. Darts and shove halfpenny. Facilities
for the disabled. It will become a free house selling
Watney beers! Open all permitted hours.

Uncle Sams: 438 Kingsland Road (A2/57) *Belhaven.*
No real ale! Formerly the Swan.

Victoria: 451 Queensbridge Road. (A1/58) *Bass Charrington.*
No real ale!

THE VILLAGE AT DALSTON: 512 Kingsland Road. (A2/59) *Free House.*
*COURAGE BEST BITTER, JOHN SMITH'S BITTER, DIRECTORS
BITTER.* Large one-bar pub which for a short time (1990)
was the Flock & Firkin and the Lamb (Roses) before that.
Guest beers promised. Food at all times. Pool. Open all
permitted hours. Owned by Wessex Taverns.

WHITE HORSE: 76 Wilton Way. (B1/60) *Ind Coope Taylor Walker.*
BASS. Basic pub currently for sale. Darts and pool. Open
all permitted hours.

Lord Truro: 180 Dalston Lane. *Grand Met-Trumans.*
No longer a pub.

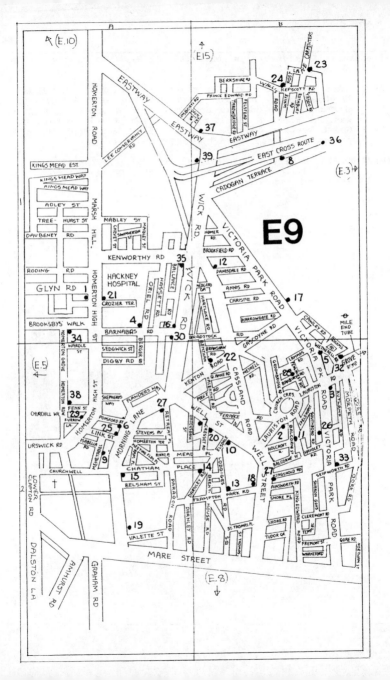

E9

Stations – Homerton and Hackney Wick (BR North London).

It has been said that few people know where Homerton is and even fewer really want to. However, that is a little unfair given that the area – the part of Hackney extending north from Victoria Park – represents a microcosm of East London housing developments. Going south from Homerton High Street blocks of soulless postwar flats give way to surviving Victorian terraces and then to the re-gentrified areas near Victoria Park. In this area there is an interesting selection of free houses, although elsewhere in the district the typical pub is a Big Four owned local, often fairly small and as likely as not under threat of closure.

Adam & Eve: 155 Homerton High Street. **(A1/1)** *Ind Coope Taylor Walker*. *No real ale!*

ALBION: 36 Lauriston Road. (B2/2) *Free House.*
RUDDLES COUNTY. Very old building with ship's beams dating from 1600s. The front part is modern – only 200 years old! It had its own brewery in late 1800s. Large skeleton of bird found in upstairs chimney. The upper part was hit by a Zeppelin in First World War. The back room includes bar billiards. Lots of prints and bric-a-brac. Pool and shove halfpenny. Snacks lunchtimes and early evenings. Very friendly. Open Monday – Saturday 11-4 and 7-11. Garden.

Alexandra: 162 Victoria Park Road. (B2/3) *Bass Charrington.*
No real ale!

Alma: 41 Barnabas Road. **(A1/4)** *Whitbreads.*
No real ale!

BEDFORD HOTEL: 220 Victoria Park Road. (B2/5) *Bass Charrington.*
CHARRINGTON IPA. Two-roomed pub full of hanging nick-nacks and curios. Darts, pool and shove halfpenny. Function room. Open all permitted hours. Facilities for the disabled.

Bridge House: 179 Ponsford Street (A2/6) *Free House.*
No real ale!

Brunswick Arms: 237 Well Street. (B2/7) *Bass Charrington.*
No real ale!

Butlers: 69 Cadogan Terrace. (B1/8) *Grand Met-Trumans.*
No beer – closed.

E9

CHESHAM ARMS: 15 Mehetabel Road. (A2/9) *Free House.*
WHITBREAD WETHERED, FULLERS LONDON PRIDE. Rare free house with good beer in an area swamped by keg beer. Victorian pub now with one large bar. Shove halfpenny. Cooked food and snacks lunchtime. Open Monday – Saturday 11-4 and 5.30-11.

Claddagh: 171 Well Street. (B2/10) *Grand Met-Watneys.*
No real ale! Formerly the Two Blackboys.

Clarendon: 86 Balcorne Street. (B2/11) *Courage.*
No beer - closed.

Dagmar Arms: 47 Danesdale Road. (B1/12) *Belhaven.*
No real ale!

Duke of Cambridge: 28 Loddiges Road. (B2/13) *Belhaven.*
No real ale!

DUKE OF DEVONSHIRE: 72 Darnley Road. (B2/14) *Belhaven.*
COURAGE BEST BITTER, DIRECTORS BITTER. Strange wedge-shaped building with more beams than a sunny day – none of them real. Occasional DJ and live music. Darts and pool. Open Monday – Thursday 12-3 and 5-11, Friday and Saturday 11-11.

Duke of Wellington: 90 Morning Lane. (A2/15) *Ind Coope Taylor Walker. No real ale!*

Eagle: 103 Wick Lane. (A1/16) *Grand Met-Watneys.*
No real ale!

FALCON & FIRKIN: 274 Victoria Park Road. (B1/17) *Free House.*
DOGBOLTER, HACKNEY BITTER, FALCON BITTER, ERIC THE STOUT. REAL CIDER. Ciders are Westons Old Rosie and Taunton Traditional. Also has guest beers. A Firkin pub since 1986. Previously the Queens Hotel (Truman). Large open-plan pub with its own brewery. The three house beers are brewed on the premises. Darts and garden. Childrens room. Cooked food lunchtimes and snacks till 8.30. Open all permitted hours during the summer and Monday – Friday 11-3 and 5.30-11, Sat 11-11 in winter.

Follies: 130 Lauriston Road. *Ind Coope Taylor Walker.*
No longer a pub.

Frampton Arms: 47 Well Street. (B2/18) *Courage.*
No real ale!

GLOBE: 20 Morning Lane. (A2/19) *Whitbreads.*
WHITBREAD FLOWERS ORIGINAL. One bar locals' estate pub with video screen for satellite TV and numerous boxing photographs. Beware Scrumpy Jack Cider on fake handpump – it is keg! Darts and pool. Garden. Lunchtime food. Open

Mon and Tues 11-3 and 7.30-11, Wed and Thurs 11-3 and 5-11 with Fri and Sat 11-11.

Gun: 235 Well Street. (B2/20) *Whitbreads.*
No real ale!

JACKDAW & STUMP: 224 Homerton High Street. (A1/21) *Free House.*
RUDDLES COUNTY, FULLERS LONDON PRIDE. Island bar with unusual decor. Mixture of modern and traditional eg large collection of plates around the walls and Coke drinking-mannequin behind bar. Pool. Garden. Live music Saturday evenings and discos, karaoke. Open all permitted hours. Formerly the Spread Eagle.

KENTON ARMS: 38 Kenton Road. (B2/22) *Bass Charrington.*
CHARRINGTON IPA. Island bar. Traditional exterior belies the modern pink interior. Built 1858 by Sir Benjamin Kenton. It has been in the same family since 1973. The interior could have been designed by Liberace, including the bejewelled fire! Darts. Garden. Open Monday - Saturday 11-3 and 5-11.

LEA TAVERN: 90 White Post Lane. (B1/25) *Free House.*
RUDDLES COUNTY. Darts and pool. Former Trumans pub. Lunchtime food.

Lord Napier: 25 White Post Lane. (B1/24) *Free House.*
No real ale!

Lord Nelson: 143 Morning Lane. (A2/25) *Belhaven.*
No beer - closed.

McCANNS: Victoria Park Road (B2/26) *Free House.*
JOHN SMITH'S BITTER, DIRECTORS BITTER. Also sells McCanns Bitter. Opened in 1989. One-bar young persons' pub with traditional wood and mirrors. Jazz every other Thursday. Cooked food at all times. Open all permitted hours.

Northumberland Arms: 78 Well Street. (B2/27) *Courage.*
No beer - closed.

Penshurst Arms: 25 Penshurst Road. (B2/28) *Ind Coope Taylor Walker. No real ale!*

Plough: 23 Homerton High Street. (A2/29) *Belhaven.*
No real ale!

PRINCE EDWARD: 97 Wick Lane. (A1/30) *Grand Met-Trumans.*
RUDDLES BEST. Very friendly Victorian two-bar locals' pub with original etched glass and excellent collection of mirrors. Very active charity fund raiser. Darts and shove halfpenny. Food at all times. Open all permitted hours. Facilities for the disabled.

Retreat: 226 Morning Lane. (A2/31) *Whitbreads.*
No beer - closed.

Royal Hotel: Lauriston Road. (B2/32) *Belhaven.*
No real ale!

ROYAL STANDARD: 84 Victoria Park Road. (B2/33) *Free House.*
COURAGE BEST BITTER, DIRECTORS BITTER, MARSTONS PEDIGREE.
Also sells Merrie Monk, the only pub in the East End to do
so. Friendly two-bar locals' pub. The tenant has now
bought the lease from Courage. Monthly gourmet evening.
Darts. Open Monday - Friday 12-3 and 5.30-11. Lunchtime
food.

Stag: 37 Brooksby's Walk. (A1/34) *Belhaven.*
No real ale!

TIGER: 245 Wick Lane. (A1/35) *Whitbreads.*
*WHITBREAD WETHERED, WHITBREAD FLOWERS ORIGINAL, MARSTONS
PEDIGREE.* Basic locals' pub. One basic bar with a small
bar at the back. Tatty at time of survey. Previously
leased by Youngs. Darts. Lunchtime snacks. Open all
permiitted hours.

Top o' the Morning: 129 Cadogan Terrace. (B1/36) *Free House.*
No real ale!

VICTORIA : 359 Wick Road. (B1/37) *Whitbreads.*
WHITBREAD FLOWERS ORIGINAL. Darts and pool. Garden. Open
all permitted hours.

WELSH HARP: 32 Homerton Row. (A2/38) *Shepherd Neame.*
SHEPHERD NEAME MASTER BREW. Friendly one-bar locals' pub.
Unusual windows in the bar allow you to see the beer
engines operating. It was in the same family for nearly
100 years until the early 1980's. Darts and shove
halfpenny. Lunchtime snacks. Open Monday - Saturday 11-3
and 5.30-11.

WHITE LION: 331 Wick Road. (B1/39) *Grand Met-Trumans.*
WEBSTERS YORKSHIRE BITTER, RUDDLES BEST. Large two-bar
locals' pub with excellent wood panelling. Raised darts
area has an enormous wooden spoon . Lunchtime food. Live
piano Sat/Sun. Open Monday - Friday 11-3 and 5-11,
Saturday 11-11.

E10

Stations - Leyton (Central), Leyton Midland (BR Barking line).

Leyton forms part of the amorphous mass of Victorian terraces extending out from Stratford, in this case in a generally northerly direction until Walthamstow is reached at the Lea Bridge - all of which is in the E10 district. On the west side it is bordered by the Hackney and Leyton Marshes, where bear hunting is said to be more rewarding than beer hunting. The area around the church is a redeeming feature and they also have a famous football club, which since the last Guide has even made the Third division. Leyton Orient is said to be the friendliest club in London - it has to be really, there are enough supporters for them all to be on first name terms.

The pubs are a bit of a mixture but you should find some good free houses, which have done a great deal for the beer range and a number of corner locals remain.

ALMA: 50 Church Road. **(B2/1)** *Bass Charrington.*
CHARRINGTON IPA. Pleasant one bar pub. Darts. Garden. Lunchtime food. Surveyor requests no explanation of pub name. 'Who the bloody hell do you think it refers to Alma Cogan??' he asks. This from a man that 'Can't Tell a Waltz From a Tango' (Ed). Open all permitted hours.

Antelope: 201 Church Road. **(A2/2)** *Ind Coope Taylor Walker.*
No real ale!

BAKERS ARMS: 575 Lea Bridge Road. **(A1/3)** *Ind Coope Taylor* Walker. *TETLEY BITTER.* One room with large oval-shaped bar in the centre. Darts and pool. Lunchtime snacks. Open all permitted hours.

Beaumont Arms: 31 Beaumont Road. **(A1/4)** *Bass Charrington.*
No real ale!

Coach & Horses: 391 High Road. **(B2/5)** *Bass Charrington.*
No real ale!

DRUM: 557 Lea Bridge Road. **(A2/6)** *Free House.*
YOUNGERS SCOTCH, GREENE KING IPA, THEAKSTONS XB, ELDRIDGE POPE ROYAL OAK, GREENE KING ABBOT ALE. Formerly Nancys. Split-level pub that sadly may become victim of a new road scheme which will no doubt move the traffic jam a few miles down the road. Food lunchtimes. Cheap pints and cheaper beer offers. Open all permitted hours.

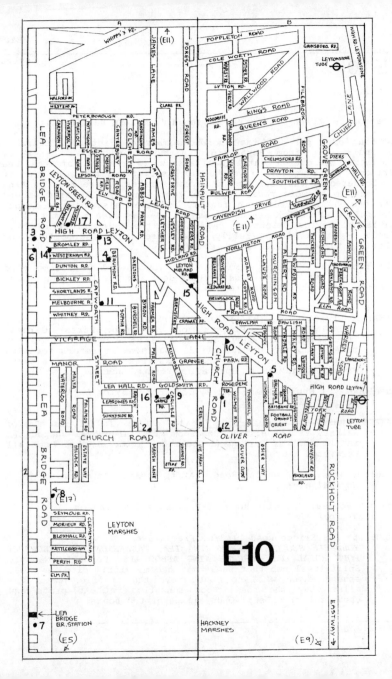

Greyhound: 91 Lea Bridge Road. **(A2/7)** *Free House.*
No real ale!

HARE & HOUNDS: 282 Lea Bridge Road. **(A2/8)** *Bass Charrington.*
CHARRINGTON IPA, FULLERS LONDON PRIDE. Family pub just in
front of Leyton Wingate Football Ground. Better than most
pubs in the area. Garden. Darts and pool. Lunchtime food.
Open all permitted hours.

HOLLY BUSH: 32 Grange Road. **(A2/9)** *Free House.*
GREENE KING IPA, GREENE KING ABBOT ALE. Now a one-bar pub
with snacks lunchtime. Darts and pool. Definately the best
bet for Leyton Orient FC and a pity the players don't get
in there before matches, it might improve their
performances. Open Monday to Saturday 11.30-3.00 and 7-11.

LION & KEY: 475 High Road. **(B2/10)** *Bass Charrington.*
CHARRINGTON IPA, BASS. Renovated in 1988. Artifacts
include red phone box, old clock and bric-a-brac. Snacks
at all times. Note the Lions with keys in their mouth on
the roof. Opens Monday to Saturday 12-3 and 5.30-11.

Lord Clyde: 175 Capworth Street. **(A1/11)** *Ind Coope Taylor
Walker.* *No real ale!*

Oliver Twist: 90 Church Road. **(B2/12)** *Whitbreads.*
No beer – closed.

Prince of Wales: 777 High Road. **(A1/13)** *Bass Charrington.*
No real ale!

TAP & SPILE: 596 Lea Bridge Road. **(A1/14)** *Free House.*
*TOLLY COBBOLD MILD, GALES XXX DARK MILD, RINGWOOD XX
PORTER, GREENE KING ABBOT ALE, WINTER WARMER (WINTER
ONLY), WILTSHIRE OLD DEVIL, ESB.* Formerly the Auctioneers.
Brent Walker free house with eight handpumps. Enthusiastic
landlord. Bar billiards, nine pin skittles and dice.
Snacks lunchtime. Open Monday to Thursday 11-3.30 and
5.30-11, Friday and Saturday 11-11.

THREE BLACKBIRDS: 640 High Road. **(A1/15)** *Grand Met-Trumans.*
WEBSTERS YORKSHIRE BITTER, RUDDLES BEST RUDDLES COUNTY.
Large three-bar pub with pool in two of the bars. Darts.
Cooked food lunchtime and snacks at other times. Open
Monday to Saturday 11-3 and 5-11.

Wakefield Arms: 14 Park Road. **(A2/16)** *Grand Met-Trumans.*
No real ale!

WILLIAM IV: 816 High Road. **(A1/17)** *Ind Coope Taylor Walker.*
OLD BREWERY BITTER. Striptease Thursday pm and Friday and
Saturday lunchtime. Busy, cosmopolitan. Darts and pool.
Open Tuesday and Wednesday 11-3 and 5.30-11, Monday,
Thursday, Friday and Saturday 11-11.

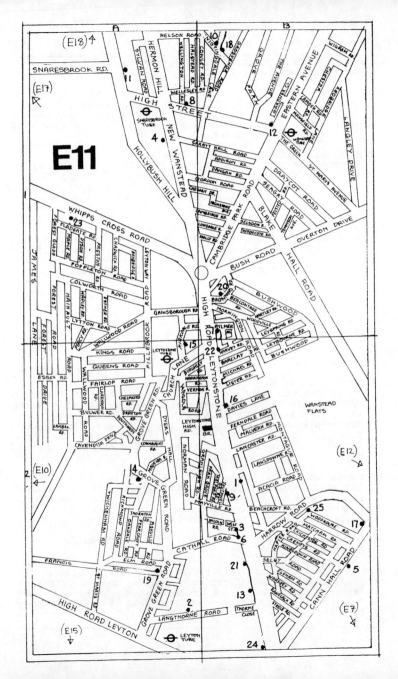

Stations — Leytonstone, Wanstead and Snaresbrook (Central),
Leytonstone High Street (BR Barking line).

The postal district covers two areas, Leytonstone proper is in
the north eastern projection of the Victorian terraces which
start in Stratford and push their way up to the Green Man
roundabout to meet the outliers of Epping Forest and Wanstead
flats. Across the roundabout Wanstead is a separate area and
considered a little more exclusive by some of its inhabitants,
for which privilege they pay a bit more in the pubs.

The beer range is generally dominated by the larger brewers but a
sprinkling of guest beers (especially in some of the managed
houses) have added to the range available. Free houses are few
and from the west of the Central line up to Whipps Cross there is
very little of anything — thanks to the Quakers who built a
number of "dry" estates here in the nineteenth century.

BELL: 468 High Road. **(B2/1)** *Bass Charrington.*
        CHARRINGTON IPA, BASS. Pub with three distinct rooms
        games (darts, pool and shove halfpenny) small lounge and
        largish saloon. Snacks and cooked meals at lunchtime. Open
        all permitted hours.

BIRKBECK **TAVERN:** 45 Langthorne Road. **(A2/2)** *Bass Charrington.*
        CHARRINGTON IPA. A real basic and friendly back street
        local. No frills but a good pint. Open Monday to Saturday
        11-3 and 5.30-11.

BRITANNIA: 493 High Road. (B2/3) *Whitbreads.*
        FLOWERS IPA, WHITBREAD FLOWERS ORIGINAL. Pedigree the
        current 'guest' beer. Darts and pool. Open all permitted
        hours.

THE BRITISH QUEEN TAVERN: 63 New Wanstead. **(A1/4)** *Grand*
        Met-Watneys. *WEBSTERS YORKSHIRE BITTER, RUDDLES BEST,*
        RUDDLES COUNTY. One bar pub with lunchtime food. Opens
        11-3 and 5.30-11 Monday to Friday and 11-4 and 5.30-11 on
        Saturday.

COLEGRAVE ARMS: 145 Cann Hall Road. **(B2/5)** *Bass Charrington.*
        CHARRINGTON IPA, GREENE KING IPA. Friendly three bar pub.
        Snacks at all times. Darts and pool. IPA at 116p has to be
        a bargain as does the Greene King variety at 120p. Open
        Monday to Friday 12-11 Saturday 11-11.

COWLEY ARMS: 483 High Road. **(B2/6)** *Bass Charrington.*
CHARRINGTON IPA. Corner pub with two comfortable bars. Darts, pool and shove halfpenny. Cooked meals lunchtime and snacks other times. Opens Monday to Saturday 11-3 and 6-11.

CROWN: 692 High Road. **(B1/7)** *Bass Charrington.*
CHARRINGTON IPA, GREENE KING IPA. Over 21's smart dress. Upstairs pool room doubles as a function room. Interesting wooden crown still standing showing when pub had three bars. Darts. Food lunchtime only. Open all permitted hours.

THE CUCKFIELD: 31 High Street Wanstead. **(A1/8)** *Bass Charrington.*

CHARRINGTON IPA, BASS. Guest beer policy which when surveyed were Greene King IPA and London Pride. Busy pub with inter-connecting doors. Strictly over 21's policy. Plenty of brik-a-brac and prints. Snacks at all times. Open Monday to Saturday 11-4 and 5-11.

Dirty Nellies: 575 High Street. **(B2/9)** *Free House.*
No real ale!

DUKE OF EDINBURGH: 79 Nightingale Lane. **(B1/10)** *Ind Coope Taylor Walker.* *TETLEY BITTER IND COOPE BURTON ALE ADNAMS BITTER.* Two bars (one doubles as a function room). Real locals' pub always popular. Plently of prints, plates etc with an aquarium in the bigger front bar. Lunchtime food is all homemade. Open all permitted hours. Garden.

EAGLE HOTEL: 76 Holly Bush Hill. **(A1/11)** *Bass Charrington.*
CHARRINGTON IPA, BASS. Mr Toby's Carvery. Games (darts and pool) in separate bar. Large pub popular with visitor (of all types) from the nearby Crown Courts. Garden and car park. Open Monday to Friday 11-3 and 5-11, Saturday 11-3 and 6-11.

George Hotel: High Street Wanstead. **(B1/12)** *Grand Met-Trumans.*
No real ale!

Halfway House: 345 High Road. **(B2/13)** *Grand Met-Watneys.*
No real ale!

HEATHCOTE ARMS: 344 Grove Green Road. **(A2/14)** *Bass Charrington.*
CHARRINGTON IPA, GREENE KING IPA. Large pub divided into three areas, public, saloon and games room (four pool tables). Various bric-a-brac, photos decorate. IPA's are 4p cheaper at 116p in the public. Outside extensively tiled with various sculptures on upper parts. Darts. Function room. Opens Monday to Friday 12-11, Saturday 11-11.

KIRKDALES WINE BAR: Kirkdale Road **(A2/15)** *Free House.*
GREENE KING ABBOT ALE. Basically a popular restaurant that
has an extensive menu. Open Monday to Saturday 12-11.

THE LINCOLN: 566 High Road. **(B2/16)** *Grand Met - Clifton Inn FH.*
RUDDLES BEST, RUDDLES COUNTY. Over 21's split-level pub
with two pool tables. Snacks and cooked food at lunchtime.
Car park.Originaly the Elms. Opens Monday to Saturday 11-3
and 5-11.

Lord Rookwood: 314 Cann Hall Road. **(B2/17)** *Bass Charrington.*
No real ale!

NIGHTINGALE: 51 Nightingale Lane. **(B1/18)** *Courage.*
*COURAGE BEST BITTER, DIRECTORS BITTER, WADWORTH 6X, YOUNGS
SPECIAL.* One bar but two distinct rooms. Busy lunchtimes
when cooked meals are available as they are at all times.
Darts. Open all permitted hours.

NORTHCOTE: 110 Grove Green Road. **(A2/19)** *Bass Charrington.*
CHARRINGTON IPA. Darts and pool and strong on dominoes.
Friendly. Snacks at all times. Open Monday to Saturday
12-11.

NORTH STAR: 24 Browning Road. **(B1/20)** *Bass Charrington.*
CHARRINGTON IPA, GREENE KING IPA. Loads of railway photos
adorn the pub, including a rare picture of the Great
Eastern 'Decapod'. Unfortunately the decor is the result
of a Charrington refurbishment and the pub is actually
named after a ship called the North Star. Very much a
locals pub, two small bars, can be lively in the evenings.
Darts and shove halfpenny. Lunchtime meals and snacks at
other times. Open all permitted hours.

Plough & Harrow: 419 High Road. **(B2/21)** *Courage.*
No real ale!

RED LION: 640 High Road. **(B2/22)** *Ind Coope Taylor Walker.*
TETLEY BITTER, IND COOPE BURTON ALE. Formerly Luthers.
Central to the shopping area with plenty of comfortable
seating. Pool and darts in the upstairs room. Food at
lunchtime. Both beers the same price which should make the
Burton a bargain at 130p. Open all permitted hours.

SIR ALFRED HITCHCOCK HOTEL: 145 Whipps Cross Road. **(A1/23)** *Free
House. FLOWERS IPA, WHITBREAD FLOWERS ORIGINAL, CASTLE
EDEN, BODDINGTONS BITTER, FULLERS LONDON PRIDE.* One of the
few pubs in the East London area with accommodation.
Overlooking Epping Forest. Real log fires. Various alcoves
leading off from the bar. Photos of 'The Master' (who was
born in Leytonstone) and stars of his films on the walls.
Open all permitted hours.

Thatched House: 245 High Road. (B2/24) *Bass Charrington*.
Large corner pub with one central bar and games room
separate from saloon. Strictly over 21's. Darts and pool.
Patio. Stop Press: no longer sells real ale.

WOODHOUSE TAVERN: 119 Harrow Road. (B2/25) *Bass Charrington*.
CHARRINGTON IPA. Tidy, large two bar pub with club room.
Ex Savill's pub about to sold off by Charrington and the
governor trying to buy it. It will then become a free
house. Facilities: Darts, pool, shove halfpenny and
function and childrens rooms. Open Monday to Thursday 11-3
and 5-11, Friday 11-4 and 5-11, Saturday 11-4 and 7-11.

Beehive E14.*Demolished*

Stations – Manor Park (BR Liverpool Street), East Ham (District).

Located on the west side of Ilford just over the River Roding (the stream below the enormous Relief Road), this area extends from Wanstead flats in the north as far as the District line in the south. It is mainly suburban, from the late 1800s on, and has pubs to match – dominated by the Big Four and regrettably not too well off for real ale.

Avenue Hotel: 90 Church Road. (B2/1) *Bass Charrington.*

No beer – closed.

BLAKESLEY ARMS: 53 Station Road. (A1/2) *Bass Charrington.*
CHARRINGTON IPA, FULLERS LONDON PRIDE. Friendly two-bar pub next to Manor Park BR Station. Darts in public bar, shove halfpenny in the saloon. Snacks lunchtime. Open all permitted hours.

Burnell Arms: 241 High Street North. (A2/3) *Bass Charrington.*
No real ale!

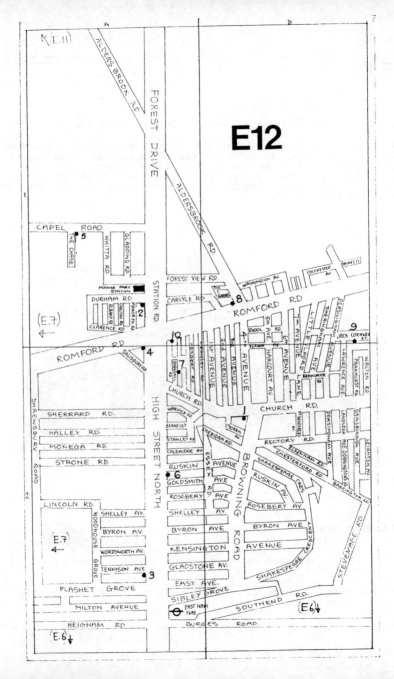

EARL OF ESSEX: 616 Romford Road. (A2/4) *Courage.*
COURAGE BEST BITTER, DIRECTORS BITTER, RUSSIAN STOUT (BOTTLED). Large street corner pub popular with local Irish community. Darts and pool. Management refused to co-operate with our surveyor. Open all permitted hours. Shows videos of hurling and gaelic football on Mondays and Tuesdays.

GOLDEN FLEECE: 166 Capel Road. (A1/5) *Grand Met-Watneys.*
WEBSTERS YORKSHIRE BITTER, RUDDLES BEST, RUDDLES COUNTY. Plush Victorian pub overlooking Wanstead Flats with beer garden. Very busy in the summer when it is popular with famlies. The interior is wood panelled and beamed and has a comfortable atmosphere. Handy for the cementries. Open Monday to Friday 12-3 and 5.30-11, Saturday 12-3 and 7-11 but may stay open in the afternoon if there sufficient demand. Lunchtime food.

Ruskin Arms: 386 High Street North. (A2/6) *Bass Charrington.*
No real ale!

STAR: 30 Snowshill Road. (A2/7) *Belhaven.*
COURAGE BEST BITTER, DIRECTORS BITTER, JOHN SMITH'S BITTER. Friendly locals pub which has changed hands several times in recent years. Now owned by Belhaven whose London pubs are currently supplied by Courage. Darts and pool. Garden. Open all permitted hours.

Three Rabbits: 833 Romford Road. (B1/8) *Bass Charrington.*
No real ale!

Victoria Cross: Jack Cornwell Street. (B1/9) *Ind Coope Taylor Walker. No real ale!*

William the Conqueror: 628/630 Romford Road. (A1/10) *Grand Met-Watneys. No real ale!*

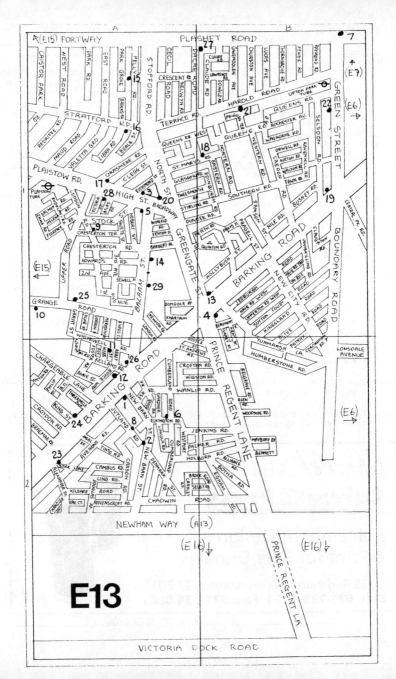

E13

E13

Stations — Plaistow (District), West Ham (BR North London/District).

The World Guide to Beer locates Plaistow in the depths of rural Sussex, but unfortunately the reality is a little different and it actually lies south of Stratford, athwart the Barking Road and Northern Outfall Sewer (along which you can cycle). Part of the borough of West Ham, it lacks any centre since all the civic facilities are at Stratford. In the 1870s it was noted for potato fields and sheep farming, but now is partly industrial but mainly covered by rows of Victorian terraces, perhaps a little more complete than in other parts of East London and complemented by a reasonable range of pubs with some breaks from the Big Four. Entertainment is most likely to be found in those along the Barking Road.

Abbey Arms: 384 Barking Road. (A2/1) *Ind Coope Taylor Walker.*
No real ale!

Army & Navy: 12 New Barn Street. (A2/2) *Ind Coope Taylor Walker.*

No real ale!

BLACK LION: 59 Plaistow High Street. (A1/3) *Courage.*
COURAGE BEST BITTER, DIRECTORS BITTER, RUSSIAN STOUT (BOTTLED), WETHEREDS. Large pub with two contrasting bars. Restaurant. Bar billiards. Garden. Open Monday — Thursday 11-3 and 5-11, Friday and Saturday 11-11.

CASTLE: 546 Barking Road. (B1/4) *Bass Charrington.*
.CHARRINGTON IPA. Two comfortable spacious bars. Darts and pool. Lunchtime food. Open all permitted hours except between 3.30 and 7 on Saturday.

Coach & Horses: 100 High Street. (A1/5) *Grand Met-Watneys.*
No real ale!

Duke of Cumberland: 101 Cumberland Road. (B2/6) *Free House.*
No real ale!

DUKE OF EDINBURGH: 299 Green Street. (B1/7) *Bass Charrington.*
FULLERS LONDON PRIDE. Nasty pub — decor has seen better days. Darts and pool. Open Monday — Friday 11-11.

Duke of Edinburgh: 9 Jutland Road. (A2/8) *Bass Charrington.*
No real ale!

EARL DERBY: 119 London Road. (A1/9) *Ind Coope Taylor Walker.*
TAYLOR WALKER BEST BITTER. Pricey pub with plush lounge
bar and basic public. Lively unpretentious local. Pool.

EARL OF BEACONSFIELD: 211 Grange Road. **(A1/10)** *Bass Charrington.*

CHARRINGTON IPA. Modern two bar local. Quiet neighbourhood
pub with not much atmosphere. Darts and pool.

Foresters Arms: 9 Whitwell Road. **(A2/11)** *Ind Coope Taylor*
Walker. *No real ale!*

Golden Lion: 343 Barking Road. (A2/12) *Grand Met-Watneys.*
No real ale!

Green Gate: 523 Barking Road. (B1/13) *Bass Charrington.*
No real ale!

GREYHOUND & HARE: 174 Balaam Street. (A1/14) *Grand Met-Watneys.*
RUDDLES COUNTY. Mock Tudor beams on the inside walls and
horse brasses. Darts and pool. Garden. Snacks at lunchtim.
Open Monday - Friday 11-3 and 5-11, Saturday 11-11.

Lamb: 85 Pelly Road. (A1/15) *Ind Coope Taylor Walker.*
No real ale!

Libra Arms: 53 Stratford Road. (A1/16) *Bass Charrington.*
No real ale!

Lord Raglan: 9 High Street. (A1/17) *Courage.*
No real ale!

LORD STANLEY: 15 St Mary's Road. (B1/18) *Shepherd Neame.*
SHEPHERD NEAME MASTER BREW, SHEPHERD NEAME SPITFIRE ALE.
Comfortable roomy genuine local - an excellent pub one
of the few decent pubs in Plaistow. Cooked food lunchtime
and snacks other times. Darts and pool. Garden. Open all
permitted hours and till midnight on Saturday.

Manhattens: 749 Barking Road. (B1/19) *Bass Charrington.*
No real ale! Formerly Pinkies.

Prince Albert: 135 Broadway. (A1/20) *Grand Met-Watneys.*
No real ale!

Prince of Wales: 35 Princes Terrace. (B1/21) *Grand-Met Truman.*
No beer - closed.

Queens: 410 Green Street. (B1/22) *Ind Coope Taylor Walker.*
No real ale!

Raffles: 244 Barking Road. (A2/23) *Bass Charrington.*
No real ale!

Red House: 299 Barking Road. (A2/24) *Grand Met-Trumans.*
No real ale!

Sultan: 112 Grange Road. (A1/25) *Free House.*
No real ale!

Swan: 1 Balaam Street. (A2/26) *Ind Coope Taylor Walker.*
No real ale!

Upton Manor Tavern: 48 Plashet Road. (B1/27) *Bass Charrington.*
No real ale!

Victoria Tavern: 28 High Street. (A1/28) *Grand Met-Watneys.*
No real ale!

THE VILLAGE AT PLAISTOW: 140 Balaam Street. (A1/29) *Free House.*
COURAGE BEST BITTER, DIRECTORS BITTER, RUDDLES COUNTY,
WADWORTH 6X. Formerly the Phantom and Firkin and the Red
Lion and now owned by Wessex Inns. Guest beers promised.
Plainly furnished local decorated with signs and posters
from old breweries. Cooked lunchtime food with snacks at
other times. Darts and garden. Open all permitted hours
during the summer and Monday – Thursday 11-3 and 5.30,
Friday – Saturday 11-11 during the winter.

Volunteer E14. *Demolished.*

Stations - Limehouse (formerly Stepney East, BR Fenchurch
Street/DLR), West Ferry, West India Quay, Heron Quays, Canary
Wharf, South Quay, Crossharbour, Mudchute, Island Gardens, Poplar
and All Saints (DLR).
Note: at the time of writing the Dockland Light Railway (DLR)
closes from 2130 in the evening and is not open at all at
weekends. Not very community minded is it?

Although the district is called Poplar, in fact it also embraces
most of Stepney, Blackwall and the Isle of Dogs and is what most
people mean when they talk of Docklands. It is very difficult to
miss as Canary Wharf lies in the centre, surrounded by growing
areas of modern office development and served by the Docklands
Light Railway. The DLR is well worth a trip to see the sights,
but bear in mind that the older pubs - and a good range of locals
has so far survived development - lie around the river where
people live, whilst the railway runs through the centre where the
high tech modern pubs have been built. They are small in number
and could easily have been lifted straight from the City, but do
offer an interesting range of beers. Elsewhere in the district
the range does also give some relief from the Big Four and it is
worth exploring a little.

The northern part of the area runs from Stepney east to Blackwall
and is a mixture of surviving older buildings and postwar
redevelopment. Once heavily pubbed, it has lost out badly in
recent years and there have been a number of closures -
especially from the large road schemes connected with the
Blackwall Tunnel and Docklands developments.

Two notable breweries once operated here. Taylor Walker ran the
Barley Mow Brewery in Church Lane from 1730 until taken over by
Ind Coope in 1960 whilst the London & Burton Brewery operated in
Medland Street until falling to Watney in 1929.

ABERFELDY TAVERN: 26 Aberfeldy Street. (B1/1) *Whitbreads.*
> *GREENE KING ABBOT ALE.* Recently refurbished pub with two
> bars. Pleasant and relaxing. Frequented by staff from the
> nearby Financial Times during the day and by locals in the
> evening and weekends. Canning Town BR Station is 15
> minutes walk away. Darts. Cooked food lunchtime. Outside
> drinking area. Open all permitted hours.

African Tavern: 46 Grundy Street. (B2/2) *Ind Coope Taylor
Walker. No real ale!*

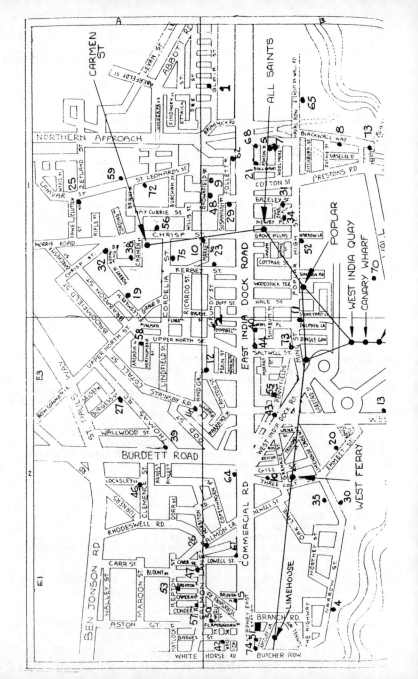

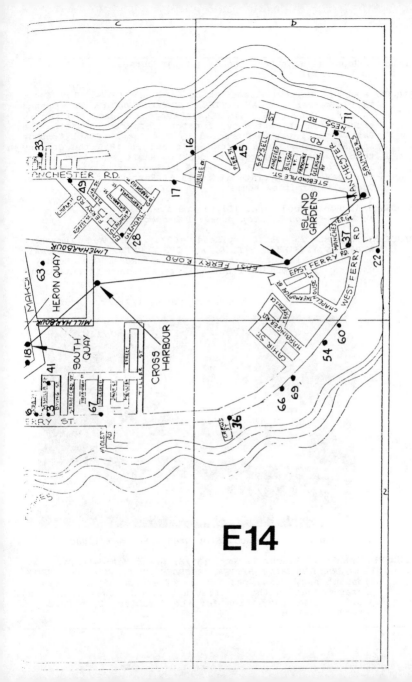

E14

Anchor & Hope: 41 West Ferry Road. (C2/3) *Courage.*
No real ale!

BARLEY MOW: 44 Narrow Street-Limehouse Basin.(B2/4) *Ind Coope*
Taylor Walker. *TETLEY BITTER, IND COOPE BURTON ALE.* Opened
in 1989. Converted from a gate keepers house. the pub is
situated on the entrance of gates to Limehouse Basin. The
Basin itself was constructed by the Regent Canal Company
in 1812, hence as a barge basin and in 1819 the company
took powers to enlarge the dock to admit sea-going ships.
It is not part of PLA but owned by the Britsh Waterways Bd
who ceased to opperate it in 1969. Restaurant and garden.
Open all permitted hours.

Beehive: 12 Robin Hood Lane. (B1/5) *Courage.*
No beer - closed. Stop press: Pub demolished.

BLACKSMITHS ARMS: 25 West Ferry Road. (C2/6) *Grand Met-Trumans.*
WEBSTERS YORKSHIRE BITTER, RUDDLES COUNTY. Unspoilt small
one bar locals pub. Darts. Lunchtime snacks. Open Monday -
Saturday 11-3 and 5-11 but will remain open if sufficient
custom.

British Oak: 28 Robin Hood Lane. (B1/7) *Free House.*

No beer - closed. Stop press: Pub demolished

BRUNSWICK ARMS: 78 Blackwall Way. (B1/8) *Grand Met-Watneys.*
WEBSTERS YORKSHIRE BITTER, RUDDLES BEST, RUDDLES COUNTY.
Pleasant easy going pub for a conversion. Specialises in
pizzas to eat in their restaurant or take away. Darts and
pool. Garden. Facilities for the disabled. Open Monday -
Saturday 11=3 and 6-11.

Buccaneer: 73 West India Dock Road.
Free House formerly the Blue Posts.

Pub demolished.

Builders **Arms**: 162 Brownfield Street. **(B1/9)** *Courage.*
No real ale!

Callaghanns: 55 Chrisp Street. **(B1/10)** *Grand Met-Watneys.*
No real ale!

CARTYS: 72 Poplar High Street. **(B2/11)** *Free House.*
YOUNGS SPECIAL. Formerly the Green Man. Darts. Meals at
lunchtime and in the evenings on request. Maps establish
that this pub existed in 1802. It was rebuilt in 1904 and
again in 1940. This latter rebuild moved the pub from the
west corner of Dolphin Lane across the road to the present
day east side. Open Monday – Saturday 11-2.30 and 5-11.
Two minutes walk from DLR Poplar Station.

Chimes: 212 Hind Grove. **(B2/12)** *Grand Met-Watneys.*
No real ale!

CITY PRIDE: 1 West Ferry Road. **(B2/13)** *Grand Met-Watneys.*
WEBSTERS YORKSHIRE BITTER, RUDDLES BEST, RUDDLES COUNTY.
Formerly the City Arms. Island shaped bar with stuffed
animals (samll mammals and birds) in cases attached to
light fixtures arund bar. Split level drinking area with
ornate bedsteads, mangles etc ie junk. Cooked food
lunchtime. Garden. Open Monday -Friday 11-11, Saturday
11-3 and 7-11.

Conant **Arms**: 41a Stainsby Road. **(A2/14)** *Grand Met-Trumans.*
No real ale!

CROWN: 667 Commercial Road. **(B2/15)** *Free House.*
WEBSTERS YORKSHIRE BITTER. Basic pub two minutes walk from

Limehouse (formerly Stepney East) BR and Docklands Light Railway Stations. Darts and pool.

Charlie Browns: 116 West India Dock Road. *Bass* Charrington.

Pub demolished.

Cubitt Arms: 262 Manchester Road. (C1/16) *Grand Met-Trumans.* *No real ale!*

DORSET ARMS: 379 Manchester Road. (C1/17) *Grand Met-Watneys.* *WEBSTERS YORKSHIRE BITTER.* Newly refurbished long bar. Darts. Garden. Cooked food lunchtime. Open Monday – Saturday 11-3 and 6-11.

Drummonds: 3 Heron Quay-Marsh Wall (C2/18) *Bass Charrington.* *No real ale!*

Earl of Ellesmere: 36 Ellesmere Street. (A1/19) *Ind Coope Taylor* Walker. *No real ale!*

Enterprise: 145 Three Colt Street. (B2/20) *Grand Met-Watneys.* *No beer – closed.*

Falcon: 202a East India Dock Road. (B1/21) *Grand Met-Trumans.* *No beer – closed. Stop press: Pub demolished.*

FERRY HOUSE: 26 Ferry Street. (D1/22) *Courage.*
COURAGE BEST BITTER, DIRECTORS BITTER, YOUNGS SPECIAL.
Pleasant small one bar pub that is two minutes walk from
DLR Island Gardens Station. Darts. Lunchtime food.

FESTIVAL INN: 71 Grundy Street. (B1/23) *Grand Met-Trumans.*
WEBSTERS YORKSHIRE BITTER. Two-bar pub in Chrisp Street
Market and near DLR All Saints station. Darts and
lunchtime snacks. Open all permitted hours.

FIVE BELLS & BLADEBONE: 27 Three Colt Street. (B2/24) *Ind Coope*
Taylor Walker. *TETLEY BITTER, IND COOPE BURTON ALE.* Near
the site of the Taylor Walker Brewery. Bar Billiards,
musak, Snacks lunchtime. Opposite St Annes church built
by Nicholas Hawksmore in 1727, burnt down in 1850. Small
one bar pub packed with nautical paraphenalia, tea chests,
model ships etc. Open all permitted hours.

Foresters Arms: 253 St Leonards Road. (A1/25) *Bass Charrington.*
No real ale!

Freemasons Arms: 96/8 Salmon Lane. (B2/26) *Ind Coope Taylor*
Walker. *No real ale!*

Galloway Arms: 43 Thomas Road. (A2/27) *Ind Coope Burton.*
No real ale!

GEORGE: 114 Glengall Grove. (C1/28) *Grand Met-Watneys.*
WEBSTERS YORKSHIRE BITTER, RUDDLES BEST. Relaxing three
bar pub with extension built on with a greenhouse effect
restaurant. Darts by arrangement. Open Monday – Saturday
11-3 and 5-11.

George IV: 7 Ida Street. (B1/29) *Grand Met-Watneys.*
No real ale!

GRAPES: 76 Narrow Street. (B2/30) *Ind Coope Taylor Walker.*
TETLEY BITTER, IND COOPE BURTON ALE. Very nice riverside
pub with views of the Thames. Grade II Listed Building
with frosted glass windows that you can imagine go back in
time, hence a reminder painted sign dated 1949 in the bar
is on show. Restaurant. Open all permitted hours.

Greenwich Pensioner: 2 Bazeley Street. (B1/31) *Ind Coope Taylor*
Walker. *No real ale!*

GUILDFORD ARMS: 93 Goldalming Road. (A1/32) *Bass Charrington.*
CHARRINGTON IPA, FULLERS LONDON PRIDE. Small triangular
pub with two bars (a good locals pub) which is worth the
five minute from Chrisp Street market. Darts and pool.
Lunchtime food. Open all permitted hours.

GUN: 27 Coldharbour. (C1/33) *Ind Coope Taylor Walker.*
IND COOPE BURTON ALE. Real ale not available when the pub

was surveyed. Darts. Garden. Lunchtime snacks. Open Monday - Saturday 11-3 and 6-11.

Hope & Anchor: 14 Newby Place. (B1/34) *Grand Met-Watneys.* *No real ale!Stop press: Renamed Anchor & Raj.*

THE HOUSE THEY LEFT BEHIND: 27 Ropemaker's Fields. (B2/35) *Grand Met-Watneys. WEBSTERS YORKSHIRE BITTER, RUDDLES COUNTY.* Formerly the Black Horse. Built in 1857 the pub has original oil paintings on the walls. Cooked meals at all times except Sat/Sun evenings. Price of beer is increased by 10p when bands are playing. Outside drinking area. Open all permitted hours.

KINGSBRIDGE ARMS: 154/6 West Ferry Road. (D2/36) *Whitbreads. FLOWERS IPA.* Unspoilt east enders pub with tiles on the ceiling similar to that of the White Horse in Poplar High Street. Lunchtime snacks. Darts. Open Monday - Thursday 11-2.30 and 5-11. Friday and Saturday the same unless there is demand then it will be open 11-11.

Lord Nelson: 1 Manchester Road. (D1/37) *Bass Charrington.* *No real ale!*

Lord Stanley: 55 Carmen Street. (A1/38) *Grand Met-Watneys.* *No beer - closed.*

LOVAT ARMS: 301 Burdett Road. (A2/39) *Grand Met-Trumans. RUDDLES BEST.* Basic one bar pub with darts. Live music. Open Monday - Friday 11-2.30 and 5-11, Saturday 7-11.

Manor Arms: 150 East India Dock Road. (B2/40) *Grand Met-Watneys.*

No real ale!

NORTH POLE: 74 Manilla Street. (C2/41) *Grand Met-Watneys. WEBSTERS YORKSHIRE BITTER.* Backstreet local with East London Fives dartboard. Friendly landlord. Relaxed atmosphere. Lunchtime snacks.

OLD SHIP: 17 Barnes Street. (B2/42) *Grand Met-Watneys. WEBSTERS YORKSHIRE BITTER, RUDDLES BEST.* Very relaxing small bar pub with prints on the walls taken from old sea battles. A stones throw from DLR and BR Limehouse station. Darts and pool. Cooked meals at lunchtime. Open Monday - Thursday 11-2.30 and 7-11, Friday and Saturday 11-11.

OPORTO TAVERN: 43 West India Dock Road. (B2/43) *Bass* Charrington. *CHARRINGTON IPA.* Smart one-bar pub still with no games room. Two minutes from DLR West Ferry station. Cooked meals lunchtime and snacks at other times. Open all permitted hours except Saturday (11-5 and 7-11).

PHOENIX: 104 East India Dock Road. (B2/44) *Ind Coope Taylor Walker*. *TETLEY BITTER, ADNAMS BITTER*. Small L-shaped bar busy at weekends. Cooked food lunchtime. Open all hours.

PIER TAVERN: 299 Manchester Road. (D1/45) *Whitbreads*.
WHITBREAD FLOWERS ORIGINAL, BODDINGTONS BITTER. Pleasant recently refurbished L-shaped bar with split-level drinking area (presumably for the business deals in mind). Frequented by the young and old alike in the evening. Ten minutes walk from DLR Island Gardens Station. Garden. Open all permitted hours.

Prince Alfred: 86 Locksley Street. (A2/46) *Grand Met-Trumans*.
No real ale!

Prince Regent: 81 Salmon Lane. (A2/47) *Ind Coope Taylor Walker*.
No real ale!

Princess of Wales: 130 Brownfield Street. (B1/48) *Belhaven*.
No real ale!

Queens: 571 Manchester Road. (C1/49) *Ind Coope Taylor Walker*.
No real ale!

QUEENS HEAD: 8 Flamborough Street. (B2/50) *Young & Co.*
YOUNGS BITTER, YOUNGS SPECIAL, WINTER WARMER (WINTER ONLY). A Grade II Listed Building situated in a conservation area. London Fives dartboard. Lunchtime food. Our surveyor kept being asked to leave.

Queens Head: 491 The Highway. *Grand Met-Watneys*.

Pub demolished.

RAILWAY TAVERN: 576 Commercial Road. (B2/51) *Bass Charrington*.
CHARRINGTON IPA. One bar pub next to Limehouse BR and DLR Station (formerly Stepney East a name that obviously did not gell with the new yuppie locals). Darts and lunchtime snacks. Open Monday - Saturday 11-2.30 and 5-11.

RESOLUTE TAVERN: 210 Poplar High Street. **(B1/52)** *Ind Coope Taylor Walker. TETLEY BITTER, IND COOPE BURTON ALE, YOUNGS BITTER.* Basic pleasant long split level bar. Two minutes walk from All Saints DLR Station. Darts. Lunchtime food. Outside drinking area. Uses the old licensing hours except Friday and Saturday (11-11).

Richard Cobden: 34 Repton Street. **(A2/53)** *Grand Met-Watneys. No real ale!*

Robert Burns: 248 West Ferry Road. **(D2/54)** *Grand Met-Trumans. No beer - closed.*

Rose & Crown: 17 Pennyfields. **(B2/55)** *Grand Met-Watneys. No real ale!*

Royal Charlie: 116 Chrisp Street. **(A1/56)** *Grand Met-Watneys. No real ale!*

Royal Navy: 53 Salmon Lane. **(A2/57)** *Belhaven. No real ale!*

Sabbarton Arms: 99 Upper North Street. **(A2/58)** *Belhaven. No beer - closed.*

St Leonards Arms: 162 St Leonards Road. **(A1/59)** *Grand Met-Trumans. No beer - closed.*

SHIP: 290 West Ferry Road. **(D2/60)** *Grand Met-Watneys. WEBSTERS YORKSHIRE BITTER.* Basic one bar pub with fives dartboard. Lunchtime meals. Open Monday - Saturday 11-2.30 and 6-11.

Sir Charles Napier: 697 Commercial Road. **(B2/61)** *Belhaven. No real ale!*

Sir John Franklin: 269 East India Dock Road. **(B1/62)** *Grand Met-Watneys. No real ale!*

SPINNAKER: Harbour Island-Marsh Wall **(C1/63)** *Greene King. GREENE KING IPA, GREENE KING ABBOT ALE.* Modern one bar pub lacking in atmsphere, seems very cold with white washed walls very bare. Not catering for the people of the area and open only from Monday to Friday 11-8, closed weekends. In that respect it keeps almost the same hours as the Docklands Light Railway.

STAR OF THE EAST: 805a Commercial Road. **(B2/64)** *Courage. COURAGE BEST BITTER.* A Grade II Listed Building. Pool tables and dart board kept very clear of drinking area. Cooked food lunchtime. Open all permitted hours.

Steamship: 24 Naval Row. **(B1/65)** *Grand Met-Watneys. No real ale!*

TELEGRAPH: 194 West Ferry Road. **(D2/66)** *Grand Met-Watneys.*
WEBSTERS YORKSHIRE BITTER, RUDDLES COUNTY. Formerly the
Magnet and Dewdrop and now named after the newspaper moved
nearby. Nautical features. Darts and shove halfpenny. Open
all permitted hours. Cooked food at all times. Outside
drinking area.

Tooke Arms: 165 West Ferry Road. **(C2/67)** *Grand Met-Watneys.*
No real ale!

Volunteer: 238 East India Dock Road. **(B1/68)** *Bass Charrington.*
No beer – closed. Stop press: Pub demolished.

VULCAN: 240 West Ferry Road. **(D2/69)** *Fullers.*
FULLERS LONDON PRIDE, ESB. No real ale when surveyed.
Darts and pool.

WATERFRONT: 187 Marsh Wall-South Quay Plaza. **(B1/70)** *Fullers.*
CHISWICK, FULLERS LONDON PRIDE, ESB. Pleasant new pub set
in a complex of modern buildings. The hugh windows give a
panoramic views of 'Dockland City'. Situated on quay
formerly operated by SW India Dock in 1870. Prior to this
its origin was the City Canal built by the Corporation. It
saved two minutes of river navigation and was unsucessful
due to the new Seamans Guide. Restaurant. Facilities for
the disabled. Two mins walk from DLR S Quay Station. Open
Mon – Fri 11-9.30 only.

WATERMANS ARMS: 1 Glenaffric Avenue. **(D1/71)** *Ind Coope Taylor*
Walker. *TETLEY BITTER, IND COOPE BURTON ALE.* A Grade II
Listed Building decorated in nautical style. Five minutes
walk from Island Gardens DLR Station. Darts and pool.
Restaurant. Open Monday – Saturday 11-3 and 6-11.

Wellington Arms: 145 St. Leonard's Road. **(A1/72)** *Grand*
Met-Watneys. *No real ale!*

WHITE HORSE: 9/11 Poplar High Street. **(B2/73)** *Grand Met-Trumans.*

WEBSTERS YORKSHIRE BITTER. Big one bar pub with specially
designed ceiling tiles. Outside statue is Listed. Fives
dartboard. Cooked lunchtime food. Outside drinking area.
Five minutes walk from Poplar DLR Station. Open Monday –
Wednesday 11-2.30 and 5-11 Thursday and Friday 11-11
Saturday 11-5 and 7-11.

White Swan: 556 Commercial Road. **(B2/74)** *Grand Met-Watneys.*
No real ale!

WHITE SWAN: 130 Blackwall Way. **(B1/74)** *Grand Met-Watneys.*
WEBSTERS YORKSHIRE BITTER. Smal pub with restaurant.
Garden. Open Monday – Saturday 11-3 and 6-11.

Young Prince: 60 Cordelia Street. (A1/75) *Whitbreads.*
No real ale!

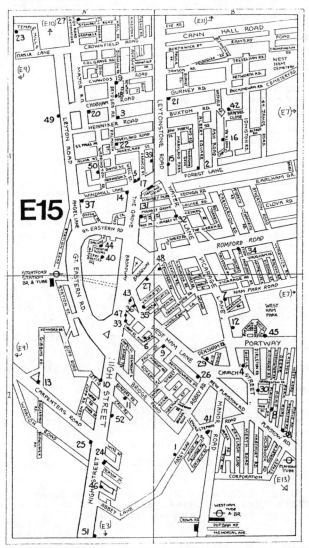

E15

Stations - Stratford (BR Liverpool Street/BR North London/Central/DLR), Maryland (BR Liverpool Street), Pudding Mill Lane (DLR - due to open during the currency of this Guide).

Once at the boundary of the Danelaw (the end of the line for Carlsberg in the 900s) and in Essex before the first round of the county re-organisations, the entry to Stratford is marked by an abrupt transition to industrial sprawl as one crosses the River Lea from Bow. The lack of pollution controls caused many industries to set up here in the 18th and 19th centuries which were not allowed in London proper. The River Lea also once marked the transition from 10.30 to 11pm evening pub closure hours for pubs, bringing extra trade from Bow for those nearer the river. Lacking a residential base, many of the pubs in this part of the area offer music in the evenings to get the punters in, although sadly real ale is not a big seller.

The centre of Stratford is home to a large shopping centre which is untainted by architectural merit but nonetheless draws in the crowds, although if you get there through the connection from the stations then you don't have to look outside anyway. You do of course if you go outside to visit one of the range of pubs in the centre - whilst many are orientated towards the younger market there should be one to suit most tastes. Going eastward rows of Victorian terraced houses mark a further change in the character of Stratford and this is where you might expect to find the street corner locals. Many pubs are Big Four, but there are exceptions and it is worth looking out for guest beers.

On Maryland Road Savills Brewery operated from 1856 until acquired by Charrington in 1925.

Adam & Eve: 126 Abbey Road. **(B2/1)** *Bass Charrington.*
  No real ale!

Albert House: 39 Forest Lane. **(B1/2)** *Bass Charrington.*
  No real ale!

AMELIA: 80 Henniker Road. **(A1/3)** *Grand Met-Watneys.*
  WEBSTERS YORKSHIRE BITTER, RUDDLES BEST. One bar pub with DJ five nights a week. Cooked meals at all times.

Angel: 21 Church Street. **(B2/4)** *Bass Charrington.*
  No real ale!

BACCHUS'S BIN: 7/9 Leytonstone Road. **(A1/5)** *Free House.*
BODDINGTONS BITTER, BRAINS SA, RAYMENTS SPECIAL, ADNAMS BROADSIDE, MORLAND SPECKLED HEN, GREENE KING ABBOT ALE. Attached to its own off licence selling real cider. Pub cum wine bar with licensed restaurant downstairs and eating area in main bar and function room. Plans for an extention. Excellent value food. Fresh flowers on the tables. Outside drinking area. Open Monday – Saturday 11-3 and 5-11.

BAKERS ARMS: 70 Pitchford Street. **(A2/6)** *Bass Charrington.*
WORTHINGTON BEST BITTER. Darts are played regularily DJ Fri and Sat nights. Hot food lunchtimes and in the evenings by request. Snacks at all times. Currently for sale. Open all permitted hours.

BAY TREE: 59 Vicarage Lane. **(B2/7)** *Bass Charrington.*
WORTHINGTON BEST BITTER. Local drinkers' pub with island bar, settees and other comfortable chairs. Makes a nice change from the ususal pub seats. Decorated in brown and light green with a collectin of old photos of Stratford around the walls. Darts and pool. Function room. Lunchtime snacks. Open Monday – Friday 12-11, Saturday 11-11.

BRITANNIA: 2 Plaistow Grove. **(B2/8)** *Ind Coope Taylor Walker.*
TETLEY BITTER, GREENE KING IPA. Wood panelled walls made to look like the side of a ship with mock port holes. A small corner street local with uncooperative landlord.

British Lion: 46 West Ham Lane. **(B2/9)** *Ind Coope Taylor Walker.*
No real ale!

BUILDERS ARMS: 302 High Street. **(A2/10)** *Grand Met-Watneys.*
WEBSTERS YORKSHIRE BITTER. Darts and pool. Open all permitted hours.

Burford Arms: 11 Burford Street. **(A2/11)** *Bass Charrington.*
No beer – closed.

Canteen: 195 Vicarage Lane **(B2/12)** *Free House.*
No real ale!

Carpenters Arms: 17 Carpenters Road. **(A2/13)** *Ind Coope Taylor Walker. No real ale!*

Cart & Horses: 1 Maryland Point. **(A1/14)** *Bass Charrington.*
No real ale!

Charleston: 16 Leytonstone Road. **(B1/15)** *Bass Charrington.*
No real ale!

Chatsworth Arms: 27 Chatsworth Road. **(B1/16)** *Grand Met-Watneys.*
No real ale!

Chevy Chase: 11 Leytonstone Road. **(A1/17)** *Ind Coope Taylor Walker. No real ale!*

Chobham Arms: 62 Chobham Road. **(A1/18)** *Grand Met-Trumans. No real ale!*

DEW DROP INN: 22 Brydges Road. **(A1/19)** *Bass Charrington. CHARRINGTON IPA.* Small local pub where the beer is well looked after. Darts. Snacks at all times. Open all permitted hours.

Eagle: 157 Chobham Road. **(A1/20)** *Free House. No real ale!*

ESSEX ARMS: 82 Leytonstone Road. **(B1/21)** *Bass Charrington. CHARRINGTON IPA, BASS.* Darts and bar billiards. Cooked meals lunchtimes and snacks at other times. Open all permitted hours.

FALMOUTH ARMS: 53 Maryland Road. **(A1/22)** *Free House. FLOWERS IPA.* Former Watney pub with ladies' dart matches Mondays and friendly Irish manager. Snacks at all times. Open all permitted hours.

Flappers: Temple Mill Lane. **(A1/23)** *Bass Charrington. No real ale!*

GREEN GATE: 225/227 High Street. **(A2/24)** *Ind Coope Taylor Walker. TAYLOR WALKER BEST BITTER, IND COOPE BURTON ALE.* Darts and pool. Cooked meals lunchtime and snacks at all times. Open Monday – Saturday 11-3.30 and 5-11.

Green Man: 196 High Street. **(A2/25)** *Grand Met-Trumans. No real ale!*

GREYHOUND: 136 West Ham Lane. **(B2/26)** *Courage. COURAGE BEST BITTER, DIRECTORS BITTER.* Pleasant well appointed pub with two bars. Darts and pool. Open all permitted hours.

KING EDWARD VII: 47 The Broadway. **(A2/27)** *Bass Charrington. CHARRINGTON IPA, GREENE KING IPA, FULLERS LONDON PRIDE, YOUNGS SPECIAL.* Formerly (pre First World War) the King of Prussia. Three bars and cooked food lunchtimes and Sundays. Open all permitted hours. It is a Listed Building and one of the original windows has the outline of Edward VII etched in it. Darts.

KING HAROLD: 116 High Road. **(A1/28)** *Bass Charrington.* Very large neighbourhood pub near Leyton Station. Real ale has been tried on more than one occasion and the present landlord seems to have found the secret of success. Darts and pool. Garden. Gym in upstairs room. Hot bar snacks at all times. Open all permitted hours.

KINGS HEAD: 11 Church Street. (B2/29) *Bass Charrington.*
CHARRINGTON IPA. One bar pub with darts and pool. Live
music Fridays. Lunchtime snacks. Open Monday – Thursday
11-3 and 5.30-11, Friday – Saturday 11-11.

Lock Stock n Barrel: 51 Church Street. (B2/30) *Belhaven.*
No real ale!

LORD HENNIKER: 119 The Grove. (A1/31) *Bass Charrington.*
CHARRINGTON IPA. Good pub for the locals. Darts and
function room. Cooked food lunchtime and snacks other
times. Open all permitted hours.

MANBY ARMS: 19 Water Lane. (B1/32) *Bass Charrington.*
CHARRINGTON IPA. Cosy one bar pub with darts and pool.
Cooked meals lunchtime. Open Monday to Thursday 11-11
Fridayand Saturday closed 3.30-5. Garden.

MULLIGANS: 13 Broadway. (A2/33) *Grand Met-Watneys.*
Formerly Moonlights Mooro's and originally the Olde
Black Bull as can be seen by the statue near the roof.
Very Irish pub as the name would indicate. A good
selection of Irish spirits. Lunchtime meals. Open all
permitted hours. Sells Mulligans Bitter which is no doubt
a dead ringer for Websters Yorkshire Bitter.

PIGEONS HOTEL: 120/122 Romford Road. (B1/34) *Bass Charrington.*
CHARRINGTON IPA. Large public house recently decorated.
Wood panelled walls. Darts and pool. Lunchtime snacks.

PRINCESS OF WALES: 25 West Ham Lane. (A2/35) *Ind Coope Taylor*
Walker. *TETLEY BITTER, IND COOPE BURTON ALE, YOUNGS*
SPECIAL. Redecorated in 1990. Comfortable pub with darts
and cooked meals lunchtime including Sundays. Beer is well
kept. Open Monday to Friday 11-11, Saturday 11-3 and 7-11.

QUEENS HEAD: 5/7 West Ham Lane. (A2/36) *Bass Charrington.*
CHARRINGTON IPA. Darts and pool. Lunchtime snacks. Open
all permitted hours.

RAILWAY TAVERN: 131 Angel Lane. (A1/37) *Bass Charrington.*
CHARRINGTON IPA, BASS, YOUNGS SPECIAL. A very pleasant
one-bar, large Victorian corner pub with games room to the
rear for darts and pool.Opens at 6am until 8am Monday to
Saturday and all permitted hours. Garden and car park.
Food lunchtime and snacks at other times.

Railway Tavern: 196 Plaistow Road. (B2/38) *Bass Charrington.*
No real ale!

ROYAL OAK: 83 Leytonstone Road. (A1/39) *Grand Met-Watneys.*
WEBSTERS YORKSHIRE BITTER. Live music Mon Thurs Sat and
Sun. Lunchtime snacks. Darts. Open all permitted hours.

SPARROWS: North Mall - Stratford Shopping Centre. (A1/40) *Bass Charrington. CHARRINGTON IPA, YOUNGS SPECIAL.* There is a small restaurant area with different set meals each day. Patio area. Open all permitted hours except Sunday when it is closed.

Spread Eagle: 1 Manor Road - Leywick Street. (B2/41) *Bass Charrington. No real ale!*

Steamship: 14 Bramall Close (B1/42) *Courage.*
COURAGE BEST BITTER. Darts and shove halfpenny. Funtion room for 50 people. Garden. Snacks at lunchtime on request. Friday quiz nights. Open all permitted hours.

SWAN: 31 The Broadway. (A2/43) *Grand Met-Watneys.*
WEBSTERS YORKSHIRE BITTER, RUDDLES BEST, RUDDLES COUNTY. Large two bar pub with darts and bar billiards. Function room. Cooked meals lunchtime and snacks other times. Open all permitted hours.

THEATRE ROYAL BAR: Gerry Raffles Square. (A1/44) *Free House.*
CHARLES WELLS EAGLE, CHARLES WELLS BOMBARDIER. Theatre bar that is open to the public. Beware sudden rushes to the bar around 9pm due to a productions interval! An exciting range of guest beers, so is worth seeking out. A rare collection of Toby jugs behind the bar. Snacks at all times. Open 11-3 and 5-11.

TOBY TAVERN: 81 Portway. (B2/45) *Free House.*
COURAGE BEST BITTER. Darts and pool. Function room for 150. Hot food lunchtime. Open all permitted hours.

Two Brewers: 197 High Street. **(A2/46)** *Bass Charrington. No real ale!*

TWO PUDDINGS: 27 The Broadway. **(A2/47)** *Grand Met-Watneys.*
WEBSTERS YORKSHIRE BITTER, RUDDLES COUNTY. Changing from a youngsters' pub to suit a wider range of client but there is a disco for them upstairs. Cooked meals lunchtime and snacks other times. Garden. Open all permitted hours.

THE VILLAGE WINE BAR: 4 Romford Road (Stratford Office Village). **(B1/48)** *Free House. COURAGE BEST BITTER.* Smart well furnished wine bar popular with office workers. Brightly lit. Lunchtime food. Not open weekends. Small function room.

Wheelers: 156 Leyton Road **(A1/49)** *Free House. No real ale!*

Windmill: 49 Waddington Road. **(A1/50)** *Grand Met-Watneys. No real ale!*

WOODMAN: 119/121 High Street. **(A2/51)** *Grand Met-Watneys.*
WEBSTERS YORKSHIRE BITTER, *RUDDLES BEST.* Games room in
public bar for darts and pool. Lunchtime snacks. Open
Monday - Saturday 11-3 and 5.30-11.

YORKSHIRE GREY: 335/337 High Street. **(A2/52)** *Bass Charrington.*
CHARRINGTON IPA. One bar pub with car park at rear. Darts
and pool table in upstairs room. Cooked meals lunchtime.
Open all permitted hours.

Fox & Anchor EC1 has an early morning licence.

Stations – Canning Town, Silvertown, Custom House and North
Woolwich (BR North London). The DLR Beckton extension is due to
open during the currency of this Guide.

Victoria Dock is a misnomer for this area, centred on the Royal
Docks and covering those parts suggested by the names of the
stations. It is the only area in this Guide with an airport,
albeit sadly under utilised and only really useful if you plan to
start your trip here in Paris. New development has been much
slower than in the Isle of Dogs and whilst some genuine industry
is still functioning (such as the Tate & Lyle refinery), many
parts appear derelict and forgotten, especially around the Docks
which were once the largest in London. This is reflected in the
pubs, which often are sadly lacking in trade – and many have been
closed in recent years.

Around Canning Town postwar rebuilding led to a range of Big Four
estate pubs although older establishments are to be found around
the docks. At North Woolwich (once part of Kent) a small
community clusters around the Woolwich Ferry and foot tunnel, and
a railway museum has been established in the station.

Anchor: 20 Star Lane. **(A2/1)** *Courage.*
No real ale!

Artful Dodger: 272 Victoria Dock Road (B2/2) *Free House.*
No beer – closed.

Barge: 271 Victoria Dock Road. **(B2/3)** *Free House.*
No real ale! Formerly Kilkenney Castle.

Beckton Arms: 8 Beckton Road. **(A2/4)** *Ind Coope Taylor Walker.*
No real ales!

British Flag: 190 Victoria Dock Road. (B2/5) *Grand Met-Watneys.*
No real ale!

CALIFORNIA: 12 Albert Road. (B1/6) *Free House.*
*COURAGE BEST BITTER, JOHN SMITH'S BITTER, DIRECTORS
BITTER.* Large corner pub with darts and two pool tables.
Food at all times. Open all permitted hours.

Chandelier: 61 Victoria Dock Road. **(A2/7)** *Grand Met-Watneys.*
No beer – closed.

CHURCHILLS: Albert Road. **(B1/8)** *Free House.*
GREENE KING ABBOT ALE. It also has a variety of guest

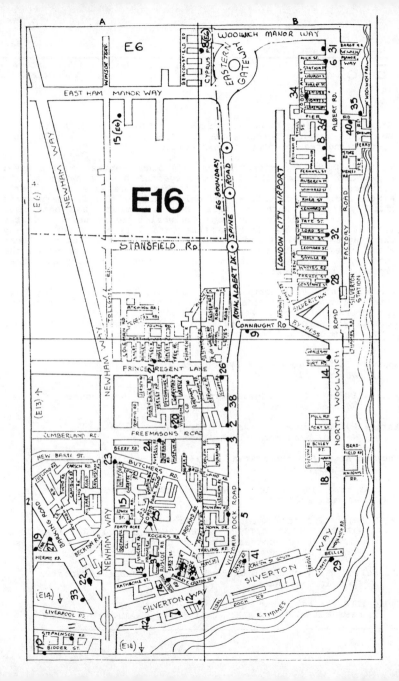

beers. The Kent Arms (Ind Coope) was formery on the site. Darts and pool. Cooked meals Mon-Fri lunchtimes. For sale in 1991. Open Monday to Friday 11-3 and 5.30-11, Saturday 11-3 and 7-11.

Connaught Tavern: 11 Connaught Road. (B1/9) *Grand-Met Truman. No beer - closed.*

Dartmouth Arms: 162 Bidder Street. (A2/10) *Bass Charrington. No real ale!*

DURHAM ARMS: 24 Stephenson Street. (A2/11) *Bass Charrington. CHARRINGTON IPA.* Back street pub a bit hard to find but well worth looking for. Friendly locals pub with pleasant glass and mirrors. Darts. Garden. Small function room. Open Monday - Friday 11-3.30 and 5-11, Saturday 11-11. Lunchtime cooked meals and snacks at all times.

ESSEX ARMS: 92 Victoria Dock Road. (B2/12) *Courage. COURAGE BEST BITTER.* Darts and pool. Food at all times. Open Monday to Friday 11-3 and 5.30-11 Saturday 12-3 and 7.30-11.

Flying Scud: 76 Rathbone Street. (A2/13) *Bass Charrington. No real ale!*

Graving Dock Tavern: 353 North Woolwich Road. (B2/14) *Grand Met-Watneys. No real ale!*

Ground Rent Tavern: 62 Rogers Road. (A2/15) *Grand-Met-Watney. No real ale!*

HALLSVILLE TAVERN: 57 Hallsville Road. (A2/16) *Free House. TETLEY BITTER.* One bar pub with darts and pool. Snacks at all times.

HENLEY ARMS: 268 Albert Road. (B1/17) *Bass Charrington. CHARRINGTON IPA.* A locals' pub with two pool teams.

Jubilee Tavern: 9 Barnwood Court. (B2/18) *Ind Coope Taylor Walker. No real ale!*

Marquis of Salisbury: 110 Hermit Road. (A2/19) *Bass Charrington.*

   No real ale!

NEW GOG: Freemasons Road. (A2/20) *Courage. DIRECTORS BITTER.* Darts and pool. Garden. Karaoke Fri and Sat evenings. Outside drinking area. Facilities for the disabled. Open all permitted hours.

Nottingham Arms: 371 Prince Regent Lane. (A2/21) *Grand Met-Watneys. No real ale!*

Ordnance Arms: 110 Barking Road. (A2/22) *Grand Met-Trumans.*
No real ale!

Pauls Head: 1 Watford Road. (A2/23) *Grand Met-Watneys.*
No real ale!

Peacock: 115 Freemasons Road. (A2/24) *Bass Charrington.*
No beer - closed.

Pitts Head: 2 Fords Park Road. (A2/25) *Bass Charrington.*
No real ale!

Prince of Wales: 388 Prince Regent Lane. (A2/26) *Whitbreads.*
No real ale!

Princess Alexandra: 219 Barking Road. (A2/27) *Courage.*
No real ale!

RAILWAY HOTEL: 2 Connaught Road. (B1/28) *Free House.*
RUDDLES BEST, RUDDLES COUNTY. Now a free house (ex Ind
Coope). Pool. Snacks at all times. Open all permitted
hours.

RAM TAVERN: 26 North Woolwich Road. (B2/29) *Grand Met-Trumans.*
WEBSTERS YORKSHIRE BITTER, RUDDLES COUNTY. Live music
Tuesday karaoke Saturdays. Darts and pool. Snacks at all
times. Open all permitted hours.

Rose of Denmark: 78 Shirley Street. (A2/30) *Grand Met-Watneys.*
No real ale!

Roundhouse: 19 Woolwich Manor Way. (B1/31) *Grand-Met-Watney.*
No real ale!

Royal Albert: 74 Albert Road. (B1/32) *Grand Met-Watneys.*
No real ale!

Royal Oak: 83 Woodman Street. (B1/33) *Belhaven.*
No real ale!

Royal Oak: 67 Barking Road. (A2/34) *Courage.*
No real ale!

ROYAL PAVILION HOTEL: 2 Pier Road. (B1/35) *Courage.*
JOHN SMITH'S BITTER, DIRECTORS BITTER WADWORTH 6X. Nicely
laid out pub with restaurant at one side that is used as a
jazz club every Monday. Music also on Saturdays. Darts. No
children's room but they are catered for. No food Mondays.
Open Monday to Saturday 11.30-3 and 7-11.

Royal Standard: 116 Albert Road. (B1/36) *Grand Met-Watneys.*
No real ale!

Shakespeares Head: 29 Ruscoe Road. **(A2/37)** *Belhaven.*
No real ale!

Spanish Steps: 277 Victoria Dock Road. **(B2/38)** *Free House.*
No beer – closed.

Streeties: 15 Shirley Street. **(A2/39)** *Grand Met-Watneys.*
No real ale!

Three Crowns: 1 Pier Road. **(B1/40)** *Bass Charrington.*
No beer – closed.

TIDAL BASIN TAVERN: 31 Tidal Basin Road. **(B2/41)** *Fullers.*
FULLERS LONDON PRIDE, ESB. Formerly Rivers. This pub is
very basic but with all the redevelopment in the area it
does well at lunchtime. The beer was good when surveyed
and cheap. Open all permitted hours and till 2am on Fri
and Sat for live music. Darts and pool. Function room.
Snacks at all times.

Windsor Castle: 73 Silvertown Way. **(A2/42)** *Free House.*
No beer – closed.

Huntingdon Arms: 66 Burke Street. *Free House.*
No longer a pub. Sold in 1986. Now a launderette!

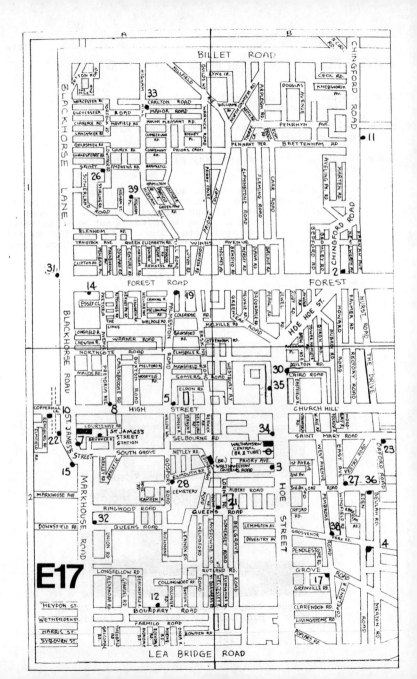

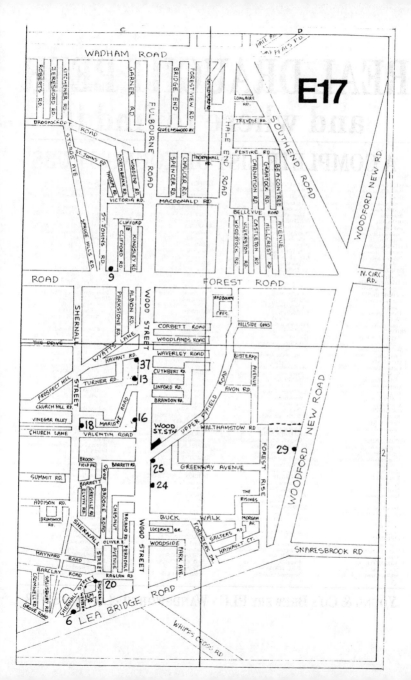

REAL DRAUGHT BEER

and where to find it

A COMPLETE LIST OF YOUNG'S PUBS

BALHAM, SW12
Duke of Devonshire .39 Balham High Rd
Grove .204 Oldridge Rd
Nightingale .97 Nightingale Lane

BARKING, Essex
Britannia. 1 Church Rd

BARNES, SW13
Bull's Head. 373 Lonsdale Rd
Coach and Horses. 27 High St
White Hart. The Terrace, Riverside

BATTERSEA, SW11
Castle. 115 Battersea High St
Duke of Cambridge.
228 Battersea Bridge Rd

BEDDINGTON, Surrey
Plough. Croydon Rd

BETCHWORTH, Surrey
Dolphin. The Street

BLOOMSBURY, WC1
Calthorpe Arms. 252 Gray's Inn Rd
Lamb. 94 Lamb's Conduit St
Three Cups. Sandland St

BOW, E3
Coborn Arms. 8 Coborn Rd

BRIXTON
Hope and Anchor. 123 Acre Lane, SW2
Trinity Arms. 45 Trinity Gardens, SW9

CARSHALTON, Surrey
Greyhound. 2 High St

CATFORD, SE6
Catford Ram. 9 Winslade Way

CHELSEA
Chelsea Ram. Burnaby St, SW10
Coopers' Arms. 87 Flood St, SW3
King's Arms. 190 Fulham Rd, SW10

CHERTSEY, Surrey
Crown. London St

CHISLEHURST, Kent
Bull's Head. Royal Parade

CHISWICK, W4
Crown and Anchor.
374 Chiswick High Rd

CITY OF LONDON
City House. 86 Bishopsgate, EC2
City Retreat. Shoe Lane, EC4
Chapman's, the Wine Lodge.
145 Fenchurch St, EC3
Dirty Dick's. 202 Bishopsgate, EC2
East India Arms. 76 Fenchurch St, EC3
Elephant. 119 Fenchurch St, EC3
Lamb Tavern. Leadenhall Market, EC3
Master Gunner.
37 Cathedral Place, EC4
Three Lords. The Minories, EC3

CLAPHAM COMMON, SW4
Windmill. South Side

CLAPHAM JUNCTION, SW11
Plough. 89 St John's Hill

CLAPTON, E5
Prince of Wales. 146 Lea Bridge Rd

CLAYGATE, Surrey
Foley Arms. Foley Rd

CLERKENWELL, EC1
London Spa. 70 Exmouth Market
Sekforde Arms. 34 Sekforde St

COVENT GARDEN, WC2
Marquess of Anglesey. 39 Bow St

CROYDON, Surrey
Dog and Bull. 24 Surrey St
Gloucester. 111 White Horse Rd
Tamworth Arms. 62 Tamworth Rd

DARTFORD, Kent
Malt Shovel. 3 Darenth Rd

DORKING, Surrey
Old House at Home. 24 West St

DULWICH, SE26
Dulwich Wood House. 39 Sydenham Hill

EAST DULWICH, SE22
Clock House. 196a Peckham Rye

EAST SHEEN, SW14
Hare and Hounds.
216 Upper Richmond Rd West

EFFINGHAM, Surrey
Plough. Orestan Lane

EPSOM, Surrey
King's Arms. 144 East St

ESHER, Surrey
Bear. 71 High St

ETON WICK, Berkshire
Pickwick. 32 Eton Wick Rd

FITZROVIA, W1
One Tun. 58 Goodge St

FULHAM, SW6
Duke of Cumberland.
235 New King's Rd

GREENFORD, Middlesex
Bridge Hotel. Western Avenue

GREENWICH, SE10
Richard I. 52-54 Royal Hill

HAMMERSMITH, W6
Brook Green. 170 Shepherd's Bush Rd
Builders. 81 King St
Thatched House. 115 Dalling Rd

HAMPSTEAD, NW3
Flask. 14 Flask Walk
Horse and Groom. 68 Heath St

HARLESDEN, NW10
Grand Junction Arms. Acton Lane

ISLEWORTH, Middlesex
Castle. 18 Upper Square
Coach and Horses. 183 London Rd

ISLINGTON, N1
Marquess Tavern. 32 Canonbury St

KENSINGTON
Britannia. 1 Allen St, W8
Britannia Tap. 150 Warwick Rd, W14

KEW, Surrey
Coach and Horses. 8 Kew Green

KILBURN, NW6
Queen's Arms. 1 High Rd

KINGSTON-UPON-THAMES, Surrey
Albert Arms. 57 Kingston Hill, Norbiton
Bishop Out of Residence.
2 Bishop's Hall, off Thames St
Grey Horse. 46 Richmond Rd
Spring Grove. 13 Bloomfield Rd

LAMBETH, SW8
Plough. 518 Wandsworth Rd
Prince of Wales. 99 Union Rd
Surprise. 16 Southville

LEE, SE12
Crown. 117 Burnt Ash Hill

LOUGHBOROUGH JUNCTION, SE5
Wickwood Tavern. 58 Flaxman Rd

MARYLEBONE, W1
Black Horse. 109 Marylebone High St
Wargrave Arms. 42 Brendon St

MAYFAIR, W1
Guinea. 30 Bruton Place
Windmill. 6-8 Mill St

MERTON, SW19
King's Head. 18 High St
Prince of Wales. 98 Morden Rd

MITCHAM, Surrey
Bull. 32 Church Rd
Cricketers. 340 London Rd
King's Arms. 260 London Rd

MORTLAKE, SW14
Charlie Butler. 40 High St
Jolly Gardeners.
36 Lower Richmond Rd

NORWOOD
Hope. 49 High St, SE27
Railway Bell. 14 Cawnpore St, SE19

NOTTING HILL, W11
Duke of Wellington. 179 Portobello Rd
Hoop. 83-85 Notting Hill Gate

OXFORD
King's Arms. 40 Holywell St

OXSHOTT, Surrey
Bear. Leatherhead Rd

PIMLICO, SW1
Morpeth Arms. 58 Millbank
Rising Sun. 46 Ebury Bridge Rd
Royal Oak. 1 Regency St

PLUMPTON GREEN, East Sussex
Fountain. Station Rd

PUTNEY, SW15
Castle. 220 Putney Bridge Rd
Duke's Head. 8 Lower Richmond Rd
Green Man. Putney Heath
Half Moon. 93 Lower Richmond Rd
Spotted Horse. 122 Putney High St

REDHILL, Surrey
Home Cottage. Redstone Hill

REGENT'S PARK, NW1
Queens. 49 Regent's Park Rd
Spread Eagle. 141 Albert St

RICHMOND-UPON-THAMES, Surrey
Fox and Goose. 327 Petersham Rd. Ham
Mitre. 20 St Mary's Grove
Old Ship. 3 King St
Orange Tree. 45 Kew Rd
Red Cow. 59 Sheen Rd
Shaftesbury Arms. 123 Kew Rd
Shakespeare. Lower Richmond Rd
Waterman's Arms. 12 Water Lane
White Cross. Riverside

ROEHAMPTON, SW15
Angel. 11 High St
Maltese Cat. Angel Square

ROTHERHITHE, SE16
Ship. 39-47 St Marychurch St

SHERE, Surrey
Prince of Wales. Shere Lane

SOUTHWARK, SE1
Founders Arms. Bankside. 52 Hopton St
Prince William Henry. 217 Blackfriars Rd

STEPNEY
Holland's. 7-9 Exmouth St, E1
Queen's Head. 8 Flamborough St, E14

STREATHAM, SW16
Bedford Park. 223 Streatham High Rd
Pied Bull. 498 Streatham High Rd

SURBITON, Surrey
Black Lion. 58 Brighton Rd
Victoria. 28 Victoria Rd
Waggon and Horses. 1 Surbiton Hill Rd

SUTTON, Surrey
Lord Nelson. 32 Lower Rd
New Town. 7 Land Rd
Robin Hood. 52 West St

SYDENHAM, SE26
Bricklayers' Arms. 189 Dartmouth Rd

TEDDINGTON, Middlesex
Abercorn Arms. 76 Church Rd
Queen Dowager. 49 North Lane

THORNTON HEATH, Surrey
Fountain Head. 114 Parchmore Rd
Lord Napier. 111 Beulah Rd
Railway Telegraph. 19 Brigstock Rd

TOOTING, SW17
Castle. 38 High St
Gorringe Park. 29 London Rd
Leather Bottle. 538 Garratt Lane
Prince of Wales. 646 Garratt Lane

TWICKENHAM, Middlesex
Old Anchor. 71 Richmond Rd
Pope's Grotto. Cross Deep

WALTON-ON-THAMES, Surrey
Royal George. 130 Hersham Rd
Swan. 50 Manor Rd

WALTON-ON-THE-HILL, Surrey
Chequers. Chequers Lane

WALLINGTON, Surrey
Duke's Head. 6 Manor Rd

WANDSWORTH, SW18
Alma. 499 York Rd
Brewery Tap. 68 Wandsworth High St
County Arms. 345 Trinity Rd
Crane. 14 Armoury Way
Gardeners' Arms. 268 Merton Rd
Grapes. 39 Fairfield St
Halfway House. 521 Garratt Lane
King's Arms. 96 Wandsworth High St
Old Sergeant. 104 Garratt Lane
Pig and Whistle. 481 Merton Rd
Queen Adelaide. 35 Putney Bridge Rd
Ship. 41 Jew's Row
Spread Eagle. 71 Wandsworth High St
Two Brewers. 147 East Hill
Wheatsheaf. 30 Putney Bridge Rd

WESTMINSTER, SW1
Buckingham Arms. 62 Petty France

WIMBLEDON, SW19
Alexandra. 33 Hill Rd
Crooked Billet. 15 Crooked Billet
Dog and Fox. 24 High St
Hand in Hand. 6 Crooked Billet
Rose and Crown. 55 High St

YOUNG & CO'S BREWERY PLC · WANDSWORTH · LONDON SW18

Stations – Blackhorse Road (BR Barking/Victoria), Walthamstow Central (BR Liverpool Street/Victoria), Walthamstow Queens Road (BR Barking), Wood Street and St James Street (BR Liverpool Street).

Victorian terraces spread across this large area, extending from the reservoirs of the Lea Valley to Epping Forest and between Chingford in the north and Leyton in the south. It grew up following the building of the railway and the originally small population was swelled by artisans from areas such as Hackney. They generally had to travel back there to work, which affected the character of the pubs and fewer were built than in other parts of East London. In recent years the number has been expanding however, as the shop conversion trend spread here from North London and a wider range of real ales has become available to relieve Big Four domination.

The only brewery of modern times in Waltham Forest Borough was Collier Brothers' Essex Brewery at St James Street. It was taken over by Tollemache of Ipswich in 1920 but closed in 1972. Most of the pubs seem to have gone to Charrington.

The Artful: 80 Brunner Road. **(A2/1)** *Grand Met-Watneys.*
No real ale!

THE BELL: 617 Forest Road. **(B1/2)** *Grand Met-Watneys.*
WEBSTERS YORKSHIRE BITTER, RUDDLES COUNTY. Large three-bar pub formerly owned by E.J. Rose. Handy for the Walthamstow Assembly Hall. Cooked meals lunchtimes and snacks in the evening. Darts andpool. Opens 11-3 and 5.30-11 Monday to Friday. Saturday from 11-11. Normal Sunday hours.

Bentleys: 300 Hoe Street. **(B2/3)** *Free House.*
No real ale!

CASTLE: 15 Grosvenor Rise East. **(B2/4)** *Bass Charrington.*
CHARRINGTON IPA. Apart from the live music this house could almost be described as a traditional East London local. Darts and pool. Outside drinking area consists of just a couple of tables. Cooked meals at all times. Open Monday – Friday 12-11 Saturday 11-4 and 7-11.

Chequers: 145 High Street. **(A2/5)** *Ind Coope Taylor Walker.*
No real ale!

CHESTNUT TREE: 757 Lea Bridge Road. **(C2/6)** *Ind Coope Taylor Walker.* *TETLEY BITTER, IND COOPE BURTON ALE.* Large well maintained house. Tends to attract youngsters Friday/Saturday nights when there is live music. Darts and pool. In 1846 it was called 'The Little Wonder'. Rebuilt in 1854. The original address was Chestnut Walk. When Lea Bridge Road was widened in 1863 the pubs name was changed to commete it. There was a pub 'next door' called 'The Volunteer' 1863-1897. Cooked food lunchtime and snacks. Function room. Open Monday – Saturday 12–11.

COACH & HORSES: 63 St James' Street. **(A2/7)** *Grand Met–Watneys.* *WEBSTERS YORKSHIRE BITTER, RUDDLES COUNTY.* Darts pool and shove halfpenny. Car park. Food at lunchtime only. Opens Monday to Thursday 11-3 and 5.30 -11, Friday and Saturday 11-11. Normal Sunday hours. Large corner house where customers are made to feel welcome.

COCK: 67 High Street. **(A2/8)** *Ind Coope Taylor Walker.* *TETLEY BITTER, IND COOPE BURTON ALE.* Darts, pool and shove halfpenney. Cooked meals lunchtime and snacks other times. Open all permitted hours. Market pub very busy during market hours.

COLLEGE ARMS: 807 Forest Road **(C1/9)** *Free House.* *GREENE KING ABBOT ALE, GREENE KING ABBOT ALE, YOUNGERS SCOTCH, ELDRIDGE POPE ROYAL OAK.* NETHERGATE OLD GROWLER. Wetherspoons free house selling the Scotch at 79p a pint! Formerly Cheeks American Bar. Open all permitted hours. Guest beers. Formerly two shops. Ale always good.

COPPERMILL: 205 Coppermill Lane. **(A2/10)** *Free House.* *TETLEY BITTER, IND COOPE BURTON ALE. MARSTONS PEDIGREE, FULLERS LONDON PRIDE, ESB.* Also currently selling Morlands Bitter. Formerly the Lord Kitchener. Darts. Snacks at all times. Open all permitted hours. Small pub converted from an off licence. Very good ale and worth seeking out.

Dog & Duck: 222 Chingford Road. **(A2/11)** *Grand Met–Watneys.* *No real ale! Formerly Racers.*

Duke of Cambridge: 178 Boundary Road. **(A2/12)** *Ind Coope Taylor Walker.* *No real ale!*

DUKES HEAD: 112 Wood Street. **(C2/13)** *Grand Met–Watneys.* *WEBSTERS YORKSHIRE BITTER.* Single bar pub with car park restaurant, garden, darts and pool. The difference in five years as far as this pub is concerned now that Grand Met brew no beer is that instead of Stag Combes and Websters at 90p a pint we now have only Websters at 1.25p a pint. Snacks at all times and cooked meals lunchtime. Opens 11-11 on Friday and Saturday.

ESSEX ARMS: 82/4 Forest Road. (A1/14) *Grand Met-Watneys.*
WEBSTERS YORKSHIRE BITTER, RUDDLES BEST. Cooked food at
lunchtime and snacks at all times.Pool. Function room.
Open Monday to Friday 11-3 and 5.30-11, Saturday 11-5 and
7-11 plus normal Sunday hours. This pub seems to be trying
to change its image from a drinkers' house to a
youngsters' pub.

Essex Brewery Tap: St James Street. (A2/15) *Bass Charrington.*
No real ale!

FLOWERPOT: 128 Wood Street. (C2/16) *Bass Charrington.*
BASS. One of the best pints of Bass anywhere in London. A
must for genuine drinkers. Snacks at all times. Built in
1863 as an Essex Brewery pub. Open 11-3 and 5.30-11 Monday
to Friday and all day Saturday. Nothing has changed in
this pub since our last guide five years ago.

GROVE TAVERN: 74 Grove Road. (B2/17) *Bass Charrington.*
CHARRINGTON IPA. Run down local serving a good drop of
IPA. Built in 1868 as 'The Britannia'. Very noisy Fri/Sat
nights with live music. Darts and bar biliards. Function
room. Lunchtime snacks. Open all permitted hours.

LORD BROOKE: 47 Shernhall Street. (C2/18) *Bass Charrington.*
CHARRINGTON IPA. Always a very good pub that has 15 dart
teams. IPA really excellent guv very friendly as are all
the staff. Facilities: Darts function room three bars
garden shove halfpenny. Snacks and cooked meals at
lunchtime. Guest beers to come. Open 11-11 Friday and
Saturday.

LORD PALMERSTON: 254 Forest Road. (A1/19) *Bass Charrington.*
CHARRINGTON IPA, GREENE KING IPA. Darts and pool. Function
room. Snacks at all times. Open all permitted hours.
Interesting architecture and windows.

LORD RAGLAN: 199 Shernhall Street. (C2/20) *Grand Met-Watneys.*
WEBSTERS YORKSHIRE BITTER. Darts and pool. Snacks at all
times. Garden. The name commemorates the Crimean War
Commander Lord Raglan who was Commander-in-Chief of the
British Expeditionary Army to the East in 1854. He died of
Crimean fever in 1855. Open Monday – Thursday 11-3 and
5.30-11, Friday – Saturday 11-11.

Lorne Arms: 64 Queen's Road. (B2/21) *Bass Charrington.*
No real ale!

Marneys: 30 St James's Street. (A2/22) *Free House.*
No real ale!

NAGS HEAD: 9 Orford Road. **(B2/23)** *Grand Met-Watneys.*
WEBSTERS YORKSHIRE BITTER, RUDDLES COUNTY, GREENE KING ABBOT ALE. Listed Building. Darts and pool. Function room. Food lunchtimes. Open all permitted hours. Shove halfpenny. Childrens room. Super pub - what a pity Grand Met own it. And what a pity they knocked it into one bar!

PIG & WHISTLE: 185 Wood Street **(C2/24)** *Free House.*
DIRECTORS BITTER, MARSTONS PEDIGREE. BORDER EXHIBITION also on and selling well. New pub with garden and food at all times. OK for the disabled. Open all permitted hours.

PLOUGH: 173 Wood Street. **(C2/25)** *Grand Met-Watneys.*
RUDDLES BEST. Darts and pool. Cooked meals lunchtime and snacks at all times. Opens all permitted hours. A run down local not quite sure what type of customer it wants.

Prince of Wales: 58 St Andrews Road. **(A1/26)** *Grand Met-Watneys.*
No real ale!

QUEENS ARMS: 42 Orford Road. **(B2/27)** *Courage.*
COURAGE BEST BITTER, JOHN SMITH'S BITTER, DIRECTORS BITTER. Darts and pool. Food lunchtime. Garden. Facilities for the disabled. Built in 1859. Open all permitted hours.

Ringwood Castle: 49 Gosport Road. **(A2/28)** *Grand Met-Trumans.*
No real ale!

Rising Sun: Woodford New Road. **(D2/29)** *Bass Charrington.*
No real ale!

Rose & Crown: 55 Hoe Street. **(B2/30)** *Grand Met-Trumans.*
No real ale!

ROYAL STANDARD: 1 Blackhorse Lane. **(A1/31)** *Ind Coope Taylor Walker. TETLEY BITTER, ADNAMS BITTER.* Very loud music every night. Not a pub for a quiet pint. This pub is more suitable for lager drinking teenyboppers. Pool, restaurant and garden. Open Monday - Thursday 12-2.30 and 5-11, Friday 12-3 and 5-11, Saturday 7-11. Music bar 8-12 every day.

SPORTSMAN: 131 Markhouse Road. **(A2/32)** *Bass Charrington.*
CHARRINGTON IPA. Formerly the Common Gate. Darts and pool. Function room. Snacks lunchtime only. Open all permitted hours. Glitter! Beer good, but it does not look or feel like a drinkers pub. Nice tiles on the south wall advertising Charringtons Stout.

TAVERN ON THE HILL: 381 Higham Hill Road. **(A1/33)** *Ind Coope Taylor Walker. TETLEY BITTER, IND COOPE BURTON ALE.* The warmth of an Irish welcome. This pub has been modified into a one-bar only house and tastefully decorated. Looks better inside than out. Darts and pool. Lunchtime food. Open all permitted hours.

TOWER HOTEL: 264 Hoe Street. **(B2/34)** *Bass Charrington.*
CHARRINGTON IPA , BASS. Current guest beer is Everards
Tiger. Darts and pool. Garden and function room. Cooked
meals lunchtime and snacks other times. Open all permitted
hours. Adjacent to Walthamstow Central Station. Tends to
change with current fashion. Formerly Flanagans Tower.

VICTORIA: 186 Hoe Street. **(B2/35)** *Free House.*
BODDINGTONS BITTER. One long T-shaped room. Open all
permitted hours. Pool. The once busy restaurant/tea room of
Theodore Komisarjesky's Granada cinema has now become a
pub. Some of the original decoration can still be seen but
drinkers should try to visit the cinema foyer at least to
sample the remaining delights of this early exercise in
fantasy architecture. In the main cinema the original
decoration with its grand Spanish features is largely
intact. (JH).

VILLAGE: 31 Orford Road. **(B2/36)** *Free House.*
*BODDINGTONS BITTER, FULLERS LONDON PRIDE, ESB, MARSTONS
PEDIGREE.* New pub that opened in 1989. Current guest beer
is Morland Old Masters. Childrens room. Food till 9pm.
Garden. Open all permitted hours. Display of over 50
cameras.

White Swan: 84 Wood Street. **(C2/37)** *Grand Met-Watneys.*
No real ale!

WINDMILL: 20 Grosvenor Park Road. **(B2/38)** *Whitbreads.*
*WHITBREAD WETHERED, WHITBREAD FLOWERS ORIGINAL,
BODDINGTONS BITTER.* The sort of pub you can go to for a
quiet drink without raising your voice. Pity about
Whitbread and their high pricing policy. Outside drinking
area. Darts, pool and snooker. Function room. Gaden.
Lunchtime snacks. Open all permitted hours.

WOODMAN: 150 Higham Place. **(A1/39)** *Courage.*
COURAGE BEST BITTER, DIRECTORS BITTER. Raises a lot of
money for Guide Dogs for the Blind Assn. Has a cabinet
with guide dog replicas on show - present total 36 dogs.
Darts and shove halfpenny. Garden. Lunchtime food. Open
Monday - Friday 12-11 Saturday 11-4 and 7-11.

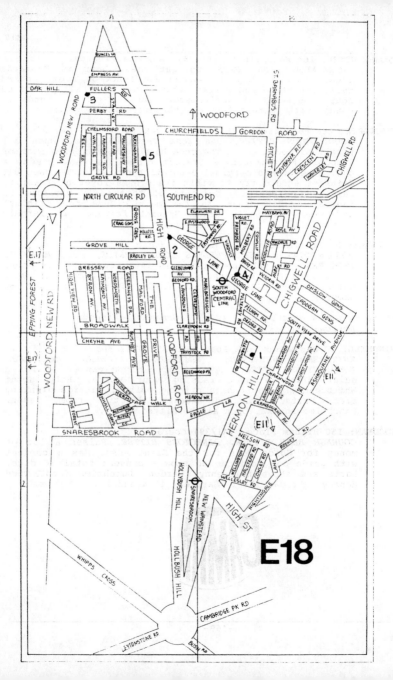

E18

Stations – South Woodford (Central).

This small district is an area of inter war suburban development at the south end of Woodford and bifurcated by the Central Line and the North Circular road. On the south side it merges imperceptibly into the Snaresbrook end of Wanstead. All the pubs are owned by the Big Four (although Woodford proper has more variety) and all have but a single bar.

BOAR AND THISTLE: 142 Hermon Hill. (B2/1) *Grand Met-Watneys.*
WEBSTERS YORKSHIRE BITTER, GREENE KING IPA. Formerly Fir Trees and Firs. Expensive one-bar pub with food at lunchtimes Monday to Saturday. No jeans or trainers. Discos most evenings. Open Monday to Friday 11-3 and 7-11, Saturday 11-3 and 7.30-11.

GEORGE: 70/74 High Road. (A1/2) *Bass Charrington.*
CHARRINGTON IPA. c/o George Lane. One-bar pub with young clientele next to the cinema. Pool and pinball machine. Outside drinking area. Live music (Irish and traditional) Sunday lunchtime. Lunchtime food. Open Friday – Saturday and Monday 11-11, Tuesday, Wednesday and Thursday 11-3 and 5-11.

NAPIER ARMS: Woodford New Road (A1/3) *Bass Charrington.*
CHARRINGTON IPA, STONES, GREENE KING IPA. Comfortable recently refurbished two bar pub with patio area. Beer range may vary. Live music on Sundays, organ, drums and floor singers (pre electronic karaoke). Occasional function nights. Darts. Snacks at all times. Open all permitted hours. Car park.

RAILWAY BELL: 87 George Lane. (B1/4) *Courage.*
COURAGE BEST BITTER, JOHN SMITH'S BITTER, DIRECTORS BITTER. Large one bar pub opposite South Woodford tube station. Occasional live music. Darts, pool and bar balliards. Barbecues in the garden in summer. Open Monday to Friday 11-3 and 5-11, Saturday 11-4 and 6-30-11.

WHITE HART: 159 High Road. (A1/5) *Bass Charrington.*
CHARRINGTON IPA, WOTHINGTON BEST BITTER, BASS, GREENE KING IPA, FULLERS LONDON PRIDE. Large split-level one bar pub opposite Queen Mary College Halls of Residence. Live music on Thursdays. Landlord gets beer in nine gallon barrels to ensure beer quality, so not all beers will be on at any one time. Darts. Garden. Cooked meals at all times. Open all permitted hours.

The beers.

Since the publication of our last guide in 1986 there have been major changes in the number of pubs breweries are allowed to own. As a consequence Grand Met (Watney/Truman) have stopped brewing (there are some that maintain they never started!). Trumans closed their Brick Lane brewery in 1989 and the history of major brewing in the East End came to a close. See article elsewhere on Brewery History. As a result the variety of real ale has diminished. Five years back a visit to a Watney and Truman pub may have resulted in the sampling of seven real ales: Combes, Stag, Ruddles County, Websters Yorkshire Bitter, Trumans Best Bitter and Sampson. Today the same visit would net but three.

Grand Met are not alone for the reducing the number of their real ales. Taylor Walker Best Bitter, Friary Meux and Benskins are becoming increasingly rare in the East End and in the main have been replaced by the bland Tetley that like Websters, is shipped down from Yorkshire.

As we went to press Charrington announced the closure of their Springfield Brewery. Charrington IPA is brewed there and already there is concern that the beer will be phased out. It must change in flavour if it is to be brewed elsewhere and again other beers are being shipped in from elsewhere. Worthington Best Bitter and Stones have already appeared in some Bass pubs.

Belhaven, (from Scotland) bought a number of pubs throughout England from Grand Met and Brent Walker but none of their real ale is supplied to them. The pubs that were real with Watney have gone keg since and any real ale sold in them is that of Courage, with who they have a trading agreement. Belhavens motives remain a mystery within CAMRA.

The Crispin EC1 as it used to be

The pubs.

As you are aware from the numerous pictures throughout this guide many of the pubs featured in our guide five years ago have been demolished or closed.
In the City in particular it has been noticed that some pub building have been demolished and replaced with pubs that are part of an office complex rather than a building in its own right.
Outside the City area many pubs have closed and there are five pubs in the E14 area (Poplar/Dockands), waiting to be demolished as part of new roads/road widening schemes. In the E1 Stepney, Whitechapel and Aldgate area instead of waiting for the demolishers balls, public houses have changed use. Two have become restaurants one a cash and carry another a joinery workshop and a fourth an off licence.

And as it is today

EAST LONDON BREWERY HISTORY

by the Brewery History Society

MAJOR BREWERIES.

ALLIED BREWERIES
Taylor Walker & Co Ltd, Barley Mow Brewery, Church Road, Limehouse.
Founded 1730 at Stepney as Salmon and Hare, later Hare and Hartford until 1796 when John Taylor acquired Hare's share. Isaac Walker became a partner in 1816. Moved to Fore Street, Limehouse by 1823 and the Barley Mow Brewery was build in 1889. Registered in March 1907. Taken over by Ind Coope Ltd in 1959 and brewing ceased in 1960.
Take-overs:
1901   John Furze and Co Ltd, St. George's Brewery, Commercial Road, Whitechapel. Founded by Joseph Ticknell at Old Castle Street in 1823 and had moved to St. George's Brewery by 1848.
1912   Highbury Brewery Ltd, 52/54 Holloway Road. Founded c1740 by a Mr Willoughby. Registered March 1896 to acquire the business of Frederick Henry and Arthur Selmes Taylor. About 40 public houses.
1927   Smith, Garrett and Co Ltd Bow Brewery, 246 Bow Road. Registered 1882. Brewery plant offered for sale on November 8th 1927. The brewery was behind the Bombay Grab public house.
1930   Cannon Brewery Co Ltd, 160 St. Johns Street, Clerkenwell. Registered in January 1895 with 110 public houses. Brewing continued until 1955 and the brewery was converted into a distillery and bonded warehouse in 1959, adjacent to Allied House, Allied-Lyons headquarters. The Cannon Brewery had in turn acquired Holt & Co of the Marine Brewery, 52 Broad Street, Ratcliffe Road, East Ham in October 1912 with 27 public houses. Founded in 1837.
1930   Glenny' Brewery Ltd, Barking Brewery, 18 Linton Road, Barking. Founded by 1871. 15 licensed houses.

Ind Coope Ltd Star Brewery, High Street, Romford and Burton-on-Trent. Founded at Romford in 1708 by Benjamin Wilson and the brewery was bought by Edward Ind in 1799 and he was joined by Octavius and George Coope in 1845 when the name was changed from Ind Smith. The Burton Brewery was established in 1856. They took over Jeremiah Hill & Co, Brentwood Brewery in 1900 with 31 public houses. Ind Coope indirectly acquired an East London brewery, the Wilmington Brewery Co, Crown Brewery, 99 Loampit Vale Lewisham was taken over by Thorne Brothers of Nine Elms in 1895, who in turn were acquired by Meux's Brewery Co Ltd of Tottenham Court Road in 1914 who were taken over by Friary, Holroyd and Healy's Brewery Ltd of Guildford in 1961 to form Friary Meux Ltd which fell to Ind Coope in 1964.

BASS
Charrington United Breweries Ltd, Anchor Brewery, Mile End. Founded in 1738 as Wastfield & Moss and became Charrington & Moss in 1766. Registered in July 1897 as Charrington & Co. Ltd. Also brewed at the Abbey Brewery, Burton-on-Trent which was founded in 1872 and was sold in 1926. Registered July 1897 as Charrington & Co. Merged with Bass, Mitchell & Butlers in 1967 to form Bass Charrington Ltd. The Anchor Brewery ceased production in January 1975.

Take overs:

1911	Chandler's Wiltshire Brewery Ltd, 505 Hackney Road, Bethnal Green. Registered in May 1900 to acquire the business carried on by George Charles Porter and William Henry Dieseldorff as Chandler & Co. Ceased brewing 1910 and was offered for sale with 35 public houses in 1911 and a half interest was acquired by Charringtons. The brewery is still standing.
1916	E.J. Brooks, 133 Hill Street, Peckham.
1925	Savill Brothers Ltd, Maryland Road, Stratford. Founded in 1856. Brewing ceased but the premises continued in use as the Taplow Distillery.
1927	Edward Tilney & Co, Alma Brewery, Spelman Street, Whitechapel. The Alma public house marks the site of the brewery.
1929	Seabrooke & Sons Ltd, Thurrock Brewery, Bridge Road, Grays, Essex. Founded by Thomas Seabrooke 1799. Registered 1891 with about 120 public houses.
1933	Hoare & Co Ltd, Red Lion Brewery, St. Katherine's Way. Founded in 1700. Registered in November 1894 to acquire Hoare & Co with 110 public houses. The Red Lion Brewery was closed on June 23rd 1934. Hoare's trademark, a toby jug still forms part of the Bass Charrington trademark. Hoare's themselves took over the following concerns:- Herbert Santer & Sons, Albion Brewery, Caledonian Road, Islington in 1918: New Cross Brewery Co. Ltd, 26 Pomeroy Street. Originally registered as the Hatcham Brewery Co. Ltd in 1888 to acquire the business of Charles Morgan & Co. This company was dissolved in 1892 and was succeeded by the South Metropolitan Brewing & Bottling Co Ltd which was also short lived. A new company, Burney's New Cross Brewery Ltd was registered in December 1898 and was closed in 1905. Finally registered as above September 1905. Their public houses only were acquired by Hoares. West's brewery Co Ltd, Three Crowns Brewery, 313/315 Hackney Road. Registered in 1895. Taken over by Hoares in November 1929 with over 60 public houses. The brewery plant was offered for sale in July 1930.
1965	Woodhead's Brewery Ltd, 112 St. Paul's Road, Islington. Registered 1915 as Edmund Woodhead & Sons Ltd and re-registered as Woodhead's Canonbury Brewery Ltd April 1936 and finally changed as above in 1946. There were no tied houses, only 2 off-licences. Woodheads' took over Albert Ward, Tower Brewery, Ashenden Road, Hackney

in 1910 and the South London Brewery Ltd, 134 Southwark
Bridge Road in 1944 founded in 1760 and was registered
in April 1937 as Jenner's Brewery Ltd. The name being
changed in 1939. All brewing was transferred to
Southwark Bridge Road in 1949.

Before their merger with Charringtons', Bass had acquired an
East London brewery; the Wenlock Brewery Co Ltd, Wenlock Road,
Shoreditch in 1961. Registered 1893 to acquire Glover, Bell &
Co. Brewing ceased in 1962.

COURAGE
Courage & Co. Ltd, Anchor Brewery. Horselydown, Bermondsey.
Brewery was bought by John Courage in 1787. Known as Courage &
Donaldson 1797-1851. Registered as above in April 1888. Merged
with Barclay, Perkins & Co. Ltd in 1955 to form Courage
Barclay & Co Ltd. From 1960 was known as Courage, Barclay &
Simonds & Co Ltd and was renamed Courage Ltd in October 1970.
Anchor Brewery closed in 1981 and brewing was transferred to a
new brewery at Worton Grange, Reading. Taken over in August
1972 by Imperial Tobacco Group Ltd which was acquired by the
Hanson Trust in 1986 which sold Courage Ltd to Elders IXL.
Take-overs:
c1898   Park Brewery Co, 54a Southampton Street, Camberwell.
         Taken over by Thomas Phillips of West Malling, Kent in
         1898 and later came under the control of Courage.
1930   Noakes & Co Ltd, Black Eagle Brewery, 27 White's
         Ground, Bermondsey. Founded in 1697 and was trading as
         Day, Noakes & Son in 1852. Registered in March 1897.
         Noakes acquired John Canning & Sons, Royal Brewery,
         Windsor in 1921 and brewing transferred to Windsor. 280
         public houses.
1956   Reffell's Bexley Brewery Ltd, Bourne Road, Bexley,
         Kent. Founded 1874. Registered December 1898 and
         acquired the London properties of Showell's Brewery Co
         Ltd. 19 tied houses.
1963   Charles Beasley Ltd, North Kent Brewery, Lakedale Road,
         Plumstead. Founded in 1845 as the Park Brewery and the
         name was change to the Lakedale Brewery by 1878.
         Registered in 1943. The brewery is still standing.

Another brewery which came under Courage control indirectly was
Thomas Norfolk & Sons Ltd, Deptford Brewery, Deptford Bridge,
registered in 1894 and was taken over by the Dartford Brewery
Co Ltd in 1904 with 55 public houses. The Dartford Brewery was
acquired by Style & Winch Ltd of Maidstone in 1924 and the
Royal Brewery Brentford Ltd in 1924 and was later uwho were
acquired by Barclay, Perkins in 1929.

WHITBREAD
Whitbread and Co Ltd, Chiswell Street, City. Founded in 1742
at the Goat Brewhouse. Old Street and moved to Chiswell Street

in 1750. Samuel Whitbread became the sole owner in 1761 and brewing ceased at Chiswell Street in 1975.

Take-overs:

1891   H. & V. Nicholl Ltd, Anchor Brewery. 170 Lewisham Road. Registered November 1887. Converted into a bottling and distribution centre.

1900   Abridge Brewery Co. Ltd, Anchor brewery, Abridge, Essex.

1924   Forest Hill Brewery Co Ltd, 61 Perry Vale, Forest Hill. Registered 1885 to acquire Morgan Brothers. The brewery was sold to United Dairies in 1927 and was converted into a bottling plant.

GRAND METROPLITAN

Mann, Crossman & Paulin Ltd, Albion Brewry, 172 Whitechapel Road.

Albion Brewery built 1808 by Richard Ivory, landlord of the Blind Beggar. Acquired by Blake & Mann 1818. Also brewed at the Albion Brewery Burton-on-Trent 1875-96. Registered October 1901. Merged with Watney, Combe, Reid & Co. Ltd. 1958 to form Watney Mann Ltd. The Albion Brewery was closed in 1979 but the building (Grade II listed) still remains in use.

Take-overs:

1925   S.R. Conron, exors of Old Hornchurch Brewery Church Hill Hornchurch. Founded 1789. Conron was listed as trading as Sweetman & Co, Francis Court Brewery, Dublin in 1889 and had moved to Hornchurch by 1905. Bought by Harman's Uxbridge Brewery Ltd 1924 and was sold to Mann's in 1925. Brewing ceased in 1929.

Reids's Brewery Co Ltd, Griffin Brewery, Liquorpond Street (now Clerkenwell Road), City. Founded 1757 when Meux & Murray acquired Jackson's Brewery, Mercer Street. Griffin Brewery built 1763. Became Reid & Co 1816. Registered 1888. Amalgamated with Watney & Combe 1898. The Griffin Brewery closed in 1899 but parts of the premises still exist as a tobacco factory.

Other breweries:

Richard Reeve, West Ham Brewery, 242 Romford Road, Forest Gate. Brewery plant was for sale April 9th 1900. Brewery still standing.

Cygnet Brewery Co Ltd, 251 Bow Road, Bow. Registered in 1906 to acquire Wonderland Co Ltd. Receiver appointed in 1908. No public houses.

Falcon Brewery Ltd, Old Ford Brewery, Paines Road, Bow. Registered in 1906 to take over the Old Ford Brewery Co. Ltd. Went into voluntary liquidation in 1903.

City of London Brewery Co Ltd, Hour Glass Brewery, Upper Thames Street. Founded by 1431 and was acquired by the Calvert family in 1759. Registered 1891 as the New City of London Brewery Co. Ltd and was renamed as above in 1895. Due to increased trade, brewing was transferred to the Swan Brewery in 1922 and the Hour Glass Brewery was used as a warehouse. Brewing continued at Fulham until 1926 when many public houses were sold to Hoare & Co. Ltd. In 1919 Nalder & Collyer's Brewery Co Ltd of Croydon was acquired. The majority of the Nalder & Collyer tied houses were sold to Ind Coope Ltd in 1936. The Hour Glass Brewery was destroyed in an air raid. The final connection with the brewing trade ended in 1968 with the sale of 20 public houses to Allied Breweries, but the company is still in existence as an investment trust.

Only one takeover, apart from the Wenlock Brewery Co Ltd, has been made by a brewery outside London. This was when Tollemache Breweries Ltd of Ipswich acquired Collier Brothers, Essex Brewery, Walthamstow in 1920. Brewing ceased in 1972.

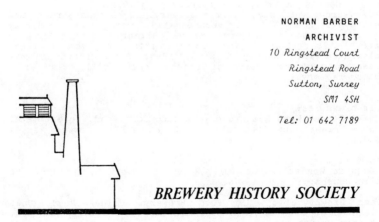

NORMAN BARBER
ARCHIVIST
10 Ringstead Court
Ringstead Road
Sutton, Surrey
SM1 4SH

Tel: 01 642 7189

BREWERY HISTORY SOCIETY

E6	PERSEVERANCE	E3	Priory Tavern
E1	Peasants Revolt	E1	PROSPECT OF WHITBY
E8	PEMBURY TAVERN	EC3	PUMPHOUSE
EC1	PENNY BLACK	EC4	PUNCH TAVERN
EC2	PENNY BLACK	E13	Queens
E2	Penny Farthing	E14	Queens
E9	Penshurst Arms	E8	QUEEN ELIZABETH
E2	Perseverance	E4	QUEEN ELIZABETH
E2	Perseverance	EC4	Queens Arms
E16	Nottingham Arms	E17	QUEENS ARMS
EC1	PHEASANT & FIRKIN	E2	Queen Victoria
E14	PHOENIX	E1	Queens Head
E14	PIER TAVERN	E1	Queens Head
E17	PIG & WHISTLE	EC4	QUEENS HEAD
E15	PIGEONS HOTEL	E15	QUEENS HEAD
E16	Pitts Head	E14	QUEENS HEAD
E3	Playwrights	E13	Raffles
E9	Plough	E1	Railway Arms
EC2	PLOUGH	E18	RAILWAY BELL
E4	PLOUGH	E16	RAILWAY HOTEL
E17	PLOUGH	E2	Railway Tavern
E11	Plough & Harrow	E14	RAILWAY TAVERN
EC2	PODIUM	EC2	RAILWAY TAVERN
EC4	POPPINJAY	E8	Railway Tavern
E1	PRIDE OF SPITALFIELDS	E7	RAILWAY TAVERN
E1	Pride of Stepney	E15	Railway Tavern
E4	PRINCE ALBERT	E15	RAILWAY TAVERN
E13	Prince Albert	E3	Railway Tavern
E14	Prince Alfred	E8	Railway Tavern
E9	PRINCE EDWARD	E16	RAM TAVERN
E8	PRINCE GEORGE	E3	Ranelagh Arms
E14	Prince Regent	EC3	RAVEN
E1	Prince Regent	EC1	RED COW
E10	Prince of Wales	E2	RED DEER
E5	PRINCE OF WALES	E13	Red House
E13	Prince of Wales	EC4	RED LION
E4	PRINCE OF WALES	E11	RED LION
E2	PRINCE OF WALES	EC3	RED LION
E2	Prince of Wales	EC2	RED LION
E1	Prince of Wales	EC3	RED LION
E17	Prince of Wales	E14	RESOLUTE TAVERN
E1	Prince of Wales	E9	Retreat
E3	Prince of Wales	E14	Richard Cobden
E8	Prince of Wales	E8	Ridley Arms
E16	Prince of Wales	E17	Ringwood Castle
E2	Prince of Wales	EC1	RISING SUN
E5	PRIORY TAVERN	E7	Rising Sun
E16	Princess Alexandra	EC4	RISING SUN
E7	PRINCESS ALICE	E17	Rising Sun
E1	PRINCESS OF PRUSSIA	E3	Rising Sun
E14	Princess of Wales	E14	Robert Burns
E15	PRINCESS OF WALES	E5	ROBIN HOOD
EC2	PRINCESS ROYAL	E8	ROBIN HOOD
EC4	PRINTERS DEVIL	E6	RODING

Pub names in capitals indicate that they sell real ale.

STATISTICS

MAJOR BREWERIES

	Keg		Real		% Real		Total	
Bass Charr	71	(72)	140	(152)	66.3	(67.8)	211	(224)
Courage	24	(32)	41	(37)	63	(53.6)	65	(69)
Allied	45	(53)	82	(79)	64.5	(59.8)	127	(132)
S&N	--	--	6	(6)	100	(100)	6	(6)
Grand Met	143	(146)	132	(195)	48	(57.3)	275	(341)
Whitbread	18	(15)	51	(47)	73.9	(75.8)	69	(62)

INDEPENDENTS

	Keg		Real		% Real		Total	
Banks & Taylor	1	–	1	–	50	--	2	–
Bateman	–	–	1	–	100	--	1	–
Belhaven	43	–	3	–	6.5	--	46	–
Eldridge Pope	–	(1)	1	(1)	100	(50)	1	(2)
Fullers	–	–	8	(7)	100	(100)	8	(7)
Gibbs Mew	–	(1)	–	(1)		(50)	–	(2)
Greene King	–	–	4	(1)	100	(100)	4	(1)
Marstons	–	–	–	(1)		(100)	–	(1)
McMullens	–	–	2	(2)	100	(100)	2	(2)
Pitfield	–	–	1	–	100	--	1	–
Sam Smiths	–	–	3	(2)	100	(100)	3	(2)
Shepherd Neame	1	–	11	(6)	91.6	(100)	2	(6)
Charles Wells	1		4		80	--	5	–
Wiltshire	–	–	1	–	100	--	1	–
Youngs	–	–	8	(10)	100	(100)	8	(10)
Free Houses	55	(37)	99	(102)	64	(72.9)	154	(139)
Totals	402_1	$(356)_2$	599	(650)	59.8	(63.9)	1001	(1006)

$_1$ includes 55 closed pubs.
$_2$ includes 17 closed pubs.

The figures in brackets are for 1986.

nb Figures correct to 1st July 1991.

Despite claims they want more pubs the independent brewers appear to be avoiding East London like the plague. At one stage Banks & Taylors had four East End pubs, but now like Gibbs Mew they appear to be doing a vanishing act on us. In 1991 Charles Wells came into the area but before the year is out we expect that Batemans and Pitfield will no longer run pubs in the area. Sam Smiths bought the Cheshire Cheese in EC4 from Marstons and promptly sold the rest of their City pubs to Greene King and built a new pub in Yuppieland. The lease on three Youngs pubs ran out and reverted to Whitbread. Fullers also want more pubs but not in the East End. 'The people of East London do not understand our beers' Mr Fuller was quoted as saying in the press. Thankfully we no longer rely on Fullers pubs to try to do so.

Do you . . .

. . . enjoy a pint of traditional ale?

. . . like the relaxed atmosphere of a good pub?

. . . believe that beer drinkers deserve a better deal?

If so, then read on—you're not alone!

Traditional beer and pubs have been under threat for decades—and remain so today.

CAMRA—the Campaign for Real Ale—exists to combat these threats. It has been called "Europe's most successful consumer movement".

CAMRA saved traditional British beer, which the brewers wanted to do away with. It has saved some breweries from takeover, and encouraged new ones to open. It has persuaded pubs to open during the afternoon, and provide an additional beer from a different brewery, through successful lobbying of Parliament. CAMRA is campaigning to save traditional Cider and Perry from extinction.

If you don't

care what

or where

you're drinking

...

DON'T

READ

THIS

BUT the

drinker's

struggle is far

from over . . .

— why is beer 30p a pint cheaper in Manchester than in London?

— do you know what goes into your pint?

Why can we not be told?

— why are we losing the heritage of so many traditional pubs?

Brewery takovers and closures are gathering momentum:

— **WATNEYS:** Norwich (closed 1985); Wilsons of Manchester (closed 1986); Drybroughs of Edinburgh (closed 1987); Ruddles (taken over 1986); Trumans, London (closed 1989).

WHITBREAD: Wethered of Marlow (closed 1988); Boddington, Manchester (taken over 1989); Chesters, Manchester (closed 1988); Higson, Liverpool (closed 1990); Fremlins, Kent (closed 1990).

SCOTTISH & NEWCASTLE: Holyrood (closed 1986); Home Ales of Nottingham (taken over 1986); Matthew Brown, Blackburn (taken over 1987), future uncertain.

GREENALL WHITLEY, having closed their subsidiary in Wem, taken over and closed Simpkiss (West Midlands) and Davenports in Birmingham, have now decided to opt out of brewing altogether. Brewing at Warrington (Greenalls) and Nottingham (Shipstones) is scheduled to cease in 1991. *We name but a few—will your local brewery be next?*

. . . CAMRA is needed today more than ever

— *the increasing stranglehold of the big brewers has led to high prices, poor choice and pub closures; and many new small breweries have been driven out of business.*

— *multi-million pound advertising promotions for weak but highly-priced 'lagers' constantly mislead drinkers.*

— *classic traditional inns continue to be destroyed in favour of theme-pub concepts. A growing number of pubs, particularly in rural areas, have been closed, often depriving a whole community of their local social centre.*

What do you get as a CAMRA member?

— *Whats Brewing,* the independent monthly newspaper for the beer drinker

— an information-packed Member's Handbook

— discounts on many products, including CAMRA's best-selling, annual *Good Beer Guide*

— up-to-date information about new beers and breweries, takeovers, closures and campaigns

— advance notice of beer festivals around the country, and discounted admission

What can you do as a CAMRA member?

— you can join in CAMRA's local and national campaigns

— you can participate in branch activities such as socials, beer festivals and brewery visits—there is a branch near you!

— you can play a part in CAMRA's Great British Beer Festival, the country's biggest beer extravaganza

CAMRA— THE PUBGOERS' CHAMPION